FLORIDA
Study Edition

my REFLECTIONS on AMERICAN HISTORY

McGraw-Hill
networks™
A Social Studies Learning System

Mc Graw Hill Education

Cover Photo Credit: SuperStock/Getty Images

www.mheonline.com

The *McGraw-Hill* Companies

 Education

Send all inquiries to:
McGraw-Hill Education
8787 Orion Place
Columbus, OH 43240

ISBN: 978-0-07-661734-0
MHID: 0-07-661734-3

Printed in the United States of America.

11 12 13 14 LOV 21 20 19 18 17

How will YOU use *My Reflections on American History*?

The *My Reflections on American History: Florida Study Edition* was created as a study edition just for you. Using this interactive textbook along with your full student edition and **netw⊙rks** will empower you to learn American history in a whole new way.

You will be able to write directly in this book! You can take notes, interact with what you read, and reflect on what you learn. As a result, you will be able to make connections between American history and your life, your community, and your world today.

Show Your Skill

1. Graphic Organizer Use the space on the graphic organizer to add details about the Plymouth colony.

Dig into the text and show what you know!

Think Critically

2. Contrast How were the views of the Anti-Federalists different from the views of the Federalists?

Analyze what you read!

Mark the Text

3. Underline the definition of a debtor.

Finally—a book you can write in!

Take the Challenge

4. Write a newspaper editorial from the perspective of a supporter of the New Jersey plan. In it, explain why you oppose the Virginia plan.

Create a unique project or do some learning on your own!

Keep Going! ▷▷

Make the Most of the *My Reflections* Activities!

Does American history matter to you today? Is it relevant to your daily life? Yes, it is!

The ideas and events you learn about in American history help you understand people and the past. As a result, you are better equipped to understand your life and the world today.

The "My Reflections" activities at the end of each chapter were created to help you make connections between the past and the present. Each activity allows you to reflect on what you have learned and how that relates to you, your community, and even the world.

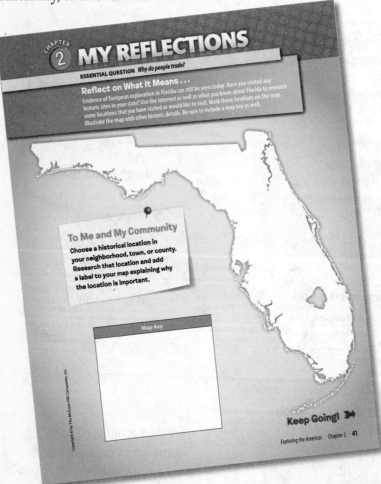

Have fun with *My Reflections on American History: Florida Study Edition!* You never know . . . you might just love American history by the time you're finished.

FLORIDA *Study Edition*

Contents

page 8

page 56

page 83

networks
Interact with your
Florida Study Edition Online!

page 116

page 191

page 199

networks
*Interact with your
Florida Study Edition Online!*

PHOTO: (t) idp eastern USA collection/Alamy; (c) Jim Lane/Alamy; (b) AAA Photostock/Alamy

page 217

page 255

page 307

netw⊛rks
Interact with your
Florida Study Edition Online!

CHAPTER
1

EXPLORING SOCIAL STUDIES

NGSSS

SS.8.A.1.4 Differentiate fact from opinion, utilize appropriate historical research and fiction/nonfiction support materials.

ESSENTIAL QUESTIONS *Why is history important? How does geography influence the way we live? Why do people make economic choices? What makes a responsible citizen?*

Madeline Albright was the first female secretary of state. In this role she handled issues between the United States and the other nations of the world. Understanding history gave her a background for the international issues she faced.

"History is a strange teacher. It never repeats itself exactly, but you ignore its general lessons at your peril."

MADELINE ALBRIGHT

general lessons

Circle which of these would be the best replacement for the phrase *general lessons*?

exams and tests   patterns and themes

books and papers

peril

What is another word for peril?

_____

_____

PHOTO: David Brauchli/Getty Images

Copyright © by The McGraw-Hill Companies, Inc.

DBQ BREAKING IT DOWN

Albright thinks that history has much to teach us. What words does she use to help us think of ourselves as "students" of history?

_____

_____

_____

You may have heard someone say, "history repeats itself." Albright does not really agree. What is her position on that?

_____

_____

_____

McGraw-Hill
networks™
There's More Online!

NGSSS

SS.8.A.1.2 Analyze charts, graphs, maps, photographs and timelines; analyze political cartoons; determine cause and effect.

SS.8.A.1.4 Differentiate fact from opinion, utilize appropriate historical research and fiction/nonfiction support materials.

SS.8.A.1.5 Identify, within both primary and secondary sources, the author, audience, format, and purpose of significant historical documents.

Essential Question
Why is history important?

Guiding Questions
1. Why do we study history?
2. What tools do we use to measure time?
3. What is a primary source?
4. What types of information can be shown in graphs, charts, and diagrams?
5. What types of thinking skills does a historian need?

Terms to Know

calendar
a system for organizing time into units and keeping track of those units

chronology
order of dates in which events happened

It Matters Because

History teaches us what has been important to others in the past and helps us understand what to expect for the future.

Your life has a history all its own. Can you recall events from your past that affect your life right now? Use the space below to write down one important event, the date it occurred, and why you believe it affects your life today.

_____

_____

_____

_____

When Did It Happen?

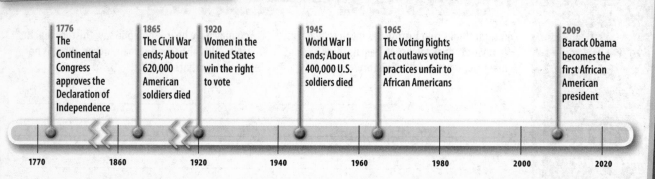

1776 The Continental Congress approves the Declaration of Independence

1865 The Civil War ends; About 620,000 American soldiers died

1920 Women in the United States win the right to vote

1945 World War II ends; About 400,000 U.S. soldiers died

1965 The Voting Rights Act outlaws voting practices unfair to African Americans

2009 Barack Obama becomes the first African American president

1770   1860   1920   1940   1960   1980   2000   2020

What Does a Historian Do?

Historians study and write about the people and events of the past. Historians find out how people lived and what happened to them. Historians also study what events were going on while those people lived. Historians look for the reasons, or causes, behind events. They also study the effects of events.

Measuring Time

A **calendar** is a tool for organizing time into units. A calendar also keeps track of those units. You can use a calendar to measure how much time has passed between events. Months and years are two common ways to measure time on a calendar.

Different groups in history have made calendars that are different from our calendars. Our calendar is called the Western calendar. In the Western calendar, a year is 365 days. The Western calendar uses the birth of Jesus as a dividing point. The years before this date are known as "B.C.," or "before Christ." The years after are called "A.D.," or anno domini. This means "in the year of the Lord" in Latin.

Historians are interested in the order in which events happened. This is called a **chronology.** An easy way to keep a chronology of events is to use or make a time line. A time line is a diagram that shows the order of events within a period of time.

Each section of a time line represents a particular period of time. A time line shows when important events happened. Each event has a label. The labels appear near the date on the time line when the event took place.

Florida History Time Line

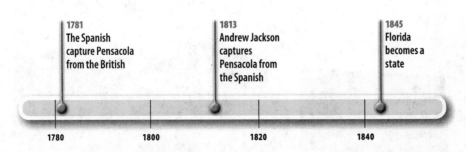

1. **Evaluate** Why do you think time lines are important to historians?

_____

_____

_____

Mark the Text

2. Underline two important tools historians use to measure time.

Copyright © by The McGraw-Hill Companies, Inc.

Thinking Like a Historian Lesson 1 **3**

3. Contrast What is the difference between a primary and secondary source?

_____

_____

_____

_____

_____

_____

4. Classify Information Is a biography considered a primary or a secondary source? Why?

_____

_____

_____

_____

5. Look around your classroom. Make a list of the primary and secondary sources you find that help you learn about history or might help future historians learn about you.

Analyzing Sources

A primary source is a source of information, such as a document, photograph, recording, or work of art, about a person or event. It contains information produced by someone who actually saw or was part of the event.

If you see a rocket launch in person and then write about it or take a picture of it, you have created a primary source. Other people who watched the rocket launch may produce primary sources, too. Their diaries, journals, videos, and eyewitness reports are types of primary sources.

To analyze primary sources, try to answer the five "W" questions:

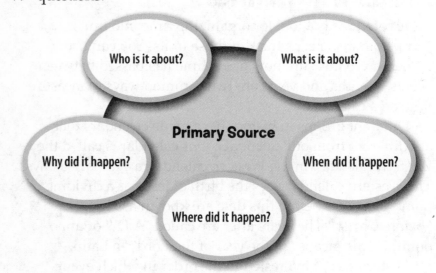

Secondary sources are based on what other people have seen and heard. They come from people who were not present at an event. A person may create a secondary source, such as a book or a video, by collecting a number of primary sources. A book about the history of the space program is a secondary source. The author of such a book may collect information from many sources. He or she would use many primary sources. The author would combine this information into something new. Biographies of famous people and histories of events are secondary sources.

This primary source photo shows a gas station near Cherry Lake, Florida in the 1930s. It provides information about the time period.

Charts, Diagrams, and Graphs

Graphs, charts, and diagrams are ways to display information such as percentages, numbers, and amounts. They are tools that help organize information and make it easier to understand.

Graphs present numbers visually. This makes the numbers easier to understand. There are three main types of graphs you will find in this textbook. They are line graphs, bar graphs, and circle graphs. To read a graph, follow these steps:

- For any kind of graph, read the graph's title. This will tell you what the graph is about.
- Bar graphs and line graphs both have a line along the bottom of the graph. This line is called the horizontal axis. The horizontal axis at the bottom of the graph tells you what is being measured.
- Bar graphs and line graphs also have a line that runs up and down, usually at the left side of the graph. This line is called the vertical axis. The vertical axis tells you the unit of measurement.
- For circle graphs, read the labels or key, which show you what each color in the graph stands for.

Bar graphs use bars to compare numbers visually:

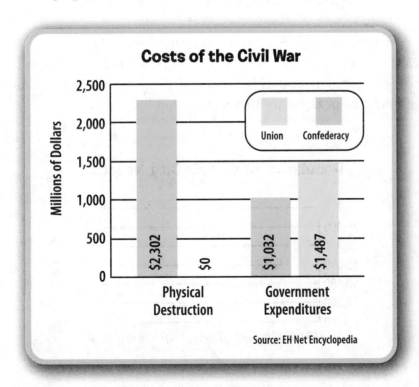

Costs of the Civil War

Source: EH Net Encyclopedia

Think Critically

6. Evaluate What is an advantage of reading information on a graph?

_____

_____

_____

Show Your Skill

7. Interpret Graphs What is one thing you can learn from the graph showing the costs of the Civil War?

_____

_____

_____

_____

_____

8. Contrast In what ways do the uses for circle graphs and line graphs differ?

_____

_____

_____

_____

_____

_____

Circle graphs are sometimes called pie graphs. Circle graphs are used when you want to show how the whole of something is divided. Each piece of the graph represents a part, or percentage, of the whole pie. The complete circle represents a whole pie—or 100 percent.

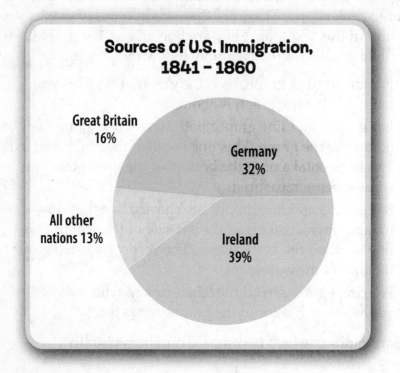

Sources of U.S. Immigration, 1841 – 1860

Great Britain 16%

Germany 32%

All other nations 13%

Ireland 39%

Line graphs help show how something changes over a period of time. Each amount being measured is placed on the graph, or grid. The amounts are usually represented by a dot. The amounts, or dots, are then connected by a line.

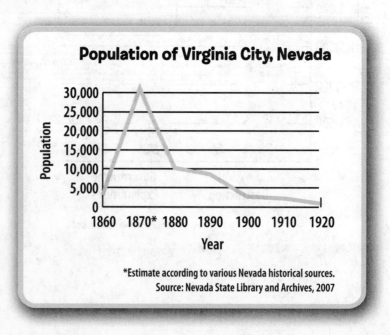

Population of Virginia City, Nevada

*Estimate according to various Nevada historical sources.
Source: Nevada State Library and Archives, 2007

Charts present facts and numbers in an organized way. One type of chart is a table. A table arranges data in rows and columns for easy reference. Charts can also be used to summarize the main ideas of a topic. This allows you to review material and compare main ideas easily.

Show Your Skill

9. Draw Conclusions Would a chart or a diagram be better for showing the parts of a cell phone? Why?

_____

_____

_____

_____

_____

Military Pay				
Army Salaries (monthly)				
Rank	Civil War	World War II 1942	Vietnam War 1965	Iraq War 2003
Private	$13	$50	$85	$1203–1543
Corporal	$14	$66	$210	$1699
Sergeant	$17	$78	$261	$1864–2339
Sergeant Major	$21	$138	$486	$4110

Source: Bureau of Economic Analysis; *Princeton Review*; www.militaryfactory.com

Diagrams are drawings that can be used to show the steps in a process. They may also be used to point out the parts of an object. They are often used to explain how something works.

1 **Torpedo tubes** were devices to launch torpedoes.

2 **Steam boilers** powered the engines.

3 Munitions were stored in the **magazine.**

4 **Cowls** provided fresh air below deck.

10. Analyze Why is it important to understand cause and effect?

_____

_____

_____

11. Interpret Images
Identify two similarities and two differences in the images.

_____

_____

_____

_____

_____

_____

Critical Thinking Skills

Historians do more than just read sources and look at pictures or graphs. Historians use many thinking skills.

Determining cause and effect is one way to link two events. A cause is something that produces something else. A cause makes something else happen. The effect is what is produced or what happens as a result of the cause.

If you want to understand the cause of an event, ask why the event happened. If you want to know the result, or effect, of an event, ask what happened after the event. Understanding cause and effect helps you see how one thing can lead to another.

Another way historians look at events or ideas is to compare and contrast them. To compare ideas, objects, or events, look for ways in which they are similar, or alike. To contrast ideas, objects, or events, look for things that make them different from each other. You might look for things that make each of them unique.

Making comparisons can help you choose among several possible alternatives. To compare and contrast ideas, objects, or events, follow these steps:

1. Decide what items to compare.
2. Determine what it is about the items you want to compare and contrast. For example, you might compare or contrast a topic, a style, or a point of view.
3. To compare the items, look for similarities between or among the items. Ask, "What makes these items alike?"
4. To contrast the items, look for differences between or among the items. Ask, "What makes these items different from each other? What makes each item unique?"

What differences do you see in these images of Chicago from the 1800s and today?

CHICAGO   IN 1858.

PHOTO: (l) Royalty-Free/CORBIS; (r) Alex L. Fradkin/Getty Images

As you think like a historian, you may need to predict the consequences of an event. Predicting future events is difficult. However, you may be able to make your predictions more accurate by gathering more information. Usually, the more information you have, the more accurate your predictions will be. The better you are able to predict what may happen, the better decisions you can make.

Historians also need to determine whether something is a fact or an opinion. It is a skill everyone should have. A fact is something you can check to prove that it is true and accurate.

An opinion is something that is based on a person's values, beliefs, or ideas. An opinion is neither true nor false. Opinions often begin with phrases such as *I believe* or *it seems to me*. They may also contain words such as *should, ought, best,* and *worst*. Often you have to evaluate what others say or write. Being able to distinguish facts from opinions will help you do that.

Fact	Opinion
The 4th of July is a national holiday.	Summer is the best season.
George Washington was the first United States president.	George Washington was the greatest president.

Another skill used by historians is making inferences and drawing conclusions. When you make an inference, you "read between the lines." That means that you use clues in the text to learn something that is not stated in the text. A conclusion is a fact or an opinion that you reach based on information that you read or hear. The ability to draw inferences and conclusions helps you understand and analyze what you are studying.

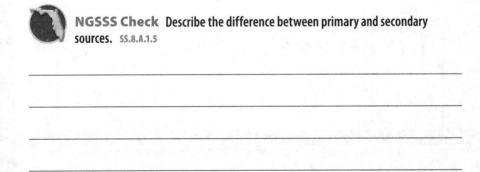

NGSSS Check Describe the difference between primary and secondary sources. SS.8.A.1.5

_____

_____

_____

_____

Show Your Skill

12. Classify Information
Give an example of a fact and an example of an opinion.

_____

_____

_____

_____

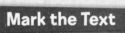

Mark the Text

13. Underline the definition of *inference.*

LESSON 2

STUDYING GEOGRAPHY

NGSSS

SS.8.G.1.2 Use appropriate geographic tools and terms to identify and describe significant places and regions in American history.

SS.8.G.3.1 Locate and describe in geographic terms the major ecosystems of the United States.

Essential Question

How does geography influence the way we live?

Guiding Questions

1. What are the five themes of geography?
2. What stories do maps and globes tell?
3. What are places and regions?
4. How do physical systems impact the world?
5. How do human systems impact our world?
6. What impact does the environment and society have on the world?

Terms to Know

globe
a round model of the Earth

map
a flat drawing of all or part of the Earth's surface

landforms
natural features on the Earth

relief
ups and downs of the Earth's surface

elevation
the height of an area above sea level

Where in the World?

Geographic Features

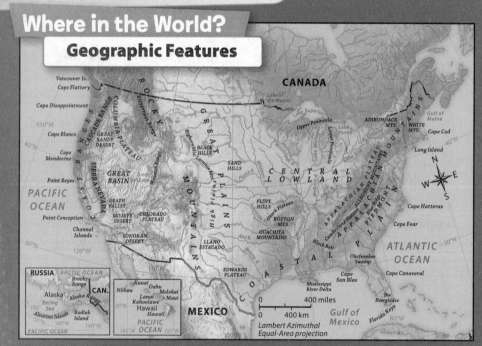

When Did It Happen?

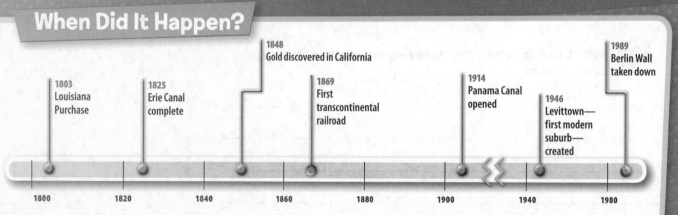

1803 Louisiana Purchase	**1825** Erie Canal complete	**1848** Gold discovered in California	**1869** First transcontinental railroad	**1914** Panama Canal opened	**1946** Levittown— first modern suburb— created	**1989** Berlin Wall taken down	

1800   1820   1840   1860   1880   1900   1940   1980

What is Geography?

Geography is the study of the Earth and its people. A geographer tries to understand everything about a place. He or she wants to know more than where the place is. The geographer wants to know what the place is like, what happens there, and how the people live there.

Geographers organize their study into different themes, or subjects. The five themes of geography are location, place, regions, movement, and human-environment interaction.

Location describes where something is. *Place* studies the physical and human features that make an area unique. *Regions* are areas that share common features, such as climate or physical features. *Movement* explains how and why people, things, and ideas move from one place to another. *Human-environment interaction* studies the relationship between people and their environment.

Maps and Globes

A **globe** is a round model of the Earth. It shows the Earth's shape and its lands. Their shapes, sizes, and locations are accurate.

A **map** is a flat drawing of all or part of the Earth's surface. Cartographers, or mapmakers, use complex formulas to transfer shapes from a round globe to a flat map. Still, all maps change the shapes of the places they show. Maps can cover small areas, cities, states, continents, or the whole world.

Because the Earth is round, a globe can represent Earth's landforms and bodies of water more accurately than a flat map can.

PHOTO: NASA/Corbis

Copyright © by The McGraw-Hill Companies, Inc.

1. List What are four things geographers want to know about a place?

_____

_____

_____

_____

2. Contrast How are maps and globes different?

_____

_____

_____

_____

Think Critically

3. Explain What features might be shown on a physical map?

_____

_____

_____

Show Your Skill

4. Draw Conclusions Why is the key, or legend, important on a map?

_____

_____

_____

_____

Geographers use many different kinds of maps. General-purpose maps show a wide range of information about an area. Physical maps and political maps are common general-purpose maps.

Physical maps show landforms and water features. Landforms are natural features on the earth. They include deserts, mountains, plains, and plateaus. The map key explains what each color and symbol stands for.

Political maps show the names and political boundaries of a place. Political maps also show human-made features, such as cities and transportation routes.

Special-purpose maps are used to show special types of information. For example, a special-purpose map might show where different Native American languages are spoken. Another special-purpose map might show what industries are found in an area.

One type of special-purpose map shows population density. Population density refers to how many people live in each square mile. A city has a high population density. Rural areas usually have a low population density.

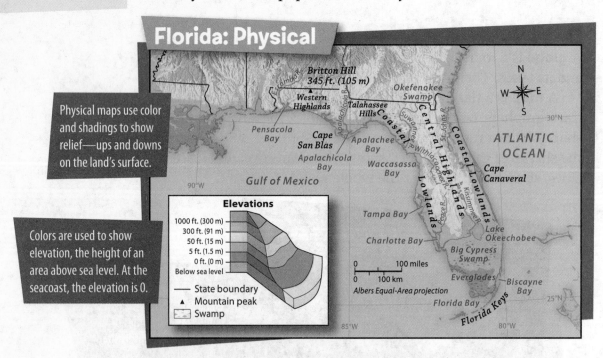

Florida: Physical

Physical maps use color and shadings to show relief—ups and downs on the land's surface.

Colors are used to show elevation, the height of an area above sea level. At the seacoast, the elevation is 0.

The Elements of Geography

Geographers studying a place want to know where it is located. Every place on Earth has an absolute location and a relative location. Absolute location refers to the exact spot on the Earth's surface where a place can be found. For example, the city of Jacksonville, Florida, is located at a specific spot on the Earth. No other place on Earth has the same absolute location as Jacksonville.

Relative location tells where a place is in relation to one or more other places. Miami, Florida, is southeast of Tampa, west of the Atlantic Ocean, and about 228 miles (367 km) north of the capital city of Havana on the island of Cuba. Your school may be down the street from your friend's house or east of the shopping mall.

Place describes the characteristics that make an area special. The characteristics can be physical features, such as mountains, climate, or unusual plant or animal life. The characteristics can also be human features, such as language or architecture. When you tell someone about your town, you are probably describing place.

Each place is unique. Still, many places share features in common with other places nearby. A group of places that share common features is called a region.

Regions can be defined by physical features, such as landforms or plant life. Regions may also be defined by human features. Human features include religion, language, and industry. For example, the South during the 1800s was a largely agricultural region.

Think Critically

5. Contrast How are absolute location and relative location different?

_____

_____

_____

_____

Mark the Text

6. Underline the sentences that define a region.

Take the Challenge

7. Write 10 clues to describe a place. Provide information about both the physical and absolute location. Describe its characteristics. Arrange the clues from most difficult to easiest and see if a partner can guess your place.

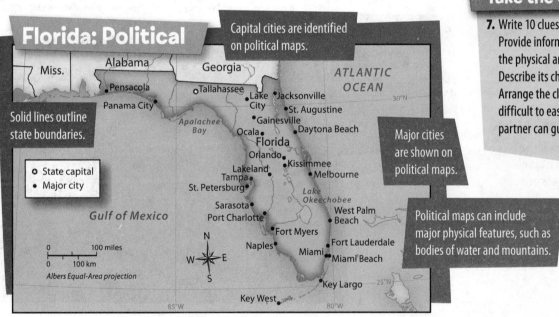

Florida: Political

Capital cities are identified on political maps.

Solid lines outline state boundaries.

Major cities are shown on political maps.

Political maps can include major physical features, such as bodies of water and mountains.

Miss.
Alabama
Georgia
ATLANTIC OCEAN
Pensacola
Tallahassee
Panama City
Apalachee Bay
Lake City
Jacksonville
St. Augustine
Gainesville
Ocala
Daytona Beach
Florida
Orlando
Kissimmee
Lakeland
Tampa
Melbourne
St. Petersburg
Lake Okeechobee
Sarasota
Port Charlotte
West Palm Beach
Fort Myers
Naples
Fort Lauderdale
Miami
Miami Beach
Key Largo
Key West
Gulf of Mexico

- State capital
- Major city

0   100 miles
0   100 km
Albers Equal-Area projection

30°N
25°N
85°W
80°W

Physical systems include the complex forces that create wind, rain, snow, and storms. There are also physical systems that move the surface of the Earth and change its shape. These systems build mountain ranges, form volcanoes, and cause earthquakes.

Physical systems affect where and how humans live. For example, people may decide not to live on the slopes of an active volcano. However, almost every place where people live feels the impact of storms, earthquakes, or other physical systems.

Think Critically

8. Contrast What is the difference between a physical system and a human system?

_____

_____

_____

_____

Show Your Skill

9. Interpret Information Describe how physical systems affect where people live.

_____

_____

_____

_____

_____

Think Critically

10. Describe What types of impacts can humans have on their environment?

_____

_____

_____

_____

_____

Ecosystems are a type of physical system. An ecosystem is a community of living things and the surroundings in which they live. A pond is an example of an ecosystem. A pond ecosystem includes the water and all the living and nonliving things in it.

A human system includes all the things humans create to live on the Earth. It includes people and their settlements. A human system also includes the cultures people form. Culture includes the way different groups deal with each other and how they settle conflicts.

People settle in certain places and change their environment to suit their needs. For example, people create cities with buildings, streets, and homes. They also build dams on rivers to generate electricity. People also adapt to the world around them. For instance, they may rely on fishing if they live near water or farming if they live on fertile land.

Human beings tend to have a great impact on the ecosystems in which they live. Some impacts may be harmful or destructive. As a result, people must find ways to balance their needs with the needs of the natural world around them.

The Everglades in Florida is a very unique ecosystem.

NGSSS Check What are some ways a place may be shown or described? SS.8.G.1.2

_____

_____

Describe the location of your hometown using several different methods.

_____

_____

STUDYING ECONOMICS

NGSSS

SS.8.E.1.1 Examine motivating economic factors that influenced the development of the United States economy over time, including scarcity, supply and demand, opportunity costs, incentives, profits, and entrepreneurial aspects.

SS.8.E.2.2 Explain the economic impact of government policies.

SS.8.E.3.1 Evaluate domestic and international interdependence.

Essential Question
Why do people make economic choices?

Guiding Questions
1. What makes up an economy?
2. How do people decide what to produce?
3. What determines the strength or weakness of a nation's economy?
4. How do nations trade with each other?
5. What influences how you make your economic decisions?

Terms to Know

opportunity cost
the cost of passing up the second choice when making a decision

capital
money and human-made goods that people use to produce goods and services

entrepreneur
a person who starts and runs a business

market economy
economic system in which buyers and sellers choose to do business with those who satisfy their needs and wants best

free enterprise system
economic system in which people are free to control and produce goods

tariff
a tax on imports

It Matters Because

Understanding economic systems also helps us understand the reasons for many actions by people and governments throughout history.

Use the Internet to research a news story about the economy in Florida. Use the space below to write the headline of the article as well as two details about Florida's economy that you read in the article.

_____

_____

_____

_____

_____

_____

When Did It Happen?

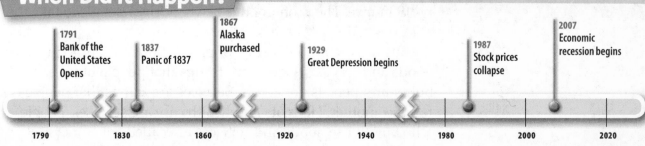

1791 Bank of the United States Opens

1837 Panic of 1837

1867 Alaska purchased

1929 Great Depression begins

1987 Stock prices collapse

2007 Economic recession begins

1790   1830   1860   1920   1940   1980   2000   2020

Think Critically

1. Conclude Why is scarcity so important in the study of economics?

_____

_____

_____

2. Describe What is an opportunity cost?

_____

_____

_____

_____

Show Your Skill

3. Make inferences Why do entrepreneurs take the risks of starting a business?

_____

_____

_____

What Is Economics?

Economics is the study of how people make choices. People have a wide variety of wants and needs. People have to choose how to use their limited resources.

Nations have to make the same kinds of choices that individuals do. Nations have limited resources. They, and their citizens, have unlimited needs and wants. Economics is the study of those choices. This involves how things are made, bought, sold, and used.

The most important idea in economics is the idea of scarcity. Scarcity means that there is not enough of something. In economics it means that there are not enough resources to make all the goods and services people want. As a result, nations and people must make choices.

For example, when you decide to buy a song online, you are making a choice. You are choosing to use your money to buy a song. You could, however, choose to save the money. Your decision to buy the song means you cannot save the money. This is called the **opportunity cost** because one choice costs you the opportunity to make another choice. There is an opportunity cost involved in every choice.

The resources needed to make goods and services are known as factors of production. The factors of production are land, labor, and capital. Many people also include **entrepreneurs** as another type of capital. They are people who start and run businesses.

Land refers to natural resources, such as farmland, that are used to make products. A nation's workforce is called labor. Labor, or human resources, includes anyone who works to produce goods and services.

Another factor of production is capital. **Capital** refers to human-made goods that are used to produce other goods and services. Capital includes machines, buildings, and tools. Money is also a type of capital.

Entrepreneurs bring together the factors of production. They organize the factors and manage a business. Entrepreneurs take the economic risks of starting a business because they hope to make money. The desire to make money, or a profit, is called the profit motive. The profit motive is what drives people to take the risks of starting a business.

Businesses use the factors of production in order to produce goods and services. Goods are things that people buy. Peanut butter and pencils are goods. Services are things that people do for one another. Haircuts and health care are services. People who buy or use goods and services are called consumers.

Market Economy

Every country has an economic system. Economic systems are the ways that people make and trade goods and services. Types of economic systems include traditional, command, and market systems.

A few places have a "traditional economy." In this system, what people do and make is based on tradition—"the way it's always been done." Traditional economies are rare today.

Some countries have a command economy. In a command economy, the government controls most economic activity. Government leaders tell people what to make and what resources to use. The government also controls the sale of the goods and services.

The United States has a market economy. Market, in this sense, means a system of buying and selling things. In a market economy, buyers and sellers are free to buy, sell, or make whatever they want. Government takes a small role in these decisions. As a result, everyone is free to take actions that make their lives better.

This freedom leads to competition. Producers compete against each other. They try to supply goods and services at prices that will win customers. Consumers make choices on how to spend their money. They try to get the best products for their money.

In a market system, the forces of supply and demand help set prices. If there is a large supply of something, the price is often low. A small supply often means a higher price. Demand affects prices, too. If the demand is great, the price is often high. If the demand is low, the price is usually low.

National Economy

The American economy is also called a free enterprise system. This means that individuals are free to own and control the means of production. For example, you may decide to go into business for yourself. You are free to choose what goods or services to produce. You are also free to choose how many goods or services to produce. You can also choose what resources you use to produce your goods and services.

This farmer in Florida chooses to take his product to the local market.

Think Critically

4. Explain What is the role of government in a command economy?

_____

_____

_____

Mark the Text

5. Underline a goal consumers share.

Take the Challenge

6. Think of a product you buy. Describe a situation that would make the price go up. Describe a situation that would make the price go down.

Think Critically

7. Analyze What are two basic freedoms involved in the free enterprise system?

_____

_____

_____

_____

Show Your Skill

8. Infer Who influences producers on what to make and what not to make in a free enterprise system?

Consumers in a free enterprise system have freedom of choice. That freedom means that buyers can choose what to buy and what not to buy. Consumer choice is important. Consumers tell producers what to make and what not to make by their choices. If consumers buy a lot of one type of thing, producers will make more of it. If consumers don't buy something, producers will stop making it.

The strength of the U.S. economic system is based on the following 5 goals:

Goal	Description
Economic Efficiency	Using limited resources wisely
Economic Stability	Reducing extreme ups and downs in the economy
Economic Fairness	Providing everyone equal opportunities in the economic system
Full Employment	Offering a job at good pay for anyone who is willing and able to work
Economic Growth	Producing an increasing amount of goods and services over the long term

International Economy

No country has all the resources, goods, and services it needs. Therefore, countries sell resources, goods, and services to each other. This creates international trade.

International trade is the exchange of goods and services across national borders. Every country imports, or buys, goods and services from other countries. Every country exports, or sells, goods and services to other countries.

Trade is based on the idea of voluntary exchange. Neither the buyer nor the seller is forced to trade. A buyer freely and willingly exchanges something—usually money—for goods or services. The seller freely and willingly trades goods or services for money.

Trade allows specialization. Many nations use their resources to produce goods or services that cannot be produced in other countries. Countries can then trade these items to other countries for goods and services they need.

Today, almost everybody uses currency, or money, for trade. However, most countries have their own currency. The United States uses the dollar. Nigeria uses the naira, Iraq the dinar, Japan the yen, and several European nations use the Euro.

People in different countries need to know the exchange rate for each currency. The exchange rate is how much one country's currency is worth in terms of another country's currency. Currency markets figure out how many yen or naira equal one dollar. This makes it possible for businesses to receive and make payments across borders.

Just like individuals and businesses, countries compete for customers and the best prices. Sometimes countries try to protect their industries from competition. They put up barriers to trade.

Three common barriers to trade are:

- **tariffs** A tariff is a tax on imports. A tariff makes the price of an imported good higher than the price of the same thing made in the home country. Companies in the home country can sell at lower prices and stay in business.
- **import quotas** An import quota sets a limit on the amount of a product that can be imported, or brought into the country.
- **embargo** An embargo is when one country prohibits its businesses from trading with another country.

In recent years, however, many countries have agreed to work toward free trade. This means they are working to reduce or eliminate trade barriers.

Economic Literacy

You and everyone around you are consumers. Consumers play an important role in the economic system. Consumers buy a wide variety of things—food, clothing, health care services, insurance, automobiles, phones, and so on. Economic literacy means being a good consumer. Good consumers ask themselves some basic questions before they spend their money.

Before you buy anything, ask yourself these questions:

1. Do I really need this item? Why? Is it something I want, but don't really need?
2. Is this item worth the time and energy I spent earning the money to pay for it?
3. Is there any better use for my money right now?
4. Instead of spending my money now, should I save for future needs or wants?

Copyright © by The McGraw-Hill Companies, Inc.

Show Your Skill

10. Generalize What is the goal of free trade?

_____

_____

_____

Think Critically

11. Infer Why do banks pay customers interest on a savings account?

_____

_____

_____

_____

_____

Think Critically

13. Evaluate Describe the positives and negatives of using credit.

_____

_____

_____

_____

_____

Saving is setting aside income, or money you have earned, so that it can be used later. You may already be saving for something you want to buy later or for continuing your education. Most people, when they save, put their money in a bank. A bank pays them interest on their money. Interest is the price the bank pays you to use the money you deposited. The bank loans that money to someone else to buy a house or a car or something else. You receive interest on your savings account while funds are in the account.

Generally, banks are a safe place to save your money. They pay a safe rate of interest. People who invest in the stock market take a larger risk. They are trying to maximize their rate of return. Because the risk is greater, the return they can get may be greater, too.

Consumers use credit when they borrow money today to buy goods and services. The amount borrowed is called the principal. The debt—the total amount owed—is equal to the principal plus interest. The consumer promises to pay back the principal, plus interest, in the future.

Most Americans borrow and buy some things on credit. When buying expensive items, such as an automobile or a house, they may consider borrowing to be necessary. Using credit can be a good way to make a purchase. At the same time, credit can lead you to spend more money than you should.

NGSSS Check List five goals of the national economy. SS.8.E.2.2

_____

_____

_____

Using credit cards can be convenient, but may also tempt people to buy more than they can afford.

4 CIVICS AND GOVERNMENT

NGSSS

SS.8.C.1.1 Identify the constitutional provisions for establishing citizenship.

SS.8.C.1.5 Apply the rights and principles contained in the Constitution and Bill of Rights to the lives of citizens today.

Essential Question
What makes a responsible citizen?

Guiding Questions
1. What are the rights of citizens?
2. What are the structures and functions of government?
3. What are the duties and responsibilities of citizens?

Terms to Know

naturalization
the legal process of becoming a citizen

due process
procedures the government must follow that are established by law

federal system
type of government in which power flows between state and local governments and the national government

What Do You Know?

Many people choose to serve our country or communities by working in government roles. In order to do so, they may run for political office or apply for a government job. Complete the chart below with the names of people who hold political office or work for the government.

My Local Government	State of Florida	United States Government

When Did It Happen?

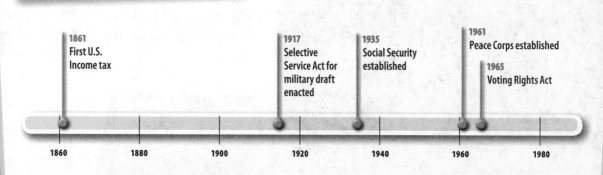

1860	1880	1900	1920	1940	1960	1980

1861 First U.S. Income tax

1917 Selective Service Act for military draft enacted

1935 Social Security established

1961 Peace Corps established

1965 Voting Rights Act

Mark the Text

1. Underline two ways to become a U.S. citizen.

Think Critically

2. **Summarize** Why does the United States government limit some rights?

_____

_____

_____

_____

_____

Rights of U.S. Citizens

Civics is the study of the rights and duties of citizens. Each country has rules for deciding who is a citizen and how people can become citizens. The U.S. Constitution lists two ways a person can become a citizen. One way is by being born in the United States. Anyone born in the United States is a U.S. citizen. A second way to become a citizen is called **naturalization.** Naturalization is a process for people born in other countries who choose to become U.S. citizens.

All U.S. citizens have certain basic rights. These rights are written in the United States Constitution. They are also guaranteed by the Constitution. As citizens, people also have specific responsibilities. In a democracy, every citizen must take part of the responsibility for deciding who will control the government. Citizens are also partly responsible for the actions the government takes.

Amendment	Meaning
First	Lists some basic freedoms guaranteed to all people in the United States. These are the freedoms of speech, religion, and the press. Also guarantees the rights to assembly and to petition the government.
Fifth	Guarantees that all citizens receive due process. Due process means that the government must follow certain rules established by the Constitution and law.
Fourteenth	Guarantees equal protection under the law. Equal protection means that Americans of all races, religions, gender, and beliefs must be treated the same as everyone else under the law.

Even the most basic rights are not unlimited. Rights need to be limited so that one person's rights do not interfere with the rights of others. The United States government can limit rights if it can show that is necessary and reasonable. For example, it limits some rights to protect people's health and safety. Any government restrictions of rights must apply to everyone equally.

At a naturalization ceremony, these new citizens take the oath of citizenship.

Government: Structures and Functions

Each country in the world has a government. Governments can generally be classified into one of three categories: unitary, confederation, or federal.

In a unitary government, all government power is controlled by a single, national government. The national government may, or may not, share power with any states, cities, or towns in the country. In a confederation, the states or other members of the confederation tightly control all government power. The member states give very limited power to the central government. Finally, in a **federal system,** the power is split between a central, national government and the state or other lower-level governments.

The U.S. Constitution sets out what the national and state governments can and cannot do. Certain powers are given to the national government. Other powers are given to state governments. Some powers are shared.

Think Critically

3. Contrast How is a unitary government different from a confederation?

Take the Challenge

4. Research the types of governments they have in five other nations. Work with your class to create a graph that shows the numbers of countries in each category.

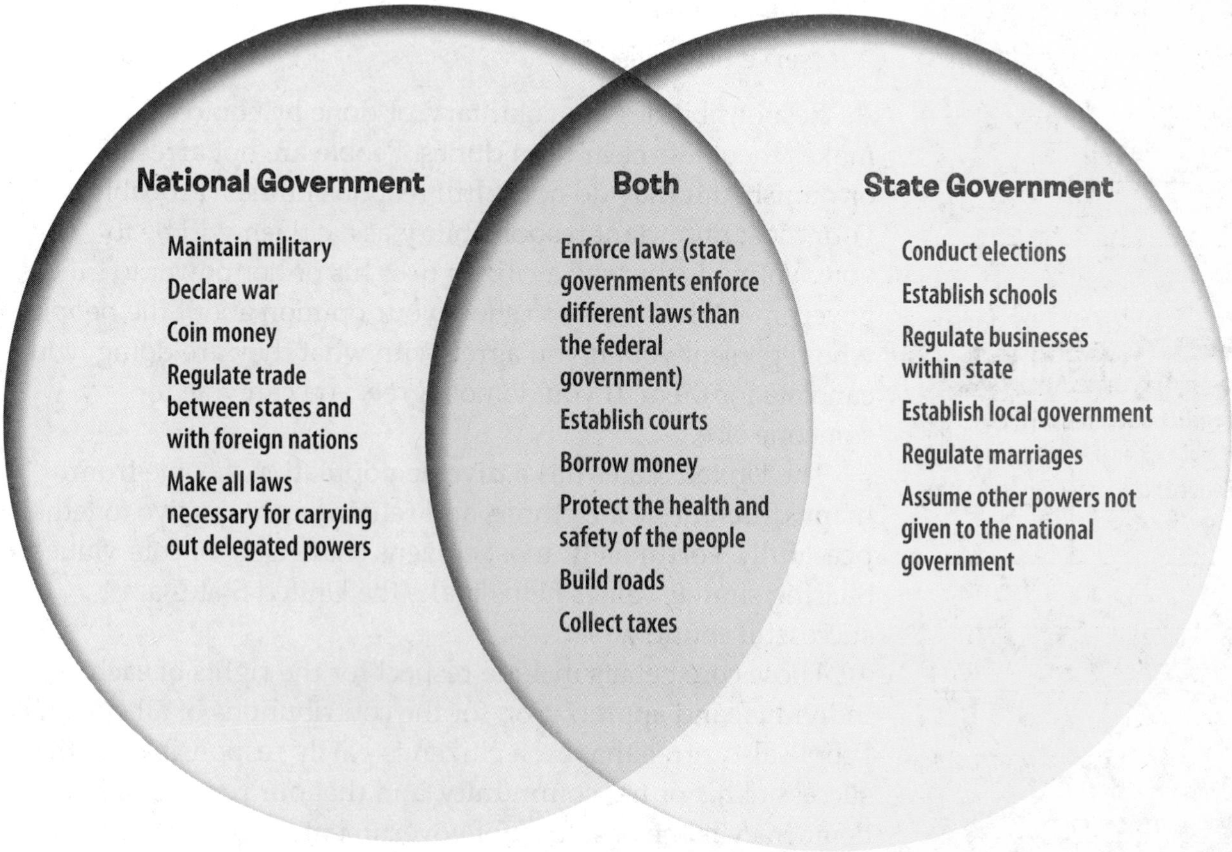

National Government
Maintain military
Declare war
Coin money
Regulate trade between states and with foreign nations
Make all laws necessary for carrying out delegated powers
Both
Enforce laws (state governments enforce different laws than the federal government)
Establish courts
Borrow money
Protect the health and safety of the people
Build roads
Collect taxes
State Government
Conduct elections
Establish schools
Regulate businesses within state
Establish local government
Regulate marriages
Assume other powers not given to the national government

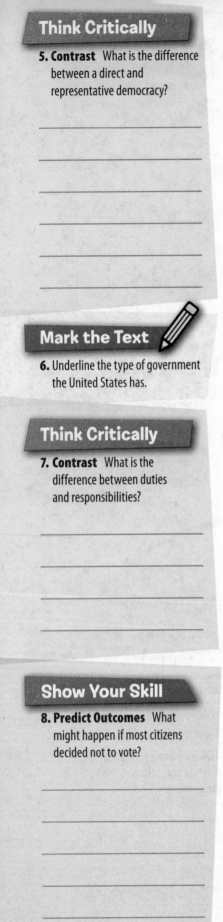

Think Critically

5. Contrast What is the difference between a direct and representative democracy?

_____

_____

_____

_____

_____

Mark the Text

6. Underline the type of government the United States has.

Think Critically

7. Contrast What is the difference between duties and responsibilities?

_____

_____

_____

_____

Show Your Skill

8. Predict Outcomes What might happen if most citizens decided not to vote?

_____

_____

_____

_____

There are two forms of democracy. The first form is direct democracy. In a direct democracy, all citizens meet to debate government matters and vote on laws. Citizens take an active, direct role in the government. The city-state of ancient Athens had a direct democracy.

Most countries have too many people to have direct democracy today. Many countries follow a second form of democracy, called a representative democracy. The United States is a representative democracy, or republic. Citizens elect representatives to make laws and govern for them.

Citizens in Action

All citizens of the United States have certain duties and responsibilities. Duties are things we are required to do by law. Responsibilities are things we should do to help our community and country. We need to meet both our duties and responsibilities to support good government and protect our rights.

Americans have four basic duties:

- obey the law
- pay taxes
- defend the nation
- serve on juries

Responsibilities are voluntary, or done by choice. This makes them less clear than duties. People are not arrested or punished if they do not fulfill responsibilities. Probably your most important responsibility as a citizen will be to vote. Voting is the way a citizen uses his or her power to guide government. It is a way to show your opinion about the people who represent you. If you agree with what they are doing, you can vote for them. If you do not agree, you can vote for someone else.

The United States has a diverse population. People from many different racial, ethnic, and religious groups live together peacefully. Fortunately, most citizens share a set of core values. Sharing similar values helps make the United States a successful country.

These core beliefs include respect for the rights of each individual and appreciation for the contributions of all citizens. People also agree that each citizen is partly responsible for the success of his or her community, and that our representative democracy is the best form of government.

One way for students to be active citizens is through service learning. Service learning helps students do things that meet community needs. A common service-learning project is to help clean and fix up local parks. Some students help teach younger children to read. Other students share their time with older people.

Service learning means using your time and your talents to make a difference. You and your team help plan a project. You decide how to use your skills and talents to make it a success.

Many students are already taking part in service learning. Most states offer service-learning programs through their state education agency. If you look at the needs of your community, you can find a way to use your skills and talents to make a difference.

NGSSS Check In what ways are people involved as citizens? Include both duties and responsibilities in your answer. SS.8.C.1.5

_____

_____

_____

_____

Think Critically

9. **Synthesize** What do people learn through service learning?

_____

_____

_____

_____

_____

_____

This family is involved in a service-learning project.

CHAPTER 1

MY REFLECTIONS

ESSENTIAL QUESTIONS ***Why is history important? How does geography influence the way we live? Why do people make economic choices? What makes a responsible citizen?***

Reflect on What It Means . . .

Today's news is tomorrow's history. History isn't just something that happened long ago. It is happening right now! Research news stories that are currently happening in your community and the world. Think about how the news is connected to history, geography, and the economy. Write your own headlines in the grid below.

Today's News = Tomorrow's History

	Community News Story	World News Story
How does this news story relate to history?		
How does this news story relate to geography?		
How does this news story relate to the economy?		

Why It Matters To Me

Pick one of the headlines from your grid. Explain how today's headline could affect you in the future.

____

____

TAKE THE CHALLENGE

As a class, create your own news show about the news in your community. You may want to invite members of the community to be interviewed on your news show.

EXPLORING THE AMERICAS

 NGSSS

SS.8.A.1.7 View historic events through the eyes of those who were there as shown in their art, writings, music, and artifacts.

SS.8.A.2.1 Compare the relationships among the British, French, Spanish, and Dutch in their struggle for colonization of North America.

ESSENTIAL QUESTIONS *Why do people trade? What are the consequences when cultures interact?*

René Goulaine de Laudonnière led an attempt by France to colonize Florida in 1564. The French built Fort Caroline along the St. John's River. However, the Spanish wanted to drive the French out of Florida and attacked Fort Caroline.

"I encountered, by chance, a great company of Spaniards, which had already repulsed our men and were now entered, which drove me back unto the court of the fort . . . and, in the meanwhile, I saved myself . . . into the woods, where I found certain of my men . . . "

RENÉ GOULAINE DE LAUDONNIÈRE

Spaniards

What words do you know that are related to the word *Spaniards*?

_____

_____

McGraw-Hill
netw⊙rks™
There's More Online!

DBQ BREAKING IT DOWN

Laudonnière founded Fort Caroline in 1564. However, he was forced to flee with his men the next year, when Spanish troops attacked the fort. Based on Laudonnière's words, what happened at the fort?

_____

_____

PHOTO: Library of Congress Rare Book and Special Collections Division Washington, D.C[LC-USZ62-374]

THE GROWTH OF TRADE

NGSSS

SS.8.A.1.7 View historic events through the eyes of those who were there as shown in their art, writings, music, and artifacts.

SS.8.A.2.1 Compare the relationships among the British, French, Spanish, and Dutch in their struggle for colonization of North America.

SS.8.E.3.1 Evaluate domestic and international interdependence.

Essential Question
Why do people trade?

Guiding Questions
1. What advances in technology paved the way for European exploration?
2. Why was the Age of Exploration a major turning point in history?

Terms to Know

technology
the use of scientific knowledge for practical purposes

compass
navigation aid that shows the direction of magnetic north

circumnavigate
to go around completely

strait
a narrow water passage between larger bodies of water

Where in the World?

Routes of Early Explorers

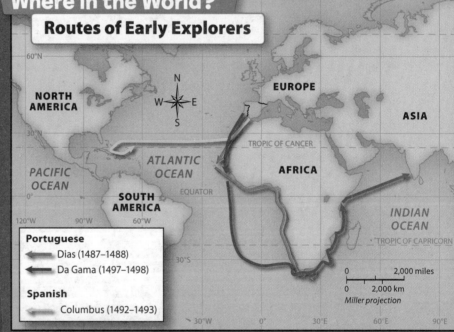

Portuguese
← Dias (1487–1488)
← Da Gama (1497–1498)

Spanish
← Columbus (1492–1493)

0   2,000 miles
0   2,000 km
Miller projection

When Did It Happen?

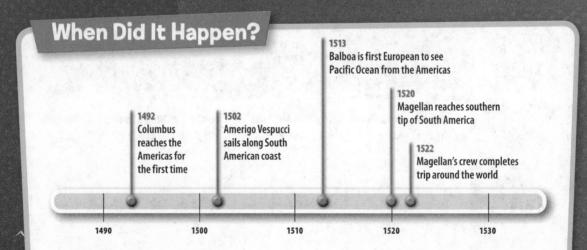

1513
Balboa is first European to see Pacific Ocean from the Americas

1520
Magellan reaches southern tip of South America

1492
Columbus reaches the Americas for the first time

1502
Amerigo Vespucci sails along South American coast

1522
Magellan's crew completes trip around the world

1490   1500   1510   1520   1530

Searching for New Trade Routes

During the 1400s, countries in Europe looked for a sea route to the Indies. The Indies are islands located to the southeast of Asia. The Indies provided spices that the Europeans wanted. Spices had three main uses:

- flavoring for food
- medicine
- a way to preserve food (Remember: There was no refrigeration.)

Early compass

Portuguese sailors were the first to find a new trade route. First, they sailed around the continent of Africa. Then they sailed to Asia. Christopher Columbus tried a different route. His plan was to sail west, across the Atlantic Ocean. He did not even know that North America and South America were there.

New **technology** made it possible for Columbus to make such a long trip. Technology is the use of scientific knowledge for practical purposes. There were new instruments for navigating, or finding the way. Examples are the **compass,** the astrolabe, and the quadrant. The compass was an instrument that shows the direction of magnetic north. There were also better maps. With these instruments and maps, sailors didn't need to see land to know where they were. Also, ships were faster and stronger.

Mark the Text

1. Underline the new technologies that aided navigation.

Take the Challenge

2. Write a speech to the people of Spain as if you are Queen Isabella. Tell your people why spending money on Columbus' voyage is a good idea.

Exploring the World

Queen Isabella of Spain agreed to pay for Columbus's expedition. She had two reasons for doing this:

- Columbus promised to bring Christianity to any lands he found.
- If Columbus found a sea route to the Indies, trade would increase. Spain would become very wealthy.

On August 3, 1492, Columbus set out from Spain. He had a crew of about 90 sailors. They had three ships, the Niña, the Pinta, and the larger *Santa María*. Columbus was captain of the Santa María. They sailed with a six-month supply of food and water. A little over two months later, on October 12, 1492, the ship's lookout saw land. The land he saw was in an island chain called the Bahamas. When Columbus went ashore, he claimed the island for Spain. He named it San Salvador.

Mark the Text

3. Chart Complete the chart. List facts about the achievements of Spanish explorers after Columbus.

Show Your Skill

4. Summarize What were three outcomes of Spanish exploration?

_____

_____

_____

_____

_____

_____

_____

_____

Columbus believed he had reached the East Indies. Maps of his day showed Europe, Asia, and Africa as one huge mass of land. The maps did not show North America or South America. Also, maps did not show the oceans as large as they were.

We now know that the place where Columbus came ashore was in the Caribbean islands. Columbus named the people he saw Indians, because he believed he was in the East Indies. When he returned to Spain, Spain's king and queen, Ferdinand and Isabella, received him with great honor. They agreed to pay for more voyages. He made three more trips: in 1493, in 1498, and in 1502. He explored the Caribbean Islands. These included what we now call Haiti, the Dominican Republic, Cuba, and Jamaica. He sailed along the coasts of Central America and South America. He made maps of the coastline of Central America.

Others followed Columbus. As a result of their voyages, the Spanish built an empire in the Americas. In 1502 Amerigo Vespucci (ves•POOH•chee) sailed along the coast of South America. He realized that South America was a separate continent. "America" is named for Amerigo Vespucci.

Vasco Núñez de Balboa explored Panama. In 1513 he saw the Pacific Ocean. He was the first European to see it from the Americas.

Ferdinand Magellan was a Portuguese sailor working for Spain. In 1520 he reached the southern tip of South America. He sailed through a **strait,** a narrow sea passage to another ocean. He noticed that the waters were very calm. *Pacifico* means peaceful in Spanish. Magellan named the ocean the Pacific. Magellan died on the journey, but his crew kept going and reached Spain in 1522. Magellan and his crew became the first people to **circumnavigate,** or sail around, the world.

Explorer	Achievement(s)

The exchange of plants and animals between the Americas and Europe was called the **Columbian Exchange.** It had a great effect on the world's cultures. The effects were both positive and negative. Exposure to new illnesses killed many people. Europeans were introduced to plants such as maize (corn) and potatoes. Rice, wheat, and bananas came to North America with the Europeans. Europeans also brought the first horses to North America.

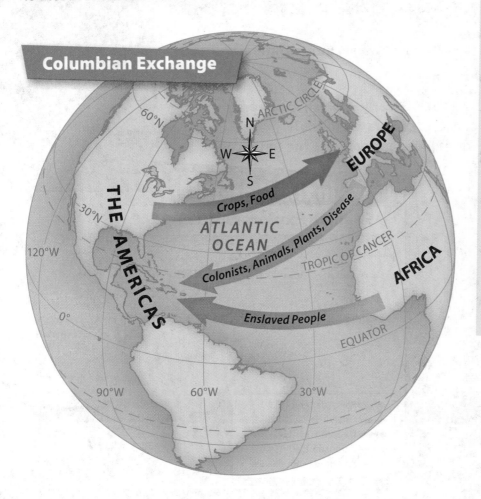

Columbian Exchange

Think Critically

5. Analyze Visuals Look at the diagram about the Columbian Exchange. What can you conclude about farming in the Americas?

_____

_____

_____

_____

_____

6. Identify Cause and Effect List at least two effects of the Columbian Exchange on life for Native Americans and Europeans.

_____

_____

_____

_____

NGSSS Check How were the goals of Spanish and Portuguese sailors the same in the 1400s? How were their routes different? SS.8.A.2.1

_____

_____

_____

_____

_____

NGSSS

SS.8.A.2.1 Compare the relationships among the British, French, Spanish, and Dutch in their struggle for colonization of North America.

SS.8.A.2.5 Discuss the impact of colonial settlement on Native American populations.

Essential Question

What are the consequences when cultures interact?

Guiding Questions

1. What were the goals of early Spanish explorers?
2. What led Spanish explorers to Florida?
3. Why did Spain explore and colonize the American Southwest?

Terms to Know

conquistador
Spanish explorer

immunity
resistance to a disease

mission
religious community made up of a small town, farmland, and a church

pueblo
town

presidio
military fort

plantation
large farm

Where in the World?

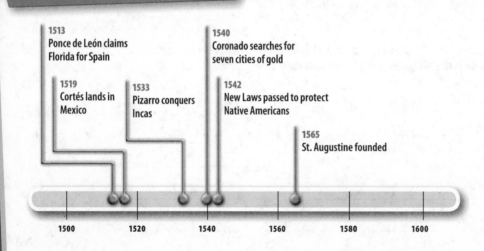

Spanish Explorers, 1513–1542

0   800 miles
0   800 km
Lambert Azimuthal
Equal-Area projection

PACIFIC OCEAN

NORTH AMERICA

ATLANTIC OCEAN

Ft. Caroline
St. Augustine

Gulf of Mexico

Caribbean Sea

CENTRAL AMERICA

SOUTH AMERICA

→ Ponce de León 1513
→ Cabeza de Vaca 1528–1536
→ De Soto 1539–1542
→ Coronado 1540–1542
— Present-day boundaries

When Did It Happen?

1513
Ponce de León claims Florida for Spain

1519
Cortés lands in Mexico

1533
Pizarro conquers Incas

1540
Coronado searches for seven cities of gold

1542
New Laws passed to protect Native Americans

1565
St. Augustine founded

1500   1520   1540   1560   1580   1600

European Explorers and Conquerors

Early Spanish explorers were known as **conquistadors,** or conquerors. Their main goal was to find riches. Spanish rulers gave them the right to explore and settle in the Americas. The conquistadors would give the rulers part of the wealth they found.

The Aztec empire, or kingdom, was in the area that is present-day Mexico. The Inca empire was in present-day Peru. Both these empires were very wealthy.

Hernán Cortés was a conquistador. He landed on the east coast of Mexico in 1519. He conquered the Aztec Empire by 1521. Cortés took the Aztecs' gold. He shipped great amounts of gold back to Spain. In 1533 conquistador Francisco Pizarro led an army into the Inca capital city, Cuzco. He killed the Inca leader and took control of the Inca Empire.

Spanish armies were much smaller than the Aztec or Inca armies. Still, they won. There were three main reasons for this:

Cause
The Spanish had weapons and animals that the Aztec and Inca had never seen, such as horses and large, dangerous dogs.

Cause
Some Native Americans did not like their Aztec rulers and helped the conquistadors to overthrow them.

Cause
The Native Americans did not have **immunity,** or protection, from diseases that the Spanish carried. Many became quite ill. They could not fight back well.

Effect
The conquistadors gained control over the Aztec and Inca Empires, and their wealth.

Copyright © by The McGraw-Hill Companies, Inc.

Show Your Skill

1. Cause and Effect Why were the Spanish able to conquer the Aztec Empire and the Inca Empire?

_____

_____

_____

_____

_____

_____

2. Identify Which Spanish conquistadors conquered the Aztec and Inca Empires?

Aztec Empire

_____

Inca Empire

_____

Mark the Text ✎

3. Number the major steps described in the text in the French attempt to set up Fort Caroline.

Spain in Florida

News of the riches that Cortés and Pizarro found spread in Europe. Other conquistadors came to explore the Americas. They searched in the southeastern and southwestern parts of North America.

Explorer	Year	Achievement
Juan Ponce de León	1513	• came ashore on Florida coast • gave Florida its name • claimed Florida for Spain • searched for the "Fountain of Youth" but did not find it
Pánfilo de Narváez	1528	• landed in Tampa Bay area • attacked by Apalachee Indians • forced to escape by sailing across Gulf of Mexico

France, too, realized that Florida was an important location. If the French controlled Florida, they could capture the riches from Spanish ships. In 1562 the French explorer Jean Ribault sailed to the St. Johns River, near present-day Jacksonville. He claimed Florida for France. In 1564 a group of French settlers arrived to set up a colony. They built a fort called Fort Caroline along the St. John's River.

King Felipe II of Spain decided that the French were trespassing on Spanish lands. He ordered the governor, Pedro Menéndez, to build a colony in Florida and drive out the French. On September 8, 1565, Menéndez set up a settlement. He called it San Agustin or St. Augustine. St. Augustine became the first permanent settlement in what would become the United States.

French ships sailed south from Fort Caroline to attack St. Augustine. The French ships ran into a hurricane. The hurricane destroyed many of their ships. Menéndez then sent soldiers to capture Fort Caroline. The Spanish victory stopped the French from trying to settle in Florida.

Menéndez established other settlements and Catholic **missions,** or religious communities. The missions were in what is today Florida, the Carolinas, and Virginia.

Ribault Monument near Jacksonville, Florida, marks the 1562 landing of Jean Ribault near the mouth of the St. Johns River.

Exploring the Southwest

Spanish conquistadors searched for quick riches. Their search took them to southwestern North America. One explorer was Álvar Núñez Cabeza de Vaca. He had been part of the expedition led by Pánfila de Narváez in 1528. After they were attacked, the few survivors sailed from Florida across the Gulf of Mexico. They landed in what is now Texas. De Vaca was one of the survivors. In 1533 he led an expedition across the Southwest. Then they headed for Mexico. When de Vaca arrived in 1536, he described seven cities of gold. Cabeza de Vaca's story inspired other explorers.

- **Hernando de Soto** led an expedition. For three years he and his men wandered throughout what is today the southeastern United States. During his expedition, he crossed the Mississippi River. He reached present-day Oklahoma.

- **Francisco Vásquez de Coronado** traveled through northern Mexico and present-day Arizona and New Mexico. He realized there was no gold there. Some members of Coronado's expedition traveled to the Colorado River. Then they reached what is now Kansas. They did not find gold.

El Adelantado Hernando de Soto.

Hernando de Soto

Francisco de Coronado

4. Identify Cause and Effect

What led Hernando de Soto and Francisco Vásquez de Coronado to explore what is now the southeastern and southwestern United States?

_____

_____

_____

_____

_____

_____

_____

Show Your Skill

5. Compare and Contrast

How were the explorations by Hernando de Soto and Francisco Vásquez de Coronado similar and how were they different?

_____

_____

_____

_____

_____

_____

_____

_____

_____

6. List Write the classes of society in New Spain, with highest at the top of the list.

_____

_____

_____

_____

_____

_____

The Spanish set up many settlements in the lands they explored. Settlements were either **pueblos, missions,** or **presidios.**

Types of Spanish Settlements	
pueblo	town, trading center
mission	religious community, including a small town, surrounding farmland, and a church; the goal of the mission was to spread the Catholic religion and the Spanish way of life among the Native Americans.
presidio	fort, usually built near a mission

There were different classes in Spain's empire. The people born in Spain, called _peninsulares_, were the top class of society. They owned land and ran the government. They served in the Catholic Church. Below them were the creoles. They were born in America to Spanish parents. Below them were the mestizos (meh•STEE•zohs). They had one Spanish parent and one Native American parent. Below them were Native Americans. At the bottom were enslaved Africans.

The conquistadors could demand taxes or labor from the Native Americans. Therefore, they also became slaves to the Spanish. A Spanish priest, Bartolomé de Las Casas, helped to convince the Spanish government to pass the New Laws in 1542. These laws made it illegal to enslave Native Americans.

Some Spanish settlers had **plantations,** or large farms. They shipped crops and raw materials to Spain. They made a lot of money.

By the 1600s, the Spanish controlled most of Mexico, the Caribbean, and Central and South America. They also controlled parts of the present-day United States. Other European powers were trying to set up colonies in North America. They included England, France and the Netherlands.

To defend its empire, Spain settled present-day New Mexico, Arizona, and Texas. France claimed land around the mouth of the Mississippi River.

NGSSS Check Compare the efforts of the French and Spanish to control Florida. SS.8.A.2.1

_____

_____

_____

_____

_____

3 COMPETING FOR COLONIES

NGSSS

SS.8.A.2.1 Compare the relationships among the British, French, Spanish, and Dutch in their struggle for colonization of North America.

SS.8.A.2.5 Discuss the impact of colonial settlement on Native American populations.

Essential Question
What are the consequences when cultures interact?

Guiding Questions
1. What were the religious motives behind the Age of Exploration?
2. How did French and Dutch settlements compare to the Spanish colonies?

Terms to Know

Protestantism
a form of Christianity that was in opposition to the Catholic Church

Reformation
sixteenth-century religious movement rejecting some Roman Catholic teachings and establishing the Protestant churches

armada
a war fleet

northwest passage
a direct water route to Asia through the Americas

tenant farmer
settler who worked for a landlord and paid him rent

Where in the World?

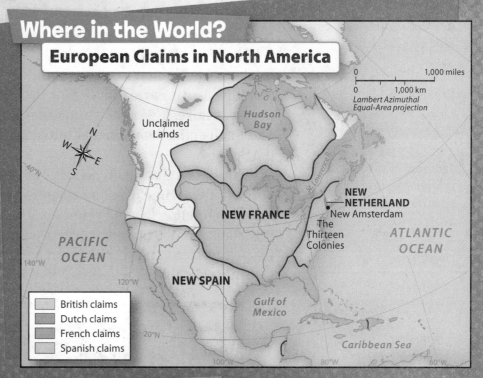

European Claims in North America

Legend:
- British claims
- Dutch claims
- French claims
- Spanish claims

When Did It Happen?

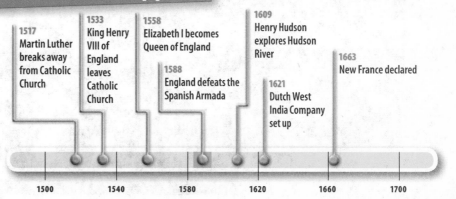

1517 Martin Luther breaks away from Catholic Church

1533 King Henry VIII of England leaves Catholic Church

1558 Elizabeth I becomes Queen of England

1588 England defeats the Spanish Armada

1609 Henry Hudson explores Hudson River

1621 Dutch West India Company set up

1663 New France declared

1500   1540   1580   1620   1660   1700

Show Your Skill

1. Cause and Effect What started the Protestant Reformation? What was the result of that action?

_____

_____

_____

_____

Think Critically

2. Identify Cause and Effect What was one major cause of conflict between England and Spain in the 1500s?

_____

_____

Show Your Skill

3. Sequence What happened right before the English started to set up colonies in North America?

_____

_____

_____

Religious Rivalries

Part of the purpose of exploring the Americas was to spread the Christian religion there. The first explorers were Roman Catholics.

In 1517 a new form of Christianity began. It opposed the Catholic Church. It was called **Protestantism.**

Protestantism started with Martin Luther, a German priest. Luther did not agree with many Church practices. In 1517 he broke away from the Church. His actions led to the **Reformation.** This religious movement took hold in many parts of Europe. It rejected some Catholic teachings and practices. It changed others.

Another important change took place in 1533. That year, King Henry VIII of England left the Catholic Church. His daughter ruled later as Queen Elizabeth I. During her rule, England became a Protestant nation.

The king of Spain, a Catholic, saw a chance to invade England. He wanted to wipe out the Protestant religion there. The king sent an **armada,** or war fleet, to attack England. The fleet was huge. It was the strongest naval force in the world. The English fleet was smaller but faster. The British defeated the Spanish.

This meant that Spain no longer ruled the seas. The English decided it was time to set up colonies in North America. English and Dutch settlers were Protestant. They set up colonies along the Atlantic coast. Spanish settlers were Catholic. They settled in southwestern and southeastern North America. The French were also Catholic. They settled in the northeast.

Even though the Spanish Armada was very large, the British were able to defeat the Spanish attempt to invade England.

Explorers mapped the coast of North America. They set up colonies and traded with the Native Americans. Explorers also wanted to discover a direct water route through the Americas to Asia. They called this the **northwest passage.** Many explorers looked for it and found other things in the process.

Searching for the Northwest Passage			
Explorer	Sailed For	Year	Found Instead
John Cabot	England	1497	Probably present-day Newfoundland
Giovanni de Verrazano	France	1524	Explored coast of North America from Nova Scotia to the Carolinas
Jacques Cartier (KAR·tyay)	France	1535	Sailed up St. Lawrence River, named the mountain that is the site of present-day Montreal
Henry Hudson	Netherlands	1609	Discovered Hudson River, sailed as far north as Albany. On his next voyage he discovered Hudson Bay.

French and Dutch Settlements

At first, the French were mainly interested in the rich natural resources of North America. They fished and trapped animals for their fur. French trappers and missionaries went far inland into North America. They traded with Native Americans. They built forts and trading posts. They generally treated the Native Americans with more respect than Spanish settlers did.

In 1663 New France became a colony. New France was made up of estates along the St. Lawrence River. Those who owned estates received land in exchange for bringing settlers. The settlers were known as **tenant farmers.** They paid rent to the estate owner. They also worked for him a set number of days each year.

French explorers gradually explored the Mississippi River. They traveled west to the Rocky Mountains and southwest to the Rio Grande. This led to New France claiming that entire territory.

Copyright © by The McGraw-Hill Companies, Inc.

Think Critically

4. Draw Conclusions Why might nations want to find a northwest passage?

_____

_____

Mark the Text

5. Chart Circle the countries in the chart that sent explorers to find a northwest passage to Asia.

Show Your Skill

6. Identify What were France's main interests in North America?

_____

_____

_____

Think Critically

7. Summarize How did the French turn the search for a northwest passage into a large landholding in North America?

_____

_____

_____

_____

_____

_____

Exploration of the Mississippi River

Marquette and Joliet
(1670s)

Fur trader Louis Joliet and priest Jacques Marquette explored the Mississippi River. They traveled by canoe until they realized the river flowed south into the Gulf of Mexico, not west to Asia.

Robert Cavelier de La Salle
(1669–1687)

De La Salle also traveled the Mississippi. He went all the way to the Gulf of Mexico and claimed the whole region for France. He called it Louisiana, after France's king, Louis XIV.

New Orleans established
(1718)

The French governor established a port where the Mississippi River meets the Gulf of Mexico. He named it New Orleans.

Think Critically

8. Compare and Contrast How were the efforts of France and the Netherlands similar and different?

_____

_____

_____

_____

_____

_____

_____

The Netherlands was a small country in Europe. It had few natural resources and a limited amount of farmland. The Dutch were the people of the Netherlands. They were attracted by the vast lands and natural resources of North America. They already had a large fleet of trading ships. They sailed all over the world. In 1621 the Netherlands set up the Dutch West India Company. Its purpose was to run trade for the Netherlands between the Americas and Africa. In 1623 this company took control of the country's North American colony, New Netherland.

The center of New Netherland was New Amsterdam. New Amsterdam was located on the tip of Manhattan Island, where the Hudson River enters New York Harbor. Governor Peter Minuit purchased the land from the Native American Manhattoes people in 1626.

 NGSSS Check What were the major North American settlement areas and explorers for each of the countries in the chart? Complete the chart with what you know. SS.8.A.2.1

	Settlement Areas	Major Explorers
England		
Spain		
France		
Netherlands		

ESSENTIAL QUESTIONS *Why do people trade? What are the consequences when cultures interact?*

Reflect on What It Means . . .

Evidence of European exploration in Florida can still be seen today. Have you visited any historic sites in your state? Use the Internet as well as what you know about Florida to research some locations that you have visited or would like to visit. Mark those locations on the map. Illustrate the map with other historic details. Be sure to include a map key as well.

To Me and My Community

Choose a historical location in your neighborhood, town, or county. Research that location and add a label to your map explaining why the location is important.

Map Key

Keep Going!

To the World

Create a historical marker to honor a place where a nation tried to colonize Florida. Include the name of the place, the country that established the colony, and some information that would be useful to a visitor.

TAKE THE CHALLENGE

As a class, make a 3-dimensional model of the state of Florida. Add historical markers that date from the colonial period, along with labels explaining the history of each marker.

CHAPTER 3

COLONIAL AMERICA

NGSSS

SS.8.A.2.4 Identify the impact of key colonial figures on the economic, political, and social development of the colonies.

ESSENTIAL QUESTIONS *How does geography influence the way people live? How do new ideas change the way people live?*

Master George Percy was 27 years old when he helped establish the Jamestown colony in 1607. Many years later, he served as the colony's governor.

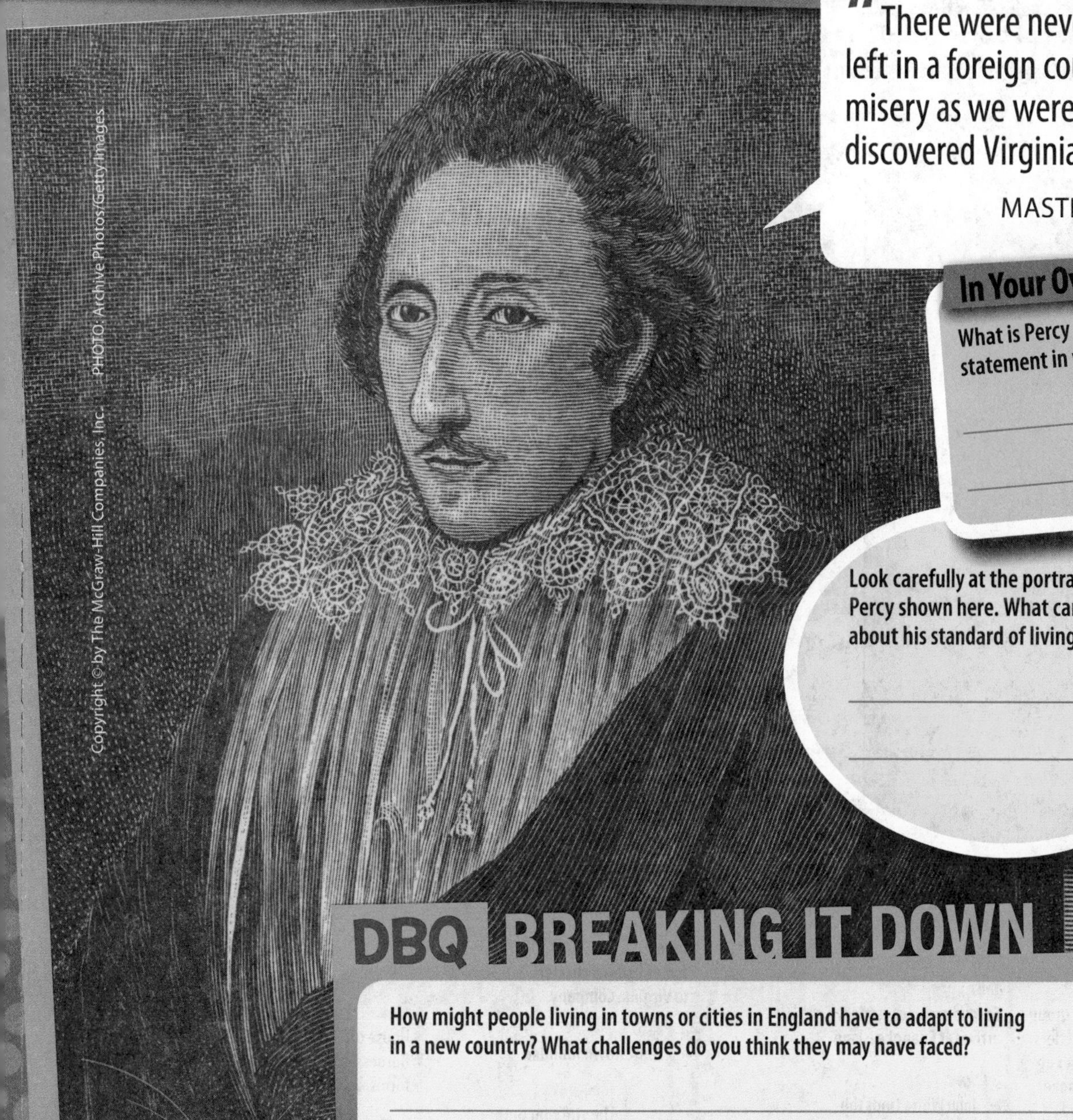

Copyright © by The McGraw-Hill Companies, Inc.   PHOTO: Archive Photos/Getty Images

" There were never Englishmen left in a foreign country in such misery as we were in this new-discovered Virginia. "

MASTER GEORGE PERCY

In Your Own Words

What is Percy trying to say? Rewrite his statement in your own words below.

_____

_____

_____

Look carefully at the portrait of Percy shown here. What can you tell about his standard of living?

_____

_____

DBQ BREAKING IT DOWN

How might people living in towns or cities in England have to adapt to living in a new country? What challenges do you think they may have faced?

_____

_____

_____

ROANOKE AND JAMESTOWN

NGSSS

SS.8.A.2.4 Identify the impact of key colonial figures on the economic, political, and social development of the colonies.

SS.8.A.2.7 Describe the contributions of key groups (Africans, Native Americans, women, and children) to the society and culture of colonial America.

Essential Question
How does geography influence the way people live?

Guiding Questions
1. What problems did the Roanoke settlers encounter?
2. Why did the Jamestown settlement succeed?

Terms to Know

charter
a document granting the recipient the right to settle a colony

joint-stock company
a company in which investors buy stock in the company in return for a share of its future profits

headright
a 50-acre grant of land given to colonial settlers who paid their own way

burgess
an elected representative to an assembly

Where in the World?

Western Northern Hemisphere

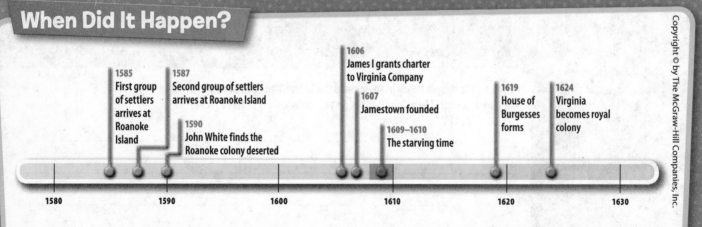

When Did It Happen?

1585 First group of settlers arrives at Roanoke Island

1587 Second group of settlers arrives at Roanoke Island

1590 John White finds the Roanoke colony deserted

1606 James I grants charter to Virginia Company

1607 Jamestown founded

1609–1610 The starving time

1619 House of Burgesses forms

1624 Virginia becomes royal colony

1580 — 1590 — 1600 — 1610 — 1620 — 1630

The Mystery of Roanoke

England wanted to settle people on land it claimed in North America. England's Queen Elizabeth gave Sir Walter Raleigh the right to start a colony there. Raleigh sent scouts to find a good place for the colony. They said Roanoke Island would be a good place. Roanoke Island is just off the coast of what is now North Carolina. The first settlers arrived in 1585. They had a difficult winter. As a result, they decided to return to England.

Raleigh sent settlers to Roanoke Island again in 1587. The leader of this group was John White. His daughter went with him. She soon had a baby named Virginia Dare. Virginia Dare was the first English child born in North America.

People Involved with Roanoke Colony	
Person	**Contribution**
Queen Elizabeth	
Sir Walter Raleigh	
John White	
Virginia Dare	

The colony needed supplies, so White returned to England to get them. He did not come right back, though. England was fighting a war with Spain and all the ships were used in the war. It took three years for White to get back to Roanoke Island.

When White arrived back at Roanoke Island, all the settlers were gone. What happened to them? The only clue was a word carved on a tree trunk. The word was *Croatoan*. That may have meant the settlers went to Croatoan Island. However, no one knows for sure because the settlers were never seen again.

Show Your Skill

1. Classify Information
Complete the chart about Roanoke.

Mark the Text

2. Circle the date the second group of settlers went to Roanoke Island. Who led that group?

_____

Show Your Skill

3. Identify Cause and Effect
Why did White return to England? Why did he not come right back?

_____

_____

_____

_____

Think Critically

4. Hypothesize What do you think happened to the colonists who disappeared from Roanoke?

_____

_____

_____

_____

_____

5. Explain Why did the English decide to settle in Roanoke?

_____

_____

_____

_____

The fort at Jamestown was built in a triangle with circular watchtowers in each of the three points.

PHOTO: MPI/Stringer/Archive Photos/Getty Images

Mark the Text

6. Underline the sentence that tells what a charter is. What company received a charter?

_____

_____

Think Critically

7. Analyze How did the Virginia Company hope its colony would make money?

_____

_____

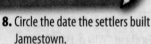

Mark the Text

8. Circle the date the settlers built Jamestown.

Success at Jamestown

The Roanoke Colony failed. However, England still wanted a colony in North America, so it decided to try again.

England had a new king, James I. He gave a business a "charter" to start a colony. A **charter** is a document that gives someone the right to start a colony. The name of the business that received the charter was the Virginia Company.

The Virginia Company was a **joint-stock company.** This meant that many people each owned a small part of the company. If the company made money, each owner would get part of the money the company made.

The people who each owned stock, or small parts, of the Virginia Company, wanted to make money. They hoped that a colony in North America would make money for the company. How? They thought the colonists would find gold, or collect and sell furs and fish.

The Virginia Company sent 144 settlers to North America. They sailed from England, across the Atlantic Ocean, and to the coast of North America. They sailed up a river and on its bank built a tiny town in 1607. They named the river the James River. They named their town Jamestown. Both names were to honor King James.

Copyright © by The McGraw-Hill Companies, Inc.

46   Chapter 3   *Colonial America*

Life was difficult in Jamestown. The colonists suffered from disease and hunger. Captain John Smith forced the settlers to work. He also made friends with the local people. They were Native Americans called the Powhatan. Their chief was also named Powhatan. He gave the colonists food and helped them survive.

Then, things got worse. The colonists and the Powhatan stopped getting along. Powhatan stopped giving the colonists food. The winter of 1609–1610 was called "the starving time." Many colonists died.

But soon after that, new colonists arrived. The colony started to do well again. The colonists started growing and selling tobacco. This made money for the owners of the Virginia Company. The relationship between the Powhatan and the colonists improved as well. A colonist named John Rolfe married a Powhatan woman. Her name was Pocahontas. She was the chief's daughter.

The Virginia Company wanted even more settlers to go to Virginia. They gave 50 acres of land free to each new settler who would go there. This land grant was called a **headright.** The headright system brought many new settlers.

Show Your Skill

9. **Make Inferences** Complete the chart to show how each event contributed to the success of Jamestown.

Mark the Text

10. Underline the sentences that explain the term *headright*.

Take the Challenge

11. Learn more about the Jamestown Rediscovery Archaeological Project. Create a simple 3-column chart that shows some of the artifacts discovered there. In the first column, write the name of the artifacts. In the middle column, describe how the artifact was used. In the final column, draw a picture of the artifact.

Reasons for Jamestown's Success	
Reason	**Why It Helped**
Leadership of Captain John Smith	
John Rolfe married Pocahontas	
Tobacco crops were planted and sold	
Headright system established	
Help from Powhatan	

12. Identify the Main Idea
What was the purpose of the burgesses? How were they chosen?

_____

_____

_____

13. Make a Connection Research to learn who represents your area in both the Florida Legislature as well as in the U.S. Senate and U.S. House of Representatives.

_____

_____

_____

_____

_____

_____

At first, the Virginia Company and the leaders it appointed made the rules for the colonists. In 1619 the company began letting the colonists make some of the rules themselves. It allowed them to choose representatives called **burgesses** to make the rules for them. These representatives met in a group called the House of Burgesses. The House of Burgesses was the first legislature in North America to be elected by the people.

Complete the Venn diagram. In each circle, list words and short phrases about each to compare the colonies.

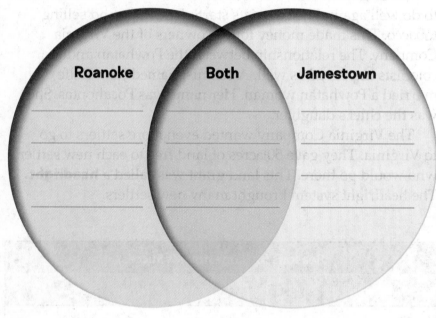

Roanoke   Both   Jamestown

NGSSS Check What role did Powhatan have in the survival of the colony at Jamestown? How did his role change over time? SS.8.A.2.7

_____

_____

_____

How did the governing of Jamestown change from when it was first established?

_____

_____

_____

_____

2 THE NEW ENGLAND COLONIES

NGSSS

SS.8.A.2.2 Compare the characteristics of the New England, Middle, and Southern colonies.

SS.8.A.2.4 Identify the impact of key colonial figures on the economic, political, and social development of the colonies.

SS.8.A.2.5 Discuss the impact of colonial settlement on Native American populations.

Essential Question
How do new ideas influence the way people live?

Guiding Questions
1. Why did the Puritans settle in North America?
2. What role did religion play in founding the various colonies?

Terms to Know

dissent
to disagree with or oppose an opinion

persecute
to mistreat a person or group on the basis of their beliefs

tolerance
the ability to accept or put up with different views or behaviors

Where in the World?

New England Colonies

New Hampshire
Mass.
Connecticut
Rhode Island

When Did It Happen?

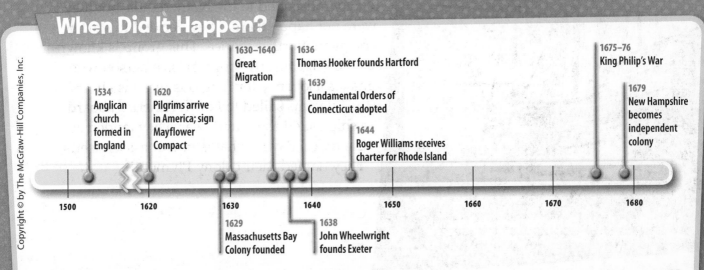

1534 Anglican church formed in England

1620 Pilgrims arrive in America; sign Mayflower Compact

1629 Massachusetts Bay Colony founded

1630–1640 Great Migration

1636 Thomas Hooker founds Hartford

1638 John Wheelwright founds Exeter

1639 Fundamental Orders of Connecticut adopted

1644 Roger Williams receives charter for Rhode Island

1675–76 King Philip's War

1679 New Hampshire becomes independent colony

1500 1620 1630 1640 1650 1660 1670 1680

PHOTO: Kenneth Wiedemann/E+/Getty Images   Copyright © by The McGraw-Hill Companies, Inc.

Mark the Text

1. Underline the sentences that tell the location of the colony of Plymouth.

Show Your Skill

2. **Interpret Information** Write a sentence about the pilgrims that uses the word *dissent*.

_____

_____

_____

Seeking Religious Freedom

Many English settlers came to North America to have religious freedom. In England, the main church was the official Anglican Church. The Anglican Church was a Protestant church. Many people who were Catholic did not want to practice the Anglican religion. Even many Protestants were unhappy with the Anglican Church. They **dissented,** or disagreed with, what the church was doing. Members of the Anglican Church who wanted to change or "purify" it were called Puritans. Persons who wanted to leave the Anglican Church, or separate from it, were called Separatists.

English Religious Groups in 1600s	
Anglicans	members of the Anglican Church
Puritans	wanted to change the Anglican Church
Separatists	wanted to separate from the Anglican Church
Catholics	members of the Roman Catholic Church

The Separatists were **persecuted,** or mistreated because of their beliefs. One group of Separatists fled to the Netherlands, but they were not happy there. They decided to start a colony in North America. This group is known as the Pilgrims. (A "pilgrim" is a person who makes a journey for religious reasons.) In 1620 the Pilgrims sailed to North America aboard a ship called the Mayflower. They landed at Cape Cod Bay in what is now Massachusetts. They named their colony Plymouth.

This replica of the Mayflower was built in England and sailed to Plymouth, Massachusetts in 1957.

Before they went ashore, the Pilgrims signed an agreement to govern themselves. The agreement was called the Mayflower Compact. By signing it, they all agreed in advance to obey whatever laws they passed for their colony. The Mayflower Compact was an important step in the development of democratic government.

The people of Plymouth governed themselves for 70 years. Later, Plymouth became part of a nearby colony called Massachusetts. Why was it called the Mayflower Compact? The Pilgrims named their document the Mayflower Compact because they were on their ship the Mayflower when they signed it. Compact means "an agreement." So the Mayflower Compact was an agreement signed on board the Mayflower.

Mark the Text

3. Underline the sentence that tells why the Mayflower Compact was important.

Show Your Skill

4. Graphic Organizer
Use the space on the graphic organizer to add details about the Plymouth Colony.

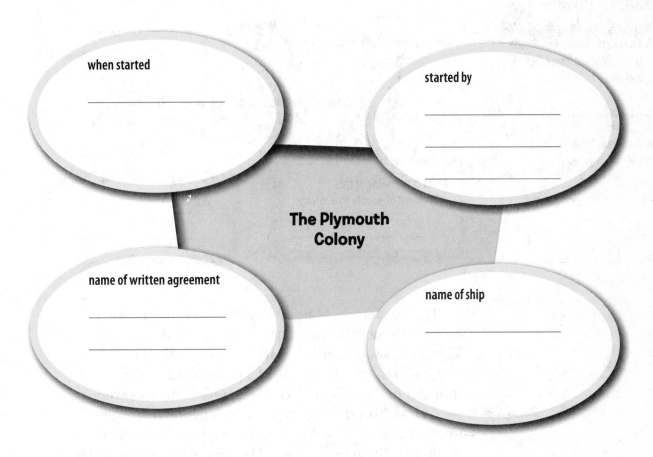

when started
_____

started by
_____
_____

The Plymouth Colony

name of written agreement
_____
_____

name of ship
_____

At first life was very difficult in the Plymouth colony. Nearly half of the colonists died during the first winter. Then, in the spring, two Native Americans befriended the Pilgrims: Squanto and Samoset. They showed the Pilgrims how to grow corn and other crops and where to hunt and fish. The Pilgrims might not have survived without their help. Squanto and Samoset also helped the Pilgrims gain acceptance by other Native Americans who lived nearby. In the fall of 1621, they all celebrated together in a great feast of thanksgiving.

Mark the Text

6. Underline the sentence that tells the name of America's first written constitution.

Think Critically

7. Contrast What made Rhode Island different from other colonies?

_____

_____

8. Analyze What did these colonies have in common?

_____

_____

_____

New Colonies

In 1629 another colony was established nearby. This was the Massachusetts Bay Colony. It was founded by Puritans. The leader of the colony was John Winthrop.

In the 1630s, more than 15,000 Puritans left England to settle in Massachusetts. They were escaping persecution and bad economic times. This movement of people is known as the Great Migration (*migration* means "movement").

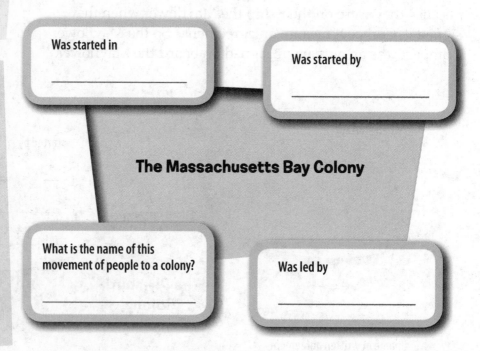

Was started in

_____

Was started by

_____

The Massachusetts Bay Colony

What is the name of this movement of people to a colony?

_____

Was led by

_____

The Puritans in Massachusetts had no **tolerance,** or acceptance, of different beliefs. This resulted in people leaving Massachusetts to start their own colonies.

One man who helped start a new colony was a minister named Thomas Hooker. He and his followers left Massachusetts to form a new colony in what is now Connecticut. In 1639 they wrote out a plan for government. It was called the Fundamental Orders of Connecticut. The Fundamental Orders of Connecticut was the first written constitution, or written plan of government, in America.

Another man who helped start a new colony was a minister named Roger Williams. He believed in religious freedom. He also believed in treating Native Americans fairly. So the Puritans expelled him from Massachusetts. He started the colony of Rhode Island in 1644. Rhode Island was the first place in America where people of all faiths could worship freely.

In 1638 John Wheelwright also left Massachusetts with a group of religious dissenters. He led them north and founded the town of Exeter in New Hampshire. New Hampshire became an independent colony in 1679.

Show Your Skill

9. Chart Use the space on the chart to organize what you learn about Connecticut, Rhode Island, and New Hampshire.

Connecticut, Rhode Island, and New Hampshire			
	Connecticut	**Rhode Island**	**New Hampshire**
Founded in year . . .			
by founder . . .			
who left . . .			
in search of . . .			

Think Critically

10. Interpret What was the cause of King Philip's War?

_____

_____

_____

Show Your Skill

11. Analyze Which colony let people of all faiths worship freely?

_____

Gradually the colonists created settlements throughout New England. The settlers and Native American peoples traded with each other. Sometimes conflicts arose. Usually, it was because settlers moved onto Native American lands without permission.

In 1675 the Wampanoag leader Metacomet waged war against settlers in Massachusetts, Connecticut, and Rhode Island. He got other Indian groups to help. The settlers called Metacomet "King Philip," so the war became known as King Philip's war. Hundreds of Native Americans and colonists died. In the end, the colonists won the war. They expanded their colonies and took even more land.

Take the Challenge

12. Sketch a map of the New England colonies that were described in this lesson. Use a map from your textbook as reference. Use colored pencils or markers to illustrate the map in order to show differences between the colonies, including their origin and the date they were established.

NGSSS Check How did fighting between colonists and the Wampanoag during King Philip's War change life for Native Americans in that area? **SS.8.A.2.5**

_____

_____

_____

THE MIDDLE COLONIES

NGSSS

S.8.A.2.2 Compare the characteristics of the New England, Middle, and Southern colonies.

SS.8.A.2.4 Identify the impact of key colonial figures on the economic, political, and social development of the colonies.

SS.8.A.2.5 Discuss the impact of colonial settlement on Native American populations.

SS.8.G.1.2 Use appropriate geographic tools and terms to identify and describe significant places and regions in American history.

Essential Question
How does geography influence the way people live?

Guiding Questions
1. Why did the Middle Colonies grow?
2. How did Pennsylvania differ from the other English colonies?

Terms to Know

patroon
landowner in the Dutch colonies who ruled over large areas of land

pacifist
a person opposed to the use of war or violence to settle disputes

Where in the World?

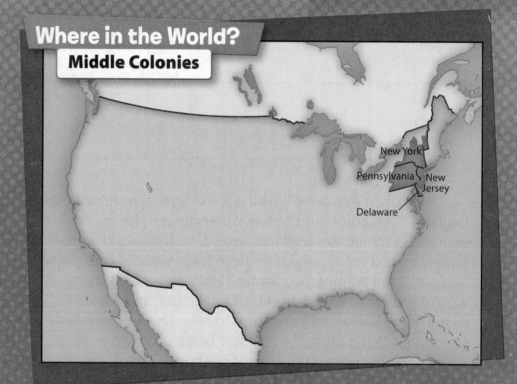

Middle Colonies

New York
Pennsylvania
New Jersey
Delaware

When Did It Happen?

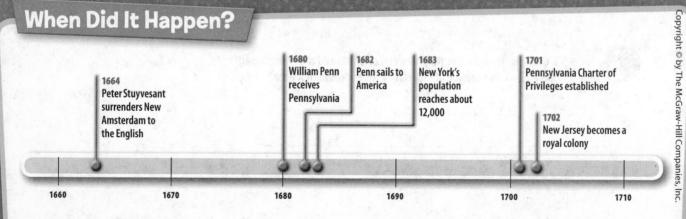

1664 Peter Stuyvesant surrenders New Amsterdam to the English

1680 William Penn receives Pennsylvania

1682 Penn sails to America

1683 New York's population reaches about 12,000

1701 Pennsylvania Charter of Privileges established

1702 New Jersey becomes a royal colony

1660   1670   1680   1690   1700   1710

New York and New Jersey

The Middle Colonies were the colonies located between New England and the Virginia colonies in the middle of the east coast of North America. Land was at first settled and controlled by the European country known as the Netherlands. The colony was called New Netherland.

The most important settlement in New Netherland was New Amsterdam. It was located at the mouth of the Hudson River. The Hudson River was a major transportation route inland. New Amsterdam was a center of shipping to and from the Americas. It was a major port.

The Dutch wanted more people to move to their colony of New Netherland. To get people to move there, they gave away land. The land giveaway worked like this: If someone could bring at least 50 new settlers to New Netherland, the Dutch would give that person a lot of free land. Not only that, but that person would get to rule the land and the settlers like a king. The landowners who got land this way were called **patroons.** Settlers were required to work for the patroon and share their crops with him.

1. Explain Why is it beneficial for a port to be situated both at the mouth of a river as well as on an ocean coast?

_____

_____

_____

2. Analyze What was the purpose of the patroon system?

_____

_____

_____

_____

The Middle Colonies had rich farmland.

Mark the Text

3. Underline the sentence that explains why New Jersey did not develop a major port.

Take the Challenge

4. You have fifteen seconds to convince a leader in England that acquiring New Netherland and New Amsterdam would help the economy of England. What will you say?

New Netherland and New Amsterdam were very successful. The English saw the success of the colony too. They wanted to take over New Netherland so they could control the valuable colony and its resources. In 1664, the English sent warships to attack New Amsterdam. The Dutch governor, Peter Stuyvesant, surrendered without a fight.

England's king gave the newly captured colony to his brother, the Duke of York. The duke changed the name of the colony from New Netherland to New York. New Amsterdam became New York City.

Dutch Control	England Takes Over	English Control
New Netherland	becomes	New York
New Amsterdam	becomes	New York City

Before long, the Duke of York decided to divide his colony. He gave part of the land to other nobles. This land became the colony of New Jersey. Unlike New York, New Jersey did not develop a major port. New Jersey had no natural harbors. Both New York and New Jersey had diverse populations. There were people of many different racial, religious, and national backgrounds in each colony.

Residents of New Amsterdam plead with Stuyvesant not to fire on the British ships in the harbor.

Pennsylvania and Delaware

The colony of Pennsylvania was founded by Quakers. The Quakers were a Protestant religious group who had been mistreated in England. They believed that everyone was equal. They were also **pacifists.** Pacifists are people who refuse to use force or fight in wars. Welsh, Irish, Dutch, and German settlers also came to Pennsylvania.

The owner of the colony was named William Penn. (In fact, the name *Pennsylvania* means "Penn's Woods.") Penn founded his colony to put his Quaker ideas into practice.

He designed the colony's main town of Philadelphia. The name means "city of brotherly love." What really makes Penn stand out is the way he treated Native Americans. Instead of just taking their land, he paid them for it. As a result, Pennsylvania had better relations with Native Americans than many other colonies.

Penn wrote Pennsylvania's constitution and he took an active role in governing his colony. In 1701, Penn issued the Charter of Privileges. This document gave the colonists the right to elect representatives to a legislature, or lawmaking body. The Charter of Privileges was important because it was another step in establishing democracy in America.

When the colonists got the right to elect people to make their laws, some colonists in southern Pennsylvania wanted to have their own legislature. Many of these colonists were from Sweden, which had started a colony there years before. Penn let these colonists have their own legislature. Eventually this region became a separate colony named Delaware.

 NGSSS Check Name two colonies that were formed from parts of other colonies and the colony from which each was formed. SS.8.A.2.2

_____

_____

Name two groups of people, besides the English, who lived in the Middle Colonies. SS.8.A.2.2

_____

_____

5. Underline the definition of pacifist. What religious group practiced pacifism?

_____

Show Your Skill

6. **Identify Cause and Effect** What was one reason Pennsylvania had a better relationship with the Native Americans?

_____

_____

_____

_____

_____

Think Critically

7. **Explain** What does a legislature do?

_____

8. **Summarize** What was William Penn's main reason for founding Pennsylvania?

_____

_____

_____

LESSON 4

THE SOUTHERN COLONIES

NGSSS

SS.8.A.2.2 Compare the characteristics of the New England, Middle, and Southern colonies.

SS.8.A.2.3 Differentiate economic systems of New England, Middle and Southern colonies including indentured servants and slaves as labor sources.

SS.8.A.2.4 Identify the impact of key colonial figures on the economic, political, and social development of the colonies

SS.8.A.2.7 Describe the contributions of key groups (Africans, Native Americans, women, and children) to the society and culture of colonial America.

Essential Question

How does geography influence the way people live?

Guiding Questions

1. What problems faced Maryland and Virginia?
2. What factors contributed to the growth of the Carolinas?

Terms to Know

indentured servant
laborer who agreed to work without pay for a certain period of time in exchange for passage to America

constitution
a written plan of government; a set of fundamental laws to support a government

debtor
person or country that owes money

Where in the World?

Southern Colonies

Maryland

Virginia · Jamestown

North Carolina

Georgia

South Carolina

When Did It Happen?

1607 Jamestown founded

1619 First enslaved Africans arrive in North America

1634 Founders of Maryland reach North America

1649 Maryland's Act of Toleration passed

1676 Bacon's Rebellion

1729 Carolina splits into North Carolina and South Carolina

1733 Georgia founded

1600　1620　1640　1660　1680　1700　1720　1740

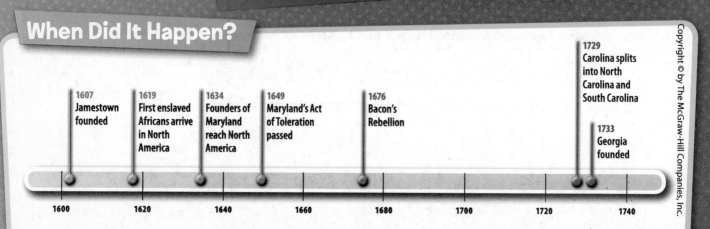

Virginia and Maryland

Jamestown was settled in 1607. Over the years, it grew into a larger colony: the Virginia Colony. Many Virginia colonists made their living by growing tobacco. It took a lot of workers to plant, take care of, and harvest this crop. Many landowners forced enslaved Africans to do this work. The first Africans arrived in Virginia in 1619.

Some workers were slaves. Many others were **indentured servants.** These were people who agreed to work for a certain number of years for no pay. In exchange, their employers paid for their voyage to the colony. Indentured servants got that name because the work agreement they signed had two parts that were divided by an *indented,* or jagged line.

In 1634 a new colony, called Maryland, began north of Virginia. Maryland was the dream of Sir George Calvert, Lord Baltimore. He wanted to found a colony where Catholics could practice their religion freely. At this time, Catholics in England were persecuted. Calvert's son, Cecilius, worked to start the colony.

Cecilius offered free land to settlers who would come to Maryland. Upper class Englishmen were given large amounts of land. Average colonists were given less land. As in Virginia, wealthy landowners used slaves and indentured servants to do the work.

Tobacco was an important crop in the colonies since Jamestown in the early 1600s. It is still grown in many Southern states today.

Think Critically

1. **Analyze** Why might a person agree to become an indentured servant and work for no pay?

_____

_____

_____

_____

_____

Show Your Skill

2. **Compare and Contrast** How was indentured service different from slavery?

_____

_____

_____

_____

_____

Mark the Text

3. Underline the sentence that tells why Maryland was founded.

Think Critically

4. **Infer** What was the law that granted religious freedom in Maryland? Why might this law have been important to the settlement of the colony?

_____

_____

_____

_____

_____

_____

Show Your Skill

5. Identify Cause and Effect
What was one effect of the tensions over the location of the boundary between Maryland and Pennsylvania?

_____

_____

Think Critically

6. Explain Why was Bacon's Rebellion important?

_____

_____

_____

Show Your Skill

7. Draw Conclusions Why did Nathaniel Bacon oppose the colonial government?

_____

_____

_____

_____

Take the Challenge

8. You are a reporter. What questions would you ask Nathaniel Bacon? Write three questions for him and exchange them with a classmate. Answer each other's questions.

Before long, there were more Protestants than Catholics living in Maryland. To protect the Catholics' religious freedom, the colony passed the Act of Toleration in 1649. However, the law did not end tension between the colony's Protestants and Catholics. The Anglican Church eventually became Maryland's official church.

Other tensions arose over Maryland's border with its northern neighbor, Pennsylvania. For many years, the two colonies argued over the exact location of the boundary between them. They finally agreed to settle the dispute once and for all. They hired Charles Mason and Jeremiah Dixon to map the border. This boundary became known as the Mason-Dixon line.

Virginia also experienced trouble during this time. James Berkeley, the governor of Virginia, promised Native Americans that settlers would not go farther west into Native American lands. Nathaniel Bacon was a farmer in western Virginia. He did not like the promise the governor had made. In fact, many people in western Virginia did not like it. They wanted to be able to move farther west. They felt that the government of the colony was controlled by people from eastern Virginia who did not care about the problems of western Virginia.

In 1676 Bacon led attacks on Native American villages. His army even marched to Jamestown and drove out Berkeley. Bacon was about to take over the colony when he died. Today, we remember this event as Bacon's Rebellion. Bacon's Rebellion was important because it showed that people wanted a government that listened to their demands.

The Carolinas and Georgia

In 1663 King Charles II created a new colony. It was called Carolina, which is Latin for "Charles's Land." The new colony needed a constitution. A **constitution** is a written plan of government. An English political thinker named John Locke wrote the constitution for Carolina. Some of John Locke's ideas about government later became part of the Declaration of Independence.

Farmers from Virginia settled in the northern part of Carolina. They grew tobacco and sold timber and tar. There was not a good harbor in northern Carolina, so the farmers used Virginia's ports. However, southern Carolina did have a good port at Charles Town (later Charleston).

Other crops were more important in southern Carolina. One of these was indigo. Indigo is a blue flowering plant. It was used to dye cloth. The other important crop was rice. Growing rice requires much labor, so the demand for slave labor increased.

In 1729 Carolina split into two separate colonies: North Carolina and South Carolina.

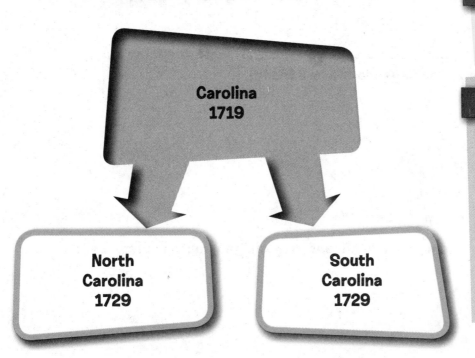

Carolina
1719

North
Carolina
1729

South
Carolina
1729

The colony of Georgia was founded in 1733. It was the last colony set up by the English in North America. The founder of Georgia was James Oglethorpe. Georgia was to be a place where poor people and debtors could get a fresh start. **Debtors** are people who owe other people money. England also hoped Georgia would protect the colonies from Spain. Spain had a colony in Florida, and Georgia stood between Spain and the other English colonies.

NGSSS Check What two things caused Bacon's Rebellion? SS.8.A.2.4

_____

_____

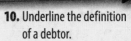

Show Your Skill

9. Classify Information
List three products that were important in North Carolina.

_____

_____

_____

Mark the Text

10. Underline the definition of a debtor.

Show Your Skill

11. Make Inferences Why was Georgia's location in relationship to Florida important?

_____

_____

_____

_____

③ MY REFLECTIONS

ESSENTIAL QUESTIONS *How does geography influence the way people live?*
How do new ideas change the way people live?

Reflect on What It Means . . .

As people moved to North America from Europe, they traveled into a totally new world. Colonists encountered new people, a new climate, new animals, and even new plants and food. In order to survive, they had to adapt to a new setting. New ideas about religion and government also shaped communities and the way people lived. Use the space below to jot down your thoughts and reflections

To Me

When I _____ , I had to adapt by:
(moved, changed schools, made a new friend)

To My Community

I can see that my community is influenced by our geography in these ways:

To the World

I believe that these new ideas are affecting people around the world:

TAKE THE CHALLENGE

If you could pick somewhere else to live, where would it be? Why does that place appeal to you? What do you expect to find there? Use a separate sheet of paper to write a letter to a friend. Describe the place you picked. Include details about the place and why you would like to live there.

CHAPTER 4

LIFE IN THE AMERICAN COLONIES

NGSSS

SS.8.E.2.3 Assess the role of Africans and other minority groups in the economic development of the United States.

ESSENTIAL QUESTIONS *How does geography influence the way people live? How do new ideas change the way people live? Why does conflict develop?*

Millions of Africans were captured and enslaved during the colonial period. They were sold to people who used them in both agricultural and business settings. Olaudah Equiano was kidnapped from his home in Nigeria in 1745. Equiano was educated and worked hard. He helped his master's business prosper and was able to buy his freedom. Equiano wrote an autobiography that details the horrors of slavery as well as the resilience and courage of enslaved persons.

" By these means I became very useful to my master; and saved him, as he used to **acknowledge**, above a hundred **pounds** a year. . . . I have sometimes heard it asserted that [an enslaved person] cannot earn his master the first cost; but nothing can be further from the truth."

OLAUDAH EQUIANO

acknowledge
What word could be used for *acknowledge* here?

_____

_____

pounds
The pound is still the currency of England today. Each pound can be divided into 100 pence. How many pence would there be in one hundred pounds?

_____

DBQ BREAKING IT DOWN

What did Equiano write that tells you that his opinion of the value of enslaved people was not what everyone thought?

_____

_____

In the space below, write a short note to a slaveholder arguing that more money could be made by freeing slaves and employing them as paid workers.

McGraw-Hill
networks™
There's More Online!

LESSON

1 COLONIAL ECONOMY

NGSSS

SS.8.A.2.3 Differentiate economic systems of New England, Middle and Southern colonies including indentured servants and slaves as labor sources.

SS.8.A.2.7 Describe the contributions of key groups (Africans, Native Americans, women, and children) to the society and culture of colonial America.

SS.8.E.2.3 Assess the role of Africans and other minority groups in the economic development of the United States.

Essential Question

How does geography influence the way people live?

Guiding Questions

1. How did the economic activity of the three regions reflect their geography?
2. Why were enslaved Africans brought to the colonies?

Terms to Know

subsistence farming
producing just enough to meet immediate needs

cash crop
a crop that can be sold easily in markets

diversity
variety, such as of ethnic or national groups

triangular trade
trade route between three destinations, such as Britain, Africa, and America

slave codes
rules focusing on the behavior and punishment of enslaved people

Where in the World?

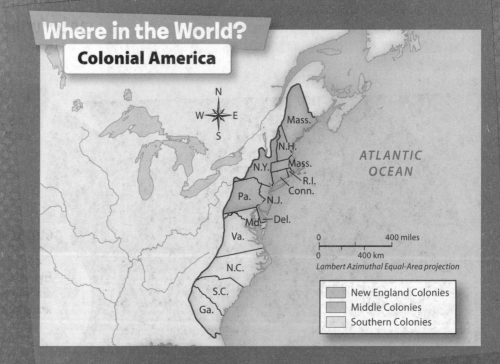

Colonial America

New England Colonies
Middle Colonies
Southern Colonies

When Did It Happen?

Slave Population in the Colonies 1650–1710

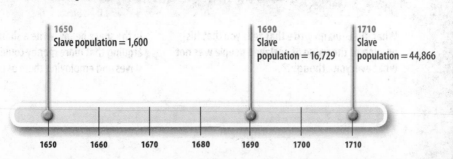

1650	1690	1710
Slave population = 1,600	Slave population = 16,729	Slave population = 44,866

1650 1660 1670 1680 1690 1700 1710

Making a Living in the Colonies

In Colonial America, most colonists were farmers or had a business linked to farming. For example, a farmer who grew wheat would need someone to mill (grind) the wheat into flour. The geography, or natural features, of a region was very important to the colonists. Understanding and using the land well would mean success for a colony. Each region was different. In each region, the colonists learned how to best use the climate and land.

In New England, winters were long. The soil was poor and rocky. This made large-scale farming difficult for the colonists. Instead, farmers practiced **subsistence farming**. This means that they produced only enough crops to feed their families. They did not have enough crops to sell or trade.

On these farms, everyone worked. Jobs included milking cows, planting crops, and harvesting (picking) crops. Women made cloth, candles, and soap. Sometimes they made extra items to sell.

New England also had many small businesses. There were mills for grinding grain and sawing lumber. In the large towns, blacksmiths, shoemakers, printers, and others set up businesses.

Building ships was an important industry in New England. The wood needed for shipbuilding came from forests in the region. New England was also a center for the shipping trade. Ships sailed from cities along the coast to other colonies and to other parts of the world. Ships and trade were an important link between all of these people and places.

Fishing and whaling were other important industries in New England. Whales were hunted for their oil and whalebone.

PHOTO: Library of Congress Prints and Photographs Division [LC-USZC2-1759]

Show Your Skill

1. Draw Conclusions Why did New England farmers practice subsistence farming?

_____

_____

_____

Mark the Text

2. In the text, underline two small businesses and two important industries in New England.

Many New Englanders from coastal towns worked as fishermen or whalers.

Think Critically

3. Contrast How did farms in the Middle Colonies differ from those in the New England Colonies?

_____

_____

_____

Show Your Skill

4. Identify Cause and Effect What makes a crop into a cash crop?

_____

_____

Think Critically

5. Contrast How were plantations in the Southern Colonies different from small farms?

_____

_____

_____

_____

Show Your Skill

6. Identify the Main Idea Why was agriculture so important to the economy of the Southern Colonies?

_____

_____

In the Middle Colonies, the soil and climate were very good for farming. The soil was richer and the climate milder than in New England. Farmers were able to plant larger areas and produce more crops. In New York and Pennsylvania, farmers grew large amounts of wheat and other **cash crops**. These were crops that could be sold easily in markets. Such markets were in the colonies and overseas.

Farmers sent their wheat and livestock (like sheep and pigs) to New York City and Philadelphia. They would be shipped to other places from there. These cities became busy ports.

Like the New England Colonies, the Middle Colonies also had industries. Some were home-based crafts like carpentry and flour making. Others were larger businesses like lumber (wood) mills and mining.

Many German, Dutch, Swedish, and other non-English settlers came to the Middle Colonies. They brought with them different ways of farming used in Europe. They also brought cultural **diversity**, or variety, to the Middle Colonies. This was not found in New England. With diversity came tolerance, or acceptance, of other religions and cultures.

The Southern Colonies also had rich soil and a warm climate. Most Southern colonists were farmers. They could plant large areas and produce large cash crops. London merchants helped them sell these crops. There was not much industry in the region.

Large farms, called plantations, were often located along rivers. This made it easier to ship crops to market by boat. The area where most of the large plantations were located was the Tidewater. This is a low-lying plain along the seacoast. Each plantation was like a small village. It could provide almost everything a person needed to live and work. Some plantations even had a school and a church.

West of the Tidewater are hills and forests. In this region, smaller farms grew corn and tobacco. There were many more of these small farms than there were plantations. Even so, the plantation owners had more money and more power. They controlled the economy and politics in the Southern Colonies.

Tobacco was the principal, or main, crop of the Maryland and Virginia colonies. Many workers were needed for growing tobacco and preparing it for sale. It cost a lot of money to hire workers. Southern farmers began using enslaved Africans.

Plantation owners grew rich from their tobacco crops. Yet sometimes they grew more tobacco than buyers wanted. For this reason, some tobacco planters switched to other crops such as corn and wheat.

The main cash crop in South Carolina and Georgia was rice. Growing and harvesting rice was hard work. Many workers were needed. Rice growers used slave labor. Farmers made more money from growing rice than from growing tobacco. Rice had become very popular in Europe. Its price kept rising. By the 1750s, South Carolina and Georgia had the fastest-growing economies in the colonies.

Show Your Skill

7. Table Complete the table to compare and contrast agriculture in the three regions of Colonial America.

	New England Colonies	Middle Colonies	Southern Colonies
Climate			
Soil			
Type of farming			

The Growth of Slavery

There was slavery in West Africa before the Europeans came to the Americas. Many West African kingdoms enslaved their enemies. Sometimes they sold the slaves to Arab slave traders. They made others work on farms or in gold mines.

In the colonies, plantation owners needed workers. The West African slave traders had workers to sell. Some Africans were taken from their villages by force. Some were captured in wars. The slave traders began shipping the enslaved people to America. Here, they were traded for goods. Slavery and the slave trade became important parts of the colonial economy.

Enslaved People in the Colonies, 1650–1710			
Year	North	South	Total
1650	880	720	1,600
1670	1,125	3,410	4,535
1690	3,340	13,389	16,729
1710	8,303	36,563	44,866

Slave traders marched the enslaved people to a European fort on the West African coast. They were traded to Europeans, branded, and forced onto a ship.

8. Identify the Main Idea What was the Middle Passage?

_____

_____

_____

9. Sequence Number these steps in the triangular trade in the order in which they happened.

_____ Slave ship travels to Europe with goods to sell and trade.

_____ Enslaved Africans are put onto the ship.

_____ Slave ship sails from West Africa to the Americas.

_____ Slave ship travels from Europe to West Africa.

10. Explain How were slave codes used to control enslaved Africans?

_____

_____

_____

The trip across the ocean from West Africa to the Americas was called the "Middle Passage." It was the second, or middle, part of a three-sided trade route. This three-sided route (shaped like a triangle) was called the **triangular trade**. The slave ships first traveled from Europe to West Africa to buy or trade for slaves. From West Africa, the ships went to the Americas. Here the slavers (people in the slave trade) sold or traded the enslaved Africans. Finally, the ships returned to Europe, now filled with trade goods.

Many Africans died during the Middle Passage. Conditions on the ships were terrible. The slave traders chained the enslaved Africans together, making it difficult for them to sit or stand. They had little food or water. If they became sick or died, the slavers threw them into the sea. If they refused to eat, the slavers whipped them.

At last, the slave ships reached the American ports. The survivors went to a slave market. Here, plantation owners looked them over and purchased them. On the plantations, most enslaved Africans worked as laborers. A few worked in the homes as servants.

The life of an enslaved person was hard. Most worked out in the fields. Often the slaveholders treated them cruelly. Many colonies had **slave codes**. These were rules that controlled the behavior and punishment of enslaved people. The rules were usually very strict, and the punishments were very harsh.

Enslaved Africans had strong family ties. Even so, slave owners often split up these families by selling a husband, wife, parent, or child to another slave owner.

Some enslaved Africans learned to be carpenters, blacksmiths, or weavers. Sometimes—with permission—they set up shops. They shared the money they made with the slaveholder. At times, a slave could earn enough to buy his or her freedom.

In the colonies, there were people who did not like slavery. They did not believe that one human had the right to own another. Puritans, Quakers, and Mennonites were among those with this point of view. In time, the question of slavery would lead to a bloody war between the North and the South.

NGSSS Check How did the geography of the colonies affect the development of farming in each region? SS.8.A.2.3

_____

_____

_____

_____

LESSON
2
COLONIAL GOVERNMENT

NGSSS

SS.8.A.2.2 Compare the characteristics of the New England, Middle, and Southern colonies.

SS.8.E.2.2 Explain the economic impact of government policies.

Essential Question
How do new ideas change the way people live?

Guiding Questions
1. Why are protected rights and representative government important principles?
2. How did the colonists react to England's economic policies?

Terms to Know

representative government
a system by which people elect delegates to make laws and conduct government

mercantilism
an economic theory whose goal is building a state's wealth and power by increasing exports and accumulating precious metals in return

export
to sell to other countries

import
to bring in from foreign markets

When Did It Happen?

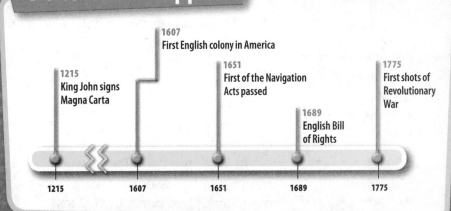

1215 King John signs Magna Carta

1607 First English colony in America

1651 First of the Navigation Acts passed

1689 English Bill of Rights

1775 First shots of Revolutionary War

1215 1607 1651 1689 1775

What Do You Know?

Directions: Read each statement. If you believe the statement is true, circle the T. If you believe the statement is false, circle the F.

Before the Lesson		Statement	After the Lesson	
T	F	The United States Constitution was the first document that protected rights.	T	F
T	F	The English Parliament is similar to our executive branch of government.	T	F
T	F	The Navigation Acts helped sailors at sea.	T	F
T	F	The colonies were allowed to export raw materials to England.	T	F

English Principles of Government

English colonists brought their ideas about government with them. Two beliefs were especially important to the English system of government. The first belief was in protected rights. The right to a trial by jury is a protected right. The second belief was in **representative government**. This is a system by which people elect delegates to make laws and conduct government. Colonists believed that their lawmakers should represent the common people. Later, these two beliefs became important parts of the U.S. Constitution.

The colonists believed that government must respect the rights of the people it governs. Laws made sure these rights were protected

The idea of protected rights began with the Magna Carta. King John signed this document on June 15, 1215. The Magna Carta protected the English people from unfair treatment by the government. This included unjust loss of life, liberty (freedom), and property. It also protected the people from unjust punishment.

Besides protected rights, the colonists believed in representative government. In a representative government, people are chosen to make laws and run the government. These people represent (act or speak for) the wishes of those who elected, or chose, them.

In England, Parliament was a representative assembly. It was made up of two parts, or houses: the House of Lords and the House of Commons. The House of Commons included commoners (everyday people). Together, as Parliament, these two houses had the power to make laws. Parliament was the model for the law-making branch of government in America.

In the mid-1600s, King James II and Parliament struggled for control. At last, in 1688, Parliament removed King James II from power. William and Mary replaced him. They promised to rule by the laws agreed upon in Parliament. From then on, rulers and lawmakers shared power.

The Magna Carta was issued in 1215.

In 1689 an important document set down clear limits on a ruler's power. This was the English Bill of Rights. It limited the ruler's ability to suspend (set aside) Parliament's laws. Rulers could no longer impose (require) taxes without Parliament's support. The bill said that members of Parliament would be freely elected (voted for). It gave citizens the right to a fair trial by jury. It banned cruel and unusual punishment.

How did these ideas of government work in the colonies? Individuals or groups owned some of the thirteen colonies. They were called proprietary colonies. These colonies set up most of their own rules. Pennsylvania was a proprietary colony. The English kings gave permission for a company to start a colony. They were called charter colonies. Massachusetts was a charter colony.

In time, some colonies in America became royal colonies. This put them under direct English control. Virginia was a royal colony. In every royal colony, Parliament appointed (chose) a governor and a council. This was called the upper house. The colonists chose an assembly, called the lower house. The upper house usually did what the king and Parliament told them to do. Often this went against the wishes of the lower house.

Not everyone in the colonies had a voice in government. Only white men who owned property could vote. Even so, a large share of the population did take part in government in some way. What they learned was useful when the colonies became independent.

In towns, people often met to talk about local issues. In time, town meetings turned into local governments. Throughout the colonies, people began to take part in government. Their belief in the right of self-government grew stronger. This helped to set the stage for the American Revolution.

English Economic Policies

In the early 1600s, many European nations followed an idea called mercantilism. **Mercantilism** is a system for building wealth and power by building supplies of gold and silver. To do this, a country must **export,** or sell, to other countries more than it **imports,** or buys. A country must also set up colonies. Colonies have two purposes. They provide raw materials and are a market for exports.

The English followed this system of mercantilism. The American colonies provided raw materials such as tobacco, rice, lumber, and fur. They also bought English-made goods such as tools, clothing, and furniture.

5. Making Connections
Which branch of the United States government is most like Parliament: the executive branch (president), the judicial branch (courts), or the legislative branch (Senate and House of Representatives)?

Mark the Text

6. Underline the sentence that tells whose wishes the upper house usually represented?

Think Critically

7. Conclude Why might a decision by the upper house upset the lower house?

Show Your Skill

8. Classify Information Name two exports from the colonies.

9. Summarize If a colonist bought cloth from France, what happened to it under rules of the Navigation Act?

_____

_____

_____

10. Draw Conclusions Why would Parliament want the Navigation Acts?

_____

_____

_____

_____

11. Write a letter to Parliament from the viewpoint of a merchant in the colonies. Express your opinion on the Navigation Acts.

In the 1650s, the English passed laws to control this trade. These were the Navigation Acts. They forced colonists to sell their raw materials to England. They also controlled trade between the colonies and Europe. If a colonist bought goods from a country in Europe, those goods went first to England. Here they were taxed, then shipped to the colony. In addition, all ships carrying trade goods had to be built in England or the colonies. The crews on these ships also had to be English.

At first, the colonists welcomed the trade laws. The laws made sure that the colonists had a place to sell their raw materials. Later, the colonists felt the laws limited their rights. They wanted to make their own products to sell. Also, they wanted to sell their products to countries other than England. Many colonial merchants began smuggling—shipping goods without paying taxes or without government approval. Later, controls on trade would cause problems between the colonies and England.

Colonial towns and merchants, like those shown in this scene in Philadelphia, depended on trade. As Britain passed new trade laws to regulate trade, colonists became frustrated.

 NGSSS Check How did Parliament's regulations, such as the Navigation Acts, affect the economy of the colonies? SS.8.E.2.2

_____

_____

_____

_____

NGSSS

SS.8.C.1.3 Recognize the role of civic virtue in the lives of citizens and leaders from the colonial period through Reconstruction.

Essential Question

How do new ideas change the way people live?

Guiding Questions

1. What was life like for people living in the thirteen colonies?
2. What values and beliefs were important to the American colonists?

Terms to Know

immigration
the permanent movement of people into one country from other countries

epidemic
an illness that affects a large number of people

apprentice
a young person who learns a trade from a skilled craftsperson

civic virtue
the democratic ideas, practices, and values that are at the heart of citizenship in a free society

When Did It Happen?

1607
First English colony in America

1647
Massachusetts public education law

1730s to 1740s
The Great Awakening

1775
Revolutionary War begins

| 1607 | 1647 | 1730s to 1740s | 1775 |

What Do You Know?

Directions: Sometimes we hear a lot about the issues about which Americans disagree. List some of the values and beliefs that you think all Americans share. After you finish reading this lesson, come back and circle the values and beliefs that were also held in colonial times.

Show Your Skill

1. Identify Cause and Effect
List two reasons why the population of the colonies was growing.

_____

_____

_____

2. Make Connections What reasons do people have for moving to a new country today?

_____

_____

_____

_____

_____

_____

Think Critically

3. Infer How would an epidemic affect population numbers?

_____

_____

networks Read Chapter 10 Lesson 1 in your textbook or online.

Life in the Colonies

In 1700 there were about 250,000 people living in the colonies. By the mid-1770s, there were about 2.5 million colonists. The number of African Americans grew from 28,000 to more than 500,000. Immigration was important to this growth. **Immigration** is the permanent moving of people from one country to another.

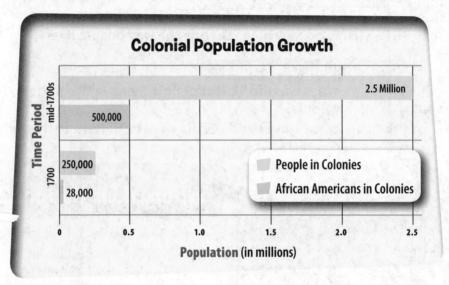

Colonial Population Growth

There was another reason for the growing number of people in the colonies: large families. Colonial women often married young and had many children. Also, America was a very healthy place to live, especially New England.

Even so, sickness took many lives. Many women died in childbirth. There were outbreaks of smallpox and other serious diseases. Some outbreaks affected large numbers of people. This is called an **epidemic**. Many people died in these epidemics.

People came to the colonies from many other countries. They spoke different languages. They had different ways of thinking. However, coming to the colonies changed them. They became something new and different. They became Americans.

The American spirit of independence began in these early years. Settlers had left their home countries far behind. In America they found conditions of life that were new. The old ways of doing things no longer worked. For this reason, they began to do things in a different way—their own way. In other words, colonists adapted to, or tried to fit in with, these new conditions of life.

The family was the basis of colonial society. Men were the official heads of the family. They ran the farm or business. They also represented the family in the community. Sons might work on the family farm or in the family business. They could also work for other people. A young man might become an **apprentice**—a person who trains under a skilled craftsman.

Women ran their homes and cared for the children. On farms, many worked in the fields with their husbands. A young, unmarried woman might work as a maid or cook for a wealthy family. A widow (a woman whose husband has died) might sew, teach, or nurse for a living. Widows and unmarried women also could run businesses and own property.

Even children worked. By the time they were four or five years old, they often had jobs. Even so, they did have time to play games and play with simple toys.

American Beliefs

Life in the colonies was built upon a strong, two-part foundation: the spirit of independence and the family. Americans also valued education, religion, and new ideas. These values shaped the character of the colonists.

Parents often taught their children to read and write at home. In New England and Pennsylvania, people set up schools. In 1647 Massachusetts passed a public education law. It said that communities with 50 or more homes must have a school.

The result of this was a high level of literacy (the ability to read and write) in New England. By 1750 about 85 percent of the men and half of the women could read.

Widows and unmarried women ran many of the schools. In the Middle Colonies, religious groups like Quakers ran some of them. Another kind of school was run by craftspeople. In these schools, apprentices learned a skill. Colleges in the colonies had a special purpose: to train ministers (people who lead religious worship).

Think Critically

4. Describe How could a young man learn to be a blacksmith?

_____

_____

_____

Mark the Text

5. Underline two ways in which unmarried women could earn a living.

Think Critically

6. Contrast How were colleges in the colonies different from colleges today?

_____

_____

Take the Challenge

7. Make a poster encouraging colonial parents to teach their children to read and write. Be certain to include reasons why those skills are important.

These reenactors from Colonial Williamsburg demonstrate what a music lesson may have been like. Students often did studies at home and were taught by parents or tutors.

8. Identify the Main Idea
What was the Great Awakening?

_____

_____

_____

Think Critically

9. Contrast How was the Enlightenment different from the Great Awakening?

_____

_____

_____

_____

Show Your Skill

10. Draw Conclusions How can censorship affect a free society?

_____

_____

_____

_____

_____

_____

Religion shaped much of colonial life. In the 1730s and 1740s, ministers were asking people to renew their faith—to return to the strong faith of earlier days. This renewal, or revival, of religious faith was called the Great Awakening.

The Great Awakening inspired many new types of churches. These churches had new ideas about faith. Their emphasis (special stress) was on personal faith rather than on church ceremonies.

The most important effect of the Great Awakening was greater religious freedom. More colonists began to choose their own faith. The older, more established churches lost power within the colonies.

The Great Awakening also broke down walls between the colonies. From north to south, the colonists were united by this revival of faith. They began to share other ideas—political ideas. In time, the colonies would also share the ideas of revolution and independence.

By the mid-1700s, another new idea was spreading through the colonies. It began in Europe and was called the Enlightenment. It was the idea that knowledge, reason, and science could improve society. In the colonies, interest in science grew. More people began to study nature, try experiments, and write about the results.

Freedom of the press was also important in the colonies. Newspapers in cities carried news about politics. Often the government did not like what was written. The newspapers were told they could not publish the information. The newspapers fought against this censorship—the banning of printed texts because they contain ideas that are unpopular or offensive. Fighting censorship helped the growth of a free press.

How should a citizen think, feel, and act in a free and self-ruled society? This is a question that colonists were beginning to think about. They began to wonder what **civic** (public or community) **virtues** (values) would be important to a free and democratic society. In time, the answers—the civic virtues—would define Americans. These civic virtues would become the building blocks of a new nation.

NGSSS Check Which of the following values and beliefs were important to the colonists? (Check all that apply.) SS.8.C.1.3

☐ a. free press

☐ b. religious freedom

☐ c. immigration

☐ d. education

☐ e. worker's rights

NGSSS

SS.8.A.2.6 Examine the causes, course, and consequences of the French and Indian War.

SS.8.A.3.1 Explain the consequences of the French and Indian War in British policies for the American colonies from 1763 – 1774.

Essential Question
Why does conflict develop?

Guiding Questions
1. How did competition for land in North America lead to the French and Indian War?
2. What was the turning point in the French and Indian War?

Terms to Know

militia
a military force made up of ordinary citizens

Iroquois Confederacy
five Native American nations that joined together in North America

alliance
partnership

Where in the World?

French Territory Before 1763

QUÉBEC
Québec
Ft. Louisburg
Montréal
NEW ENGLAND COLONIES
NEW FRANCE
Ft. Duquesne
Mississippi River
Ohio River
APPALACHIAN MOUNTAINS
MIDDLE COLONIES
ATLANTIC OCEAN
SOUTHERN COLONIES

N W E S

0   400 miles
0   400 km
Lambert Azimuthal Equal-Area projection

When Did It Happen?

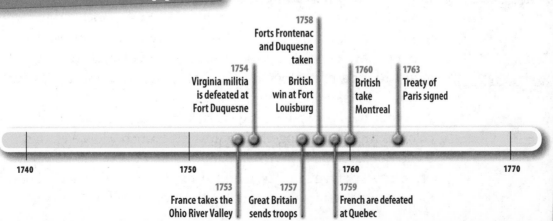

1758
Forts Frontenac and Duquesne taken

1754
Virginia militia is defeated at Fort Duquesne

British win at Fort Louisburg

1760
British take Montreal

1763
Treaty of Paris signed

1740   1750   1760   1770

1753
France takes the Ohio River Valley

1757
Great Britain sends troops

1759
French are defeated at Quebec

networks Read Chapter 4 Lesson 4 in your textbook or online.

Rivalry Between the French and British

In the 1700s, Britain and France were top world powers. In North America, the rivalry, or competition, between them was very fierce.

The Appalachian Mountains were west of the colonies. Beyond them was the Ohio River Valley. This large area was rich in natural resources. Both the British and French claimed rights to the region. Already, the French were trading for fur with the Native Americans in the area. They did not want to share this business with the British.

To protect their claims, the French built a number of forts. The British took action. They built a fort in what is now western Pennsylvania. Before it was finished, the French moved in and took over the area. They built their own fort and called it Fort Duquesne.

In the spring of 1754, the Virginia colony fought back. It sent a **militia** to Fort Duquesne. A militia is a military force made up of everyday citizens. This militia was led by a young Virginian named George Washington. The militia reached Fort Duquesne. Washington set up his own fort nearby. He called it Fort Necessity.

The French attacked. Native Americans joined them in the fighting. Together, they defeated Washington and his militia. Even so, Washington was called a hero. He had struck the first blow against the French.

The fight for rights had begun. Now both the French and British looked to the Native Americans for help. In this, the French had the advantage. The Native Americans trusted them. The French were interested mostly in fur trading. They did not want to take over Native American land. On the other hand, the British wanted land. They had already taken much from the Native Americans and were not trusted. For these reasons, Native Americans often helped the French and attacked British settlements.

Because of this, the British tried to make a treaty with the Iroquois. The **Iroquois Confederacy** was the most powerful group of Native Americans in eastern North America. Delegates (representatives) from seven colonies met with Iroquois leaders at Albany, New York, in June of 1754. The Iroquois would not agree to an **alliance,** or partnership. However, they did promise to stay neutral—to take no side in the fighting.

While in Albany, the delegates also talked about ways the colonies might work together against the French. However, they could not agree on a plan. No colony wanted to give up power in order to work together. The plan to unify the colonies failed. Soon all were involved in a full-out war: the French and Indian War.

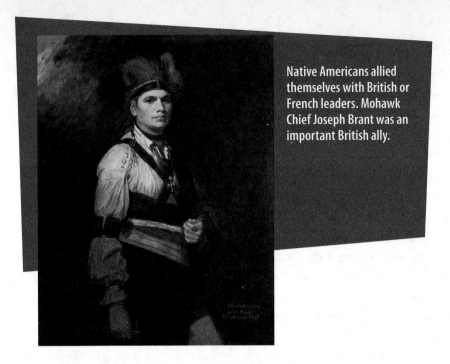

Native Americans allied themselves with British or French leaders. Mohawk Chief Joseph Brant was an important British ally.

The French and Indian War

Early in the war, the French were winning. They captured many British forts. Their Native American allies were attacking colonists along the frontier, or edges, of the colonies.

In 1757 William Pitt took over leadership of Great Britain. He became prime minister. Pitt was a very good military planner. He decided to send more trained British soldiers to fight in North America. He also decided that Great Britain would pay the high cost of fighting the war—for now. Higher taxes on the colonies would pay for it later.

In North America, Pitt had two goals. The first was to secure British rights to the Ohio River Valley. The second was to take over French Canada.

The British had a number of victories in 1758. The first was at Fort Louisburg, in present-day Nova Scotia. They also took Fort Frontenac at Lake Ontario and Fort Duquesne. This they renamed Fort Pitt.

In September of 1759, the British won a major victory. Outside of the city of Quebec—the capital of New France—the British troops surprised and defeated the French army. This happened on a field called the Plains of Abraham.

The following year, the British took Montreal. This ended the war in North America. However, the war continued in Europe. It finally ended with the Treaty of Paris in 1763. Great Britain was given Canada, Florida, and French land claims east of the Mississippi River. Spain—an ally of France—was given the Louisiana Territory.

France no longer held power in North America. This now belonged to Great Britain and Spain.

Think Critically

5. Explain Why was William Pitt successful at managing the war for Britain?

_____

_____

_____

_____

_____

_____

Mark the Text

6. Underline in the text William Pitt's goals in the war with the French.

Show Your Skill

7. Interpret Information What event marked the turning point in the war?

_____

_____

_____

_____

Mark the Text

8. Underline the sentence that tells what happened to Florida at the end of the French and Indian War.

9. Conclude How could the Proclamation of 1763 calm the fighting between colonists and Native Americans?

_____

_____

_____

_____

_____

_____

Show Your Skill

10. Identify Cause and Effect Why did the Proclamation of 1763 cause colonists to distrust the government?

_____

_____

_____

_____

_____

Take the Challenge

11. Work with a partner. One partner should take the viewpoint of a colonist and the other should take the viewpoint of Pontiac. Discuss the Proclamation of 1763 and how it might affect you.

New British Policies

The British now controlled the Ohio River Valley. Native Americans had to do business with them. The British raised the prices of their goods. They would not pay for the use of Native American land. British settlers began moving west.

Pontiac, chief of an Ottawa village near Detroit, decided to fight back. In 1763 he gathered a force of Native Americans. They attacked the British fort at Detroit as well as other British settlements. During Pontiac's War, Native Americans killed settlers along the Pennsylvania and Virginia frontiers.

Then something surprising happened in Britain. King George III ruled that colonists could not settle west of the Appalachian Mountains. This Proclamation of 1763 was useful to the British. It calmed the fighting between colonists and Native Americans. Also, it stopped colonists from leaving their colonies on the coast—where the important markets and businesses were. Ten thousand British troops in America would enforce the new rule.

Colonists were alarmed. They thought the proclamation limited their freedom of movement. They feared that British troops might be used to take away their liberties. The colonies began to distrust their British government.

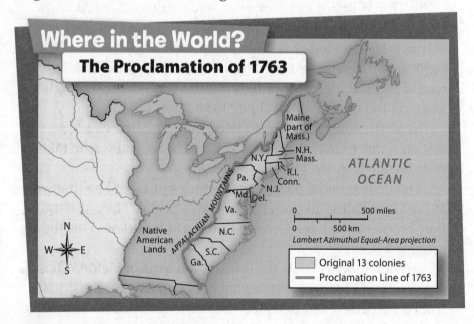

Where in the World?

The Proclamation of 1763

 NGSSS Check Number these events in the French and Indian War. SS.8.A.2.6

_____ British victory on the Plains of Abraham

_____ Treaty of Paris signed

_____ Prime Minister Pitt sends British troops to North America

_____ French defeat at Montreal

ESSENTIAL QUESTION *How does geography influence the way people live?*

Reflect on What It Means . . .

In colonial times, the economy of a region was shaped in part by the geography of the region. Is that true today? Reflect on the types of jobs and businesses you have in your community. Are they affected by the location and resources of your area?

To My Community

Compare and contrast Florida's colonial economy with Florida's economy today.

Florida's Economy	
Colonial Florida	**Florida Today**

To the World

How is Florida's economy connected with the rest of the country and the world? Add a few lines to your chart noting connections such as imports and exports between Florida and other countries.

To Me

How does Florida's economy affect the people of your neighborhood, town, or county? Add a call-out label to your chart explaining how you and the people of your community fit into the rest of Florida's economy.

Keep Going! ➤➤

TAKE THE CHALLENGE

As a class, produce a news radio show about Florida's economy. You may want to present your radio show over the Internet as an audio podcast. Write the script for the program in the space below.

THE SPIRIT OF INDEPENDENCE

NGSSS

SS.8.A.3.3 Recognize the contributions of the Founding Fathers (John Adams, Sam Adams, Benjamin Franklin, John Hancock, Alexander Hamilton, Thomas Jefferson, James Madison, George Mason, and George Washington) during American Revolutionary efforts.

SS.8.A.3.5 Describe the influence of individuals on social and political developments during the Revolutionary era.

ESSENTIAL QUESTIONS *What motivates people to act? Why does conflict develop?*

The Declaration of Independence was originally supposed to be drafted by a committee—but the committee pushed Jefferson to do the writing. Below is an excerpt from the letter Adams wrote to Jefferson explaining why Jefferson should write the Declaration.

PHOTO: Library of Congress, Prints and Photographs Division (LC-USZC4-9904)

" Reason first—You are a Virginian, and a Virginian ought to appear at the head of this business. Reason second— I am obnoxious , suspected, and unpopular. You are very much otherwise. Reason third—you can write ten times better than I can. "

—FROM THE WRITINGS OF THOMAS JEFFERSON

obnoxious

Write another word (synonym) for obnoxious?

_____

DBQ BREAKING IT DOWN

Why do you think Adams felt it was important for the Declaration of Independence to be written by a Virginian?

_____

_____

_____

_____

Why might the person who presents an idea be as important as the idea itself?

_____

_____

_____

_____

McGraw-Hill
networks™
There's More Online!

NO TAXATION WITHOUT REPRESENTATION

NGSSS

SS.8.A.3.1 Explain the consequences of the French and Indian War in British policies for the American colonies from 1763–1774.

SS.8.A.3.2 Explain American colonial reaction to British policy from 1763–1774.

SS.8.A.3.4 Examine the contributions of influential groups to both the American and British war efforts during the American Revolutionary War and their effects on the outcome of the war.

SS.8.A.3.8 Examine individuals and groups that affected political and social motivations during the American Revolution.

SS.8.A.3.16 Examine key events in Florida history as each impacts this era of American history.

Essential Question

Why does conflict develop?

Guiding Questions

1. Why did the British government establish new policies?
2. How did the American colonists react to British policies?

Terms to Know

revenue
incoming money from taxes or other sources

writs of assistance
court documents allowing customs officers to enter any location to search for smuggled goods

resolution
an official expression of opinion by a group

effigy
a mocking figure representing an unpopular individual

boycott
to refuse to buy items as a protest

repeal
to cancel an act or law

Where in the World?

The Proclamation of 1763

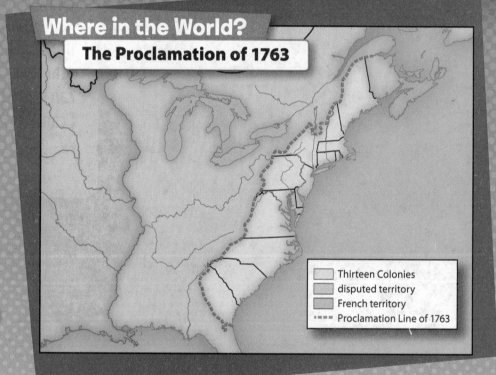

Thirteen Colonies
disputed territory
French territory
Proclamation Line of 1763

When Did It Happen?

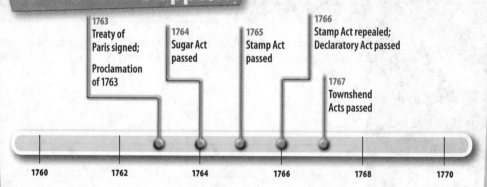

1763 Treaty of Paris signed; Proclamation of 1763

1764 Sugar Act passed

1765 Stamp Act passed

1766 Stamp Act repealed; Declaratory Act passed

1767 Townshend Acts passed

1760   1762   1764   1766   1768   1770

Dealing with Britain

After the French and Indian War, the British gained a lot of land in North America. They also ran up a big debt. To control the land, the king issued the Proclamation of 1763. This order:

- prohibited, or stopped, colonists from moving west of the Appalachian Mountains to avoid conflict with Native Americans,
- allowed the British to control the fur trade, and
- kept colonists near the Atlantic coast. This was good for British trade.

To protect its interests, Britain kept 10,000 troops in the colonies. The British government needed **revenue,** or incoming money, to pay the troops. It also needed money to pay its debt from the war. To raise money, Britain placed new taxes on the colonists and enforced old tax laws more strictly.

To avoid paying taxes, some colonists smuggled goods. Smuggling means bringing goods into a place secretly and illegally. In 1763 George Grenville was the British prime minister. He knew that American juries often found smugglers innocent. Grenville got Parliament to pass a new law. It sent smugglers to courts without juries. Parliament also approved **writs of assistance.** These documents allowed officers to search any location for smuggled goods.

In 1764 Parliament passed the Sugar Act. It lowered the tax on molasses. The British government hoped that colonists would pay a lower tax instead of smuggling. The law also allowed officers to take smuggled goods without going to court.

Colonists believed that these new laws violated their rights as British citizens. Those rights included the right to a jury trial and the right to be safe in their own homes. Many colonists also thought they should not be taxed if they did not agree to it.

As a young man, George Washington earned a living as a surveyor. He took measurements of land areas and traveled the frontier. Information from surveyors helped create maps of the frontier beyond the Appalachians.

Mark the Text

1. Underline the reason why some colonists took part in smuggling.

Show Your Skill

2. **Draw Conclusions** Why did Parliament pass the Sugar Act?

_____

_____

_____

Think Critically

3. **Generalize** Why were the colonists angry about many of the laws Parliament passed?

_____

_____

_____

_____

Take the Challenge

4. Discuss why taxation by the British to help cover the cost of the war was fair or unfair. Flip a coin to decide which side you will take in the discussion.

Heads = Fair

Tails = Unfair

5. Evaluate Was the boycott by colonial merchants effective? Why or why not?

_____

_____

_____

_____

_____

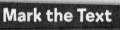

Show Your Skill

6. Compare and Contrast How did the Townshend Acts differ from the Stamp Act? How were they alike?

_____

_____

_____

_____

_____

_____

_____

Mark the Text

7. Underline the words that explain what the Daughters of Liberty encouraged people to do to protest the taxes.

New Taxes on the Colonies

In 1765 Parliament passed the Stamp Act. This law taxed printed items, such as newspapers. It angered colonists and interfered in colonial affairs. In Virginia, Patrick Henry convinced the House of Burgesses to pass a **resolution,** a formal declaration, against the Stamp Act. It said that only the Virginia assembly had the power to tax the citizens of Virginia.

In Boston, Samuel Adams helped start the Sons of Liberty. This group also protested the Stamp Act. Protesters burned **effigies,** or rag figures, that represented tax collectors.

Patrick Henry was known for his persuasive speeches.

PHOTO: Bettman/Corbis

In October delegates from nine colonies met in New York. The meeting was called the Stamp Act Congress. The delegates sent a resolution to Parliament and the British king. It said that only assemblies in the colonies could tax the colonists. Colonial merchants decided to **boycott,** or refuse to buy, British goods. Many merchants signed promises not to buy or use goods imported from Britain.

British merchants began to lose money. They asked Parliament to **repeal,** or cancel, the Stamp Act. Parliament did repeal the law, but it passed another called the Declaratory Act. This act stated Parliament had the right to tax the colonists.

In 1767 Parliament passed the Townshend Acts. These were more taxes on goods imported to the colonies. By this time, any British taxes angered the colonists. Groups like the Daughters of Liberty encouraged Americans to make their own goods instead of buying them from Britain.

NGSSS Check Name three ways that colonists protested the tax laws passed by Parliament. SS.8.A.3.2

_____

_____

_____

2 UNITING THE COLONISTS

NGSSS

SS.8.A.3.1 Explain the consequences of the French and Indian War in British policies for the American colonies from 1763–1774.

SS.8.A.3.2 Explain American colonial reaction to British policy from 1763–1774.

SS.8.A.3.8 Examine individuals and groups that affected political and social motivations during the American Revolution.

Essential Question
Why does conflict develop?

Guiding Questions
1. How did the American colonists react to the Boston Massacre?
2. How did the British government react to the actions of the colonists?

Terms to Know

rebellion
open defiance of authority

propaganda
ideas or information spread to harm or help a cause

committee of correspondence
an organization that spread political ideas and information through the colonies

Where in the World?

Boston, 1770

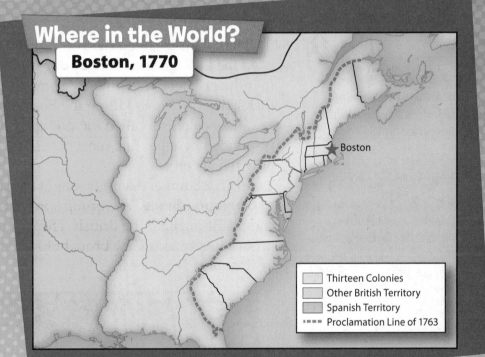

Thirteen Colonies
Other British Territory
Spanish Territory
Proclamation Line of 1763

When Did It Happen?

1770 Boston Massacre

1772 Boston committee of correspondence revived

1773 Boston Tea Party

1774 Parliament passes Coercive Acts

1770   1771   1772   1773   1774   1775

Think Critically

1. Explain What is propaganda?

_____

_____

_____

Show Your Skill

2. Draw Conclusions Why did the people of Boston resent the British soldiers?

_____

_____

_____

Mark the Text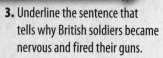

3. Underline the sentence that tells why British soldiers became nervous and fired their guns.

Take the Challenge

4. Come to the defense of the soldiers in the Boston Massacre. Use 20 words or fewer to persuade the judge why their actions might have been justified.

Trouble in Massachusetts

The colonists' protests made British officials nervous. They sent more troops to Boston to stop the **rebellion.** The colonists thought the British had gone too far. To make matters worse, British soldiers were rude and sometimes stole from the colonists.

On March 5, 1770, a fight broke out between a group of soldiers and Bostonians. This is what happened.

- Angry colonists gathered at the place where British taxes were collected.
- The colonists threw sticks and stones at the soldiers on duty.
- The soldiers became nervous and fired their guns into the crowd.
- Five colonists were killed. One was Crispus Attucks, a dockworker who was part African and part Native American.

The colonists called the event the Boston Massacre. They used the killings as **propaganda.** That is information used to influence people's opinions. Samuel Adams put up posters that showed soldiers killing the Bostonians.

Many colonists called for stronger boycotts. Parliament responded by repealing most of the Townshend Acts. It kept only the tax on tea.

In 1772 Samuel Adams brought back the Boston **committee of correspondence.** The group spread writings about colonists' complaints against the British. Throughout the colonies, more groups organized. They brought together colonists who were against British policies.

Colonial leaders used stories and posters about the Boston Massacre to try to persuade colonists to oppose British policies.

PHOTO: North Wind Picture Archives/Alamy

Crisis in Boston

In 1773 the British East India Company was in financial trouble. Parliament wanted to save the company, so it passed the Tea Act. It gave the company almost total control of the tea market in the colonies. It also removed some of the taxes on tea. Colonists were still angry because they did not want to pay any tax. They also did not want Parliament telling them what tea they could buy.

The royal governor ordered the ships to be unloaded. During the night of December 16, 1773, the Sons of Liberty dressed up as Native Americans. They boarded the ships and threw 342 chests of tea overboard. This event became known as the Boston Tea Party.

King George III felt that Britain was losing control of the colonies. To punish colonists, Britain passed the Coercive Acts. These laws closed Boston Harbor until the colonists paid for the tea they threw overboard. With the harbor closed, no food or supplies could get into Boston. Colonists believed that the Coercive Acts violated their rights. They called them the Intolerable Acts.

> Colonists called for a new boycott that would stop the East India Company ships from unloading their tea.
>
> ↓
>
> The Daughters of Liberty urged people to boycott tea.
>
> ↓
>
> The East India Company continued to ship tea to the colonies.
>
> ↓
>
> The colonists in New York and Philadelphia forced the tea ships to turn back.
>
> ↓
>
> Three tea ships arrived in Boston Harbor.

NGSSS Check Complete each sentence about the Boston Massacre. SS.8.A.3.2

Colonists began to spread _____ that British soldiers had killed colonists.

Colonists used committees of _____ to share information and colonists' opinions.

Complete each sentence about the Boston Tea Party.

Some colonists dressed as _____ and threw tea off British ships in

_____ .

The colonists threw the "party" to _____ the special treatment given to one tea

supplier, the _____ .

5. Cause and Effect Why did Parliament pass the Tea Act?

_____

_____

_____

Mark the Text

6. Circle the names of two cities where the colonists turned away tea ships. Underline the city where the tea ships arrived.

Show Your Skill

7. Recognize Point of View Why were the Coercive Acts also called the Intolerable Acts?

_____

_____

_____

Think Critically

8. Identify Cause and Effect List the effects of the Coercive Acts on the colonists of Boston.

_____

_____

_____

_____

LESSON 3

A CALL TO ARMS

NGSSS

SS.8.A.3.2 Explain American colonial reaction to British policy from 1763–1774.

SS.8.A.3.3 Recognize the contributions of the Founding Fathers (John Adams, Sam Adams, Benjamin Franklin, John Hancock, Alexander Hamilton, Thomas Jefferson, James Madison, George Mason, and George Washington) during American Revolutionary efforts.

SS.8.A.3.6 Examine the causes, course, and consequences of the American Revolution.

SS.8.A.3.8 Examine individuals and groups that affected political and social motivations during the American Revolution.

Essential Question

What motivates people to act?

Guiding Questions

1. What role did key individuals play in the movement toward independence?
2. Why were the battles at Lexington and Concord important?
3. What were the beliefs of the Loyalists and Patriots?

Terms to Know

minutemen
civilian soldiers who boasted they could be ready to fight with only one minute's notice

Loyalists
American colonists who remained loyal to Britain and opposed the war for independence

Patriots
American colonists who favored American independence

Where in the World?

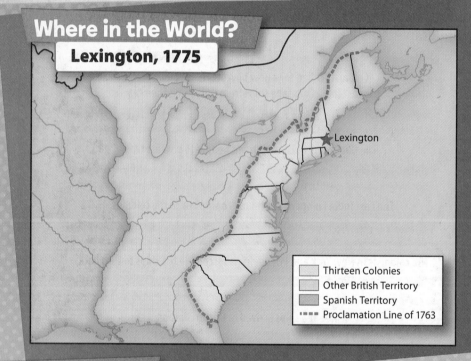

Lexington, 1775

Lexington

Thirteen Colonies
Other British Territory
Spanish Territory
----- Proclamation Line of 1763

When Did It Happen?

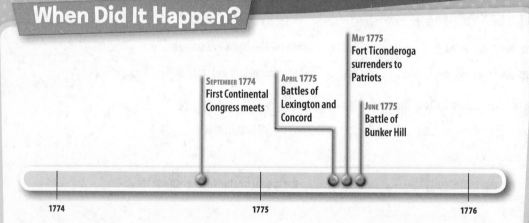

SEPTEMBER 1774
First Continental Congress meets

APRIL 1775
Battles of Lexington and Concord

MAY 1775
Fort Ticonderoga surrenders to Patriots

JUNE 1775
Battle of Bunker Hill

1774   1775   1776

A Meeting in Philadelphia

Fifty-five delegates met in Philadelphia. They came from every colony except Georgia. They met to represent all the colonies in challenging British control. The meeting was called the Continental Congress. John Adams, Samuel Adams, and Patrick Henry were delegates. John Jay, Richard Henry Lee, and George Washington were also delegates.

The delegates to the Continental Congress:

- issued a statement asking Parliament to repeal several laws that violated colonists' rights.
- voted to boycott trade with Britain. This included all goods coming into and going out of the colonies.
- decided to approve the Suffolk Resolves. These resolutions called on the colonists to arm themselves against the British.

In Massachusetts, the militia began to train and stockpile weapons. A colonial militia was a group of citizens who served as part-time soldiers to help protect the colony. Some militias claimed they could be ready to fight on a minute's notice. These groups were known as **minutemen.**

PHOTO: Joe Vogan/Alamy

The Continental Congress met in Carpenters' Hall in Philadelphia in 1774.

Fighting Begins

The British also began to prepare for a fight. King George III believed the New England colonies were rebelling. By April 1775, thousands of British soldiers were in and around Boston. The king ordered British general Thomas Gage to get rid of the militia's weapons and arrest the leaders. The general heard that the militia stored weapons at Concord, a town near Boston. On April 18, 1775, he sent 700 troops to destroy the weapons.

Mark the Text

1. Circle the names of some of the delegates to the Continental Congress.

Show Your Skill

2. Identify the Main Idea
What was the main purpose of the Continental Congress?

_____

_____

_____

Take the Challenge

3. Research a member of the Continental Congress. Find five fascinating facts about that person to share with the class.

The North Bridge at Concord was the site of an American victory against the British.

PHOTO: Bettmann/CORBIS

Think Critically

4. Sequence Place the following events in the order in which they happened.

_____ Paul Revere and Richard Dawes warn Lexington that the British are coming.

_____ Battle of Concord

_____ King George III declares that the colonies are rebelling.

_____ British troops are ordered to destroy the Massachusetts militia's weapons.

_____ Battle of Lexington

5. Evaluate What was the goal of the British troops who marched on Concord? Do you think they were successful? Why or why not?

_____

_____

_____

_____

_____

_____

6. Infer What does it mean when someone is called a "Benedict Arnold"? Why?

_____

_____

_____

_____

Colonists in Boston saw the troops march out of town. Paul Revere and William Dawes, members of the Sons of Liberty, rode to Lexington, a town near Concord. They warned colonists that the British were coming.

About 70 minutemen met the British at Lexington. Someone fired a shot, causing both sides to begin shooting. Eight minutemen were killed. The British moved on to Concord. There they found that most of the militia's gunpowder had been removed. They destroyed any supplies that were left. Then the minutemen forced the British troops to turn back.

Word quickly spread about the British movement. Along the road from Concord to Boston, colonists hid behind trees and fences. As British troops marched back to Boston, the colonists fired. By the time the British reached Boston, 73 of their soldiers had died and at least 174 were wounded.

More Military Action

After Lexington and Concord, many colonists joined militias. Benedict Arnold of the Connecticut militia enlisted 400 men. He set out to capture Fort Ticonderoga on Lake Champlain. He joined forces with Ethan Allen and the Vermont militia, known as the Green Mountain Boys. Together, the two groups caught the British by surprise. Fort Ticonderoga surrendered on May 10, 1775. Later, Arnold sold military information to the British. When it was discovered, he fled to New York City. There he commanded British troops and fought against the Americans.

Before long, there were about 20,000 militiamen around Boston. On June 16, 1775, Colonel William Prescott set up militia posts on Bunker Hill and Breed's Hill. These sites were across from Boston Harbor. The British decided to remove the colonists from the hills.

The next day, British troops charged up Breed's Hill (not Bunker Hill, although the battle is named after Bunker Hill). The Americans were running out of ammunition, so Prescott is said to have shouted, "Don't fire until you see the whites of their eyes." The militia fired, and the British retreated. Twice more the British tried but failed. Finally, the Americans ran out of gunpowder. They had to pull back. The British won the Battle of Bunker Hill, but more than 1,000 of their soldiers died or were wounded.

Colonists had to decide whether to join the rebels or stay loyal to Britain.

Colonists	
Loyalists	**Patriots**
• sided with Britain	• supported the war for independence
• did not think that unfair taxes and laws were good enough reasons to fight	• felt they could no longer live under British rule
• believed the British would win and did not want to be on the losing side	

The American Revolution was not just a war between the British and the Americans. It was also a war between American Patriots and Loyalists.

 NGSSS Check

1. Identify each battle. SS.8.A.3.6

   The first shot of the American Revolution is fired.

   _____

   The Green Mountain Boys catch the British by surprise.

   _____

   The British charge uphill.

   _____

2. Summarize the main difference between Loyalists and Patriots.

   _____

   _____

Copyright © by The McGraw-Hill Companies, Inc.

7. **Generalize** Complete the following sentences:

   Loyalists felt that

   _____

   _____

   _____

   _____.

   Patriots felt that

   _____

   _____

   _____

   _____.

Think Critically

8. **Conclude** What did the British learn from the Battle of Bunker Hill?

   _____

   _____

   _____

   _____

   _____

DECLARING INDEPENDENCE

NGSSS

SS.8.A.1.6 Compare interpretations of key events and issues throughout American History.

SS.8.A.3.3 Recognize the contributions of the Founding Fathers (John Adams, Sam Adams, Benjamin Franklin, John Hancock, Alexander Hamilton, Thomas Jefferson, James Madison, George Mason, George Washington) during American Revolutionary efforts.

SS.8.A.3.6 Examine the causes, course, and consequences of the American Revolution.

SS.8.A.3.7 Examine the structure, content, and consequences of the Declaration of Independence.

Essential Question
What motivates people to act?

Guiding Questions
1. How did individuals and events impact efforts for independence?
2. Why did the American colonies declare independence?

Terms to Know

petition
a formal request

preamble
the introduction to a formal document that often tells why the document was written

Where in the World?
Philadelphia, 1776

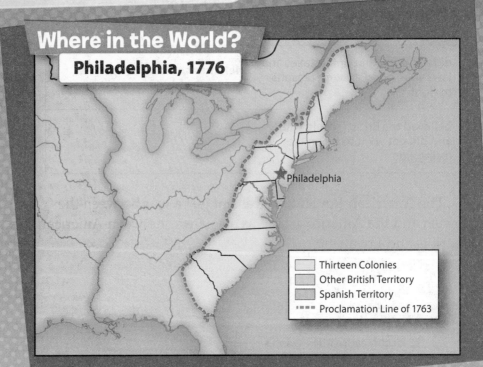

Philadelphia

Thirteen Colonies
Other British Territory
Spanish Territory
- - - Proclamation Line of 1763

When Did It Happen?

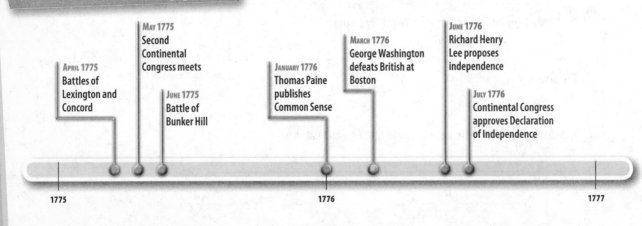

APRIL 1775
Battles of Lexington and Concord

MAY 1775
Second Continental Congress meets

JUNE 1775
Battle of Bunker Hill

JANUARY 1776
Thomas Paine publishes Common Sense

MARCH 1776
George Washington defeats British at Boston

JUNE 1776
Richard Henry Lee proposes independence

JULY 1776
Continental Congress approves Declaration of Independence

1775

1776

1777

The Second Continental Congress

On May 10, 1775, the Second Continental Congress met. The delegates included some of the greatest leaders in America. Among them were John and Samuel Adams, Patrick Henry, Richard Henry Lee, and George Washington. Several new delegates came as well.

Benjamin Franklin, one of the most respected men in the colonies, had been a leader in the Pennsylvania legislature. John Hancock of Massachusetts was a wealthy merchant. He funded many Patriot groups, including the Sons of Liberty. The delegates chose Hancock to be president of the Second Continental Congress. Thomas Jefferson, only 32, was also a delegate. He served in the Virginia legislature. Jefferson was already known as a brilliant thinker and writer.

The Congress offered Britain one more chance to avoid war. It sent a **petition,** or formal request, to King George III. The request was called the Olive Branch Petition. It explained that the colonists wanted peace and asked the king to protect their rights. The king refused to receive the petition. Instead, he prepared for war.

The Americans learned that British troops were planning to invade New York. The Americans decided to strike first. They sent troops north from Fort Ticonderoga and captured Montreal.

In July 1775, George Washington arrived in Boston. He found that the militia was not well organized, so he trained them. By March 1776, they were ready to fight. Washington placed the troops in a semicircle around Boston. This surprised the British. They realized they were within easy reach of Washington's guns. British General William Howe commanded his troops to board ships and leave Boston. On March 17, Washington led his joyful troops into the city.

The desire for independence from Britain was growing. Colonist Thomas Paine wrote a booklet called *Common Sense.* It encouraged complete independence from Britain. Paine's words had a great influence on colonists.

Think Critically

1. Evaluate Which of the early actions of the Second Continental Congress do you think was most important and why?

_____

_____

_____

2. Evaluate Was George Washington successful in training the colonial militia? Explain your answer.

_____

_____

_____

Mark the Text

3. Underline the name of the author and the name of the booklet that encouraged independence from Britain.

Show Your Skill

4. Draw Conclusions What was the purpose of the Olive Branch Petition?

_____

_____

Second Continental Congress

- authorized the printing of money
- set up a post office with Franklin in charge
- set up committees to handle relations with Native Americans and other countries
- created the Continental Army
- chose George Washington to command the army

Think Critically

6. **Infer** Why was Thomas Jefferson chosen to write the Declaration of Independence?

_____

_____

_____

7. **Describe** List the four sections of the Declaration of Independence.

_____

_____

_____

_____

Take the Challenge

8. Rewrite the Preamble to the Constitution in your own words. What parts do you think are the most important for our country today?

The United States Constitution

Declaring Independence

The delegates at the Second Continental Congress debated. Some wanted the colonies to declare independence. Other delegates did not. In June 1776, Virginia's Richard Henry Lee proposed a bold resolution. He proposed that the United Colonies should be free and independent.

While the debate went on, the Congress chose a committee to write a Declaration of Independence. John Adams, Benjamin Franklin, Thomas Jefferson, Robert Livingston, and Roger Sherman were on the committee. They asked Thomas Jefferson to write the first draft of the document.

Jefferson agreed. He was inspired by the ideas of English philosopher John Locke to explain why the colonies should be independent. Locke had said that people are born with certain natural rights to life, liberty, and property. Locke wrote that people form governments to protect those rights, and that a government interfering with those rights could rightfully be overthrown.

On July 2, 1776, the Second Continental Congress voted on Lee's proposal for independence. Then the delegates discussed and edited Jefferson's draft. They approved the Declaration of Independence on July 4. John Hancock was the first to sign it. He said that he wrote his name large enough for King George III to read without his glasses. Eventually 56 delegates signed the document announcing the birth of the United States.

The Declaration has four major sections. The **preamble,** or introduction, states that people who wish to form a new country should explain their reasons for doing so. The next two sections list the rights that the colonists believed they should have and their complaints against Britain. The final section proclaims the existence of the new nation.

NGSSS Check List two important figures from this time period and tell why each was important. SS.8.A.3.3

_____

_____

_____

_____

_____

ESSENTIAL QUESTION *What motivates people to act?*

Reflect on What It Means . . .

In 1818, as he looked back on the American Revolution, John Adams commented that the revolution was over before the war began. "The revolution," Adams explained, "was in the minds and hearts of the people." It is the <u>power</u> of words rather than the <u>number</u> of words that make them convincing.

To Me

In 20 words or fewer, tell why you would have been a Patriot or Loyalist at the beginning of the American Revolution.

To the Community

In 20 words or fewer, convince someone in your community to join your side.

To the World

In 20 words or fewer, convince someone from France why they should care about this revolution.

Keep Going! ⟫

TAKE THE CHALLENGE

Research quotations from the American Revolution that contain no more than 20 words. Choose two quotations and rewrite each of them in your own words in the space below. As a class, make a display depicting real historical writings and your rewritten versions of the quotations. Challenge each other to figure out which quotations were written around 1776 and which were written as part of this assignment.

THE AMERICAN REVOLUTION

NGSSS

SS.8.A.3.3 Recognize the contributions of the Founding Fathers (John Adams, Sam Adams, Benjamin Franklin, John Hancock, Alexander Hamilton, Thomas Jefferson, James Madison, George Mason, George Washington) during American Revolutionary efforts.

ESSENTIAL QUESTION *Why does conflict develop?*

The Revolutionary War was not George Washington's first time going into battle. During the French and Indian War, two horses were shot out from under him. He knew his troops would need to be brave.

PHOTO: SuperStock/Getty Images

Copyright © by The McGraw-Hill Companies, Inc.

" The time is now near at hand which must probably determine whether Americans are to be freemen or slaves; whether they are to have any property they can call their own...The fate of unborn millions will now depend, under God, on the courage and conduct of this army. "

GENERAL ORDERS, 2 JULY 1776, IN J. C. FITZPATRICK (ED.) WRITINGS OF GEORGE WASHINGTON VOL. 5 (1932)

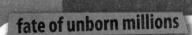

fate of unborn millions

What was Washington trying to say about the action of his men by using this phrase?

_____

_____

In this speech, Washington was addressing the Continental Army. What do you think was the purpose of his speech?

_____

_____

DBQ BREAKING IT DOWN

George Washington chose the words of his speech carefully. Imagine that you are an American general writing to inspire troops to go into battle today. What words would you use to make your troops feel inspired? In the space, write your own speech.

_____

_____

McGraw-Hill
networks™
There's More Online!

LESSON 1

THE WAR FOR INDEPENDENCE

NGSSS

SS.8.A.3.3 Recognize the contributions of the Founding Fathers (John Adams, Sam Adams, Benjamin Franklin, John Hancock, Alexander Hamilton, Thomas Jefferson, James Madison, George Mason, George Washington) during American Revolutionary efforts.

SS.8.A.3.4 Examine the contributions of influential groups to both the American and British war efforts during the American Revolutionary War and their effects on the outcome of the war.

SS.8.A.3.6 Examine the causes, course, and consequences of the American Revolution.

SS.8.A.3.8 Examine individuals and groups that affected political and social motivations during the American Revolution.

Essential Question
Why does conflict develop?

Guiding Questions
1. **Who were the opposing sides in the American Revolution?**
2. **What were significant battles in the early years of the American Revolution?**
3. **Was the British plan for victory successful?**

Terms to Know

mercenary
hired soldier

recruit
to enlist in the military

Where in the World?

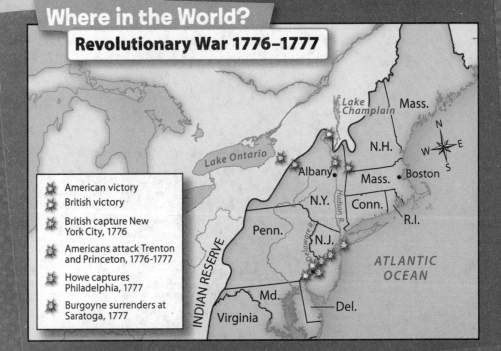

Revolutionary War 1776–1777

- American victory
- British victory
- British capture New York City, 1776
- Americans attack Trenton and Princeton, 1776-1777
- Howe captures Philadelphia, 1777
- Burgoyne surrenders at Saratoga, 1777

When Did It Happen?

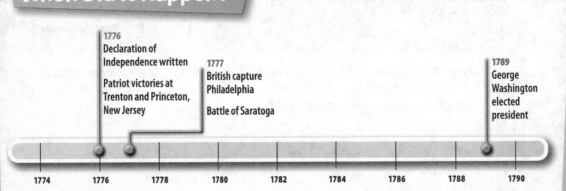

1776
Declaration of Independence written

Patriot victories at Trenton and Princeton, New Jersey

1777
British capture Philadelphia

Battle of Saratoga

1789
George Washington elected president

1774   1776   1778   1780   1782   1784   1786   1788   1790

The Two Armies Face Off

Founder John Adams predicted a "long . . . and bloody war." The British felt they would crush the colonists. The colonists, on the other hand, felt Great Britain would give up quickly after losing a few battles.

Great Britain had good reason to be confident. Some of the reasons for this included:

- Having the strongest navy in the world
- Having a well-trained army
- Having great wealth from their worldwide empire
- Having a large population (over 8 million people).

In comparison, the colonists seemed outmatched. They had

- a weak navy
- no regular army, just local militia groups
- a lack of fighting experience
- a shortage of weapons and ammunition
- people that did not support their efforts for independence.

There were some people in the colonies who were still loyal to the king of Great Britain. They were called Loyalists, or Tories. Loyalists had different reasons for supporting Great Britain. Some relied on Great Britain for their jobs. Others thought a revolution would cause too much trouble. Others did not understand why the colonists wanted to break free of Great Britain.

This disagreement caused serious problems between people. Even neighbors and family members disagreed. One example is Benjamin Franklin, who was important in helping the country begin the war for independence, and his son, William, who was a Loyalist.

Besides Loyalists, Great Britain had other people to help them fight. Some of these people were **mercenaries,** or soldiers who are paid to fight. The Americans called these soldiers Hessians.

Some African Americans also supported Great Britain and the Loyalists. Great Britain worked to get their support, sometimes promising freedom to those who helped the British cause.

The Patriots had some advantages as well. The fighting would take place on their land. The British, on the other hand, would be fighting far from home. This meant that all of the British supplies and soldiers had to come from far away.

The Patriots were also fighting for a great cause—their independence from Britain. This gave them more motivation

Think Critically

1. **Explain** Why did the British think they would win the war?

Mark the Text

2. Underline reasons that people in the colonies stayed loyal to Britain.

Show Your Skill

3. **Classify** List three advantages the Patriots had during the American Revolution.

Think Critically

4. **Infer** Why do you think some African Americans sided with the British?

5. Interpret What disadvantages did the Patriots face in fighting the British?

_____

_____

_____

_____

6. Analyze Why did Congress need to form a "real" army?

_____

_____

7. Research women involved in the American Revolution. Learn five fascinating facts about one of them and share the facts with the class.

Colonial uniforms varied in style. Many soldiers had to provide their own gear.

to fight, even when times were hard. The Patriots' greatest advantage was the leadership of George Washington. He was courageous and determined. These qualities made him an excellent leader.

After the Declaration of Independence in 1776, the Continental Congress acted as a national government for the colonies. Congress, however, had limited powers. They could not raise money by taxing everyone in the colonies. Money was needed to support the war effort. Some members of Congress, such as James Madison from Virginia, called for a stronger national government.

Not everyone agreed with this idea. After living with harsh British rule, the colonists did not want to transfer, or move, power to the new government. This made it hard for Congress to raise money and **recruit,** or enlist, soldiers.

Many of the troops were members of their local militia. A militia is usually made up of local people who are called to fight when needed. Many of them were farmers who needed to tend to their farms to provide for their families. It was important for the Patriots to form a "real" army. Soldiers would be trained and paid for their efforts. Congress established the Continental Army.

At first, soldiers signed up for a year at a time. General Washington felt soldiers should agree to stay until the war was over. It was also difficult to find good leaders for the army. Some were capable young men from the army. Others had experience in previous, or earlier, wars.

Sometimes women were involved in the fighting. Margaret Corbin, a woman from Pennsylvania, went with her husband when he signed up with the Continental Army. She took his place after he died in battle. Legend has it that another woman, Mary Ludwig Hays McCauley, also fought in the war. She was known as "Molly Pitcher" because she brought pitchers of water to the soldiers. Deborah Sampson disguised herself as a man so she could join the fight, too.

PHOTO: Niday Picture Library/Alamy

Early Campaigns

Early battles of the American Revolution were fought by smaller numbers of soldiers. At Bunker Hill, in Massachusetts, about 2,200 British soldiers fought about 1,200 Americans. Despite outnumbering the Americans, the British lost many more troops. Even though the British won the battle, they quickly realized more troops were needed to fight the war.

In 1776 Great Britain sent 32,000 more troops to fight the war. The British hoped to frighten the Americans with the size of the British force. They hoped this would make the Americans surrender.

Patriot Nathan Hale was caught spying on the British.

What the Patriots lacked in numbers they made up in determination. In August of 1776, the two armies met in the Battle of Long Island in New York. Nathan Hale, a Patriot, spied on the British. The British discovered the truth and sentenced Hale to death. Before he was hanged, Hale supposedly said, "I only regret that I have but one life to lose for my country."

The Continental Army was outnumbered at Long Island. Even though they fought hard, the British had more men and more supplies. In fact, many Patriot soldiers had no shoes, socks, or jackets. The Battle of Long Island was a serious defeat for the Continental Army. The British leader, General Howe, could have probably captured all of General Washington's troops. He chased the Continental Army across New Jersey into Pennsylvania. Then he was satisfied that Washington was defeated, and he let him go.

This was a very difficult time for the Continental Army. Even General Washington worried whether they would succeed or not. It would be difficult to win without more men and more supplies. He wrote to his brother and said, "I think the game is pretty near up."

Washington told the Continental Congress he needed more troops. Many African Americans wanted to join the fight but were not allowed to early in the war. Washington asked Congress to reconsider. Some colonies allowed African Americans to enlist despite the ban. Historians estimate that around 5,000 African Americans fought with the Patriots. Peter Salem was an enslaved African American soldier who fought at Concord and the Battle of Bunker Hill. Because of his service in the army, he won his freedom.

Show Your Skill

8. Generalize How did the number of British troops compare with the number of American troops?

_____

_____

_____

_____

9. Explain Why did Washington win in Trenton?

_____

_____

_____

_____

_____

10. Summarize Why was the winter of 1776–1777 significant?

_____

_____

_____

_____

_____

_____

11. Describe Explain the British plan in 1777.

_____

_____

_____

_____

_____

Even though the winter was cold and they had lost some battles, General Washington did not give up. On Christmas night, he and his troops crossed the icy Delaware River. His plan was to surprise a Hessian force of about 1,400 men who were camped in Trenton, New Jersey. The plan worked, and Washington's forces captured about 900 troops. Faced with more fighting, Washington decided to march on to Princeton, New Jersey. Though met there by more British troops, Washington pushed them back. The battles were a success for the Continental Army. This helped encourage the troops— they now believed that they could win.

Early Battles of the Revolution		
Battle	**Winner**	**Effect**
Battle of Bunker Hill	British	British won but sustained many losses; decided they would need more troops
Battle of Long Island	British	British outnumbered the Patriots
Battles of Trenton and Princeton	Americans	Surprise attack succeeds; raises morale of the Continental Army

British Strategy

The British had a plan to win in 1777. They wanted to cut off New England from the Middle Colonies. To do so, the British needed to gain control of the Hudson River. This meant taking Albany, New York.

The British plan involved three separate attacks. The British would come in on Albany from different directions at the same time. General Burgoyne would move south from Canada. Lieutenant Colonel St. Leger would move east from Lake Ontario. General Howe would move north up the Hudson River.

British Plan of Attack (1777)	
British Leader	**Role in Albany Attack**
General Burgoyne	Move south from Canada
Lieutenant Colonel St. Leger	Move east from Lake Ontario
General Howe	Move north up Hudson River

General Howe changed his plans, however. General Howe decided to capture Philadelphia. This was an important Patriot city because it was the home of the Continental Congress. General Howe's forces took Philadelphia, forcing the Congress to escape. Instead of going to Albany, General Howe stayed in Philadelphia for the winter.

General Burgoyne surrendered at Saratoga.

This was not the only change in the British plan. St. Leger lost to the Americans at Fort Stanwix, New York. This delayed St. Leger from reaching Albany.

General Burgoyne also had problems. He was able to capture Fort Ticonderoga in July 1777, but then he needed supplies. He sent some troops to Vermont. There was an American supply base there, which they planned to capture. However, a local militia group, called the Green Mountain Boys, attacked Burgoyne's troops. This was a win for the Patriots.

Burgoyne was really in trouble now. Low on supplies and with no other British forces to help, he retreated to Saratoga, New York. There, American general Horatio Gates surrounded Burgoyne's forces. Burgoyne surrendered on October 17, 1777.

The British plan to take Albany and the Hudson River had failed. The Americans had won a huge victory at Saratoga. The American win at the Battle of Saratoga changed the course of the war.

Show Your Skill

12. Identify Cause and Effect
How did Howe's victory in Philadelphia lead to Burgoyne's defeat at Saratoga?

_____

_____

_____

_____

_____

_____

British Defeat at Saratoga	
British Leader	**Role in Loss at Saratoga**
General Burgoyne	Left low on supplies with no support at Saratoga; forced to surrender
Lieutenant Colonel St. Leger	Never met at Albany, stopped by American forces, retreated westward
General Howe	Never arrived in New York, stayed in Philadelphia for winter of 1777

NGSSS Check Summarize why the British were unable to cut off New England from the Middle Colonies. S.8.A.3.6

_____

_____

LESSON 2

THE WAR CONTINUES

NGSSS

SS.8.A.3.3 Recognize the contributions of the Founding Fathers (John Adams, Sam Adams, Benjamin Franklin, John Hancock, Alexander Hamilton, Thomas Jefferson, James Madison, George Mason, George Washington) during American Revolutionary efforts.

SS.8.A.3.4 Examine the contributions of influential groups to both the American and British war efforts during the American Revolutionary War and their effects on the outcome of the war.

SS.8.A.3.5 Describe the influence of individuals on social and political developments during the Revolutionary era.

SS.8.A.3.6 Examine the causes, course, and consequences of the American Revolution.

Essential Question

Why does conflict develop?

Guiding Questions

1. How did America gain allies?
2. What was life like on the home front during the American Revolution?

Terms to Know

desert
to leave without permission or intent to come back

inflation
when it takes more and more money to buy the same amount of goods

Where in the World?

The Winter of 1777–1778

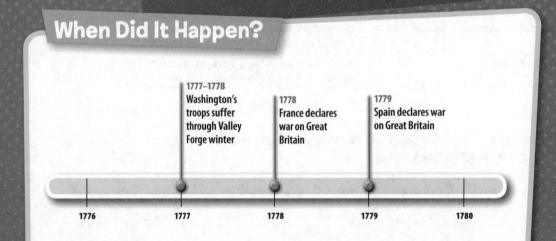

When Did It Happen?

1777–1778
Washington's troops suffer through Valley Forge winter

1778
France declares war on Great Britain

1779
Spain declares war on Great Britain

1776 — 1777 — 1778 — 1779 — 1780

Gaining Allies

The United States needed help to win the American Revolution. The Continental Congress sent Benjamin Franklin to France in 1776. Franklin was a charming, skilled statesman and was very popular in France. The Continental Congress hoped he would be able to win French support for the American war effort. Early on, the French secretly gave the Americans money to support their cause. They did not wish to openly side against Great Britain.

Some news arrived in 1777 that changed the French position, however. The Continental Congress sent Jonathan Austin of Boston to France with news of the American victory at Saratoga. When Austin arrived, Benjamin Franklin had one question: Have the British taken Philadelphia? Austin told him it had been taken. This was not the news he had been sent to deliver, though.

"But sir, I have greater news than that," Austin answered. "General Burgoyne and his whole army are prisoners of war!"

This information about the Patriot win at Saratoga was very important. France and other nations now saw that the Patriots might win the war. Soon after, in February 1778, France declared war on Great Britain. They agreed to help the Americans with money, equipment, and troops.

News of the French alliance traveled slowly back to the United States. Over the winter of 1777–1778, the Continental Army suffered through a hard winter. General Washington and his troops were camped in Valley Forge, Pennsylvania. This camp was about 20 miles away from Philadelphia. There, British General Howe and his men were comfortable and warm. Washington's troops were miserable and cold. They did not have enough food, clothing, or medicine. General Washington had to use all of his leadership skills to keep his army together at Valley Forge.

Many soldiers got sick. Many died. Some soldiers quit. Other soldiers **deserted,** or left without permission. Despite the hardships, the troops kept on. "Naked and starving as they are," General Washington wrote, "we cannot enough admire the incomparable patience and fidelity [faithfulness] of the soldiery."

The Continental Army survived the winter. As spring arrived, the troops grew stronger in mind and body. Then, in April 1778, General Washington announced that France would help them. This made everyone feel hopeful, and the army celebrated with a religious service and a parade.

Show Your Skill

1. Identify Cause and Effect
What was one effect of the American victory in the Battle of Saratoga?

_____

_____

_____

_____

_____

_____

Think Critically

2. Explain Why did some American soldiers decide to desert during the winter of 1777–1778?

_____

_____

_____

_____

Take the Challenge

3. You are a soldier at Valley Forge. What might it take to motivate soldiers to not desert during that winter at Valley Forge? Write a short speech to encourage your fellow soldiers.

Show Your Skill

4. Interpret Charts How did Lafayette help the Patriot cause?

_____

_____

_____

_____

Think Critically

5. Interpret Why might foreign-born people come and help the Patriots in their fight for freedom?

_____

_____

_____

_____

_____

_____

_____

6. Infer Why was help from Spain important?

_____

_____

_____

_____

_____

_____

Marquis de Lafayette fought at the Battle of Brandywine.

Individuals from around the world helped the Patriots. A young Frenchman named Marquis de Lafayette arrived in 1777 to help the Patriot cause. He was only 19 years old, but excited about the ideas of liberty and independence. He volunteered his services and became a trusted aide to General Washington.

Two Polish men were also important in the war effort: Thaddeus Kosciusko and Casimir Pulaski. Kosciusko helped build important defenses for the Americans. Pulaski was promoted to general. He was fatally wounded in battle in 1779.

Friedrich von Steuben was another foreign-born person who helped the Patriots. Through the harsh winter at Valley Forge, von Steuben trained the Continental Army. This made them a much more effective fighting force.

Some people helped away from the battlefield as well. Juan de Miralles arrived from Spain. He helped persuade Spain, Cuba, and Mexico to help the United States by sending money to support the war.

Foreign Supporters of the Revolution	
Marquis de Lafayette	French nobleman and Patriot volunteer; became trusted aide to General Washington
Thaddeus Kosciusko	Polish nobleman who helped build important defenses for the Americans
Casimir Pulaski	Polish man who rose to rank of general in Continental Army; died fighting for the Patriot cause
Friedrich von Steuben	Former army officer from Prussia who helped train the Continental Army
Juan de Miralles	Spanish supporter who persuaded Spain, Cuba, and Mexico to send money to help the Patriots

Even with help from many countries and individuals, the fight for independence was still not over. More battles and challenges were yet to come.

Life on the Home Front

The war had effects on the lives of everyone in the United States. The Patriot soldiers faced great difficulties on the battlefield. Those at home faced challenges as well.

Women raised their children and took care of their homes on their own. They also ran businesses and farms while their fathers, husbands, and brothers were away at war. Children lived without their fathers present.

These circumstances made some people think differently about women's roles. Perhaps equality and freedom could extend to women as well. Abigail Adams, the wife of Congressman John Adams, wrote to ask him to think about the position of women as he helped form the new nation.

For others, the fight for freedom made them question slavery. In 1778, the governor of New Jersey, William Livingstone, asked his state government to free all enslaved people. He felt that slavery disagreed with the ideas of Christianity and humanity. African Americans also argued this point. How could men seeking freedom not extend that to African Americans as well? The issue, or matter, of slavery would continue for many years to come.

The war also affected another group of people in the United States. These people were Loyalists, American settlers who supported Great Britain. Some Loyalists joined the British troops and fought against the Patriots in the war. Some were spies for Great Britain. Others fled to Canada or went back to Great Britain. The people who stayed faced trouble. Many were ignored or treated badly by their neighbors. Some were attacked or hurt. Those caught spying could be arrested or even executed.

Abigail Adams reminded Patriot leaders to "Remember the Ladies" when making decisions.

Think Critically

7. Analyze How did the American Revolution affect people other than soldiers?

_____

_____

_____

_____

Mark the Text

8. Underline the names of two people who supported more equality for women and for African Americans.

NGSSS Check How did other nations support the Americans in the American Revolution? SS.8.A.3.4

_____

_____

NGSSS

SS.8.A.3.4 Examine the contributions of influential groups to both the American and British war efforts during the American Revolutionary War and their effects on the outcome of the war.

SS.8.A.3.6 Examine the causes, course, and consequences of the American Revolution.

SS.8.A.3.16 Examine key events in Florida history as each impacts this era of American history.

Essential Question
Why does conflict develop?

Guiding Questions
1. How did the war in the West develop?
2. What was the result of the war at sea?
3. What was the result of the war in the South?

Terms to Know

blockade
measure that keeps a country from communicating and trading with other nations

privateer
privately owned ship outfitted with weapons

Where in the World?

The Revolutionary War in the West and South

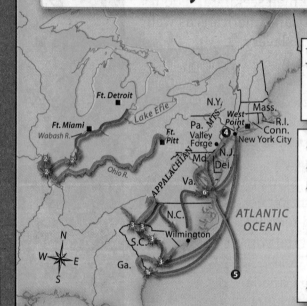

- ← American and/or allied forces
- ← British forces
- ✴ American victory
- ✴ British victory
- ■ Fort

- British capture Savannah, 1778
- Patriots victorious at Kaskaskia, Cahokia, and Vincennes
- After defeats at Charles Town and Camden, Patriots are victorious at Kings Mountain and Cowpens, 1780–1781
- ④ Washington and Rochambeau rush toward Virginia, Aug. 1781
- ⑤ French Admiral De Grasses keeps British ships away
- Cornwallis trapped; the British surrender at Yorktown, 1781

When Did It Happen?

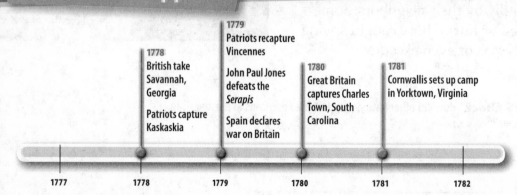

1778
British take Savannah, Georgia

Patriots capture Kaskaskia

1779
Patriots recapture Vincennes

John Paul Jones defeats the *Serapis*

Spain declares war on Britain

1780
Great Britain captures Charles Town, South Carolina

1781
Cornwallis sets up camp in Yorktown, Virginia

1777 1778 1779 1780 1781 1782

Fighting in the West

Native Americans were another group of people affected by the war. There were many Native American nations in the different colonies. Some of these nations took sides in the war between the Patriots and the British. Some helped the Patriots. More Native Americans decided to help the British, however. The Patriots had lived in North America and taken land that belonged to the Native Americans. The Patriots had fought with them and changed their way of life. To them, the British seemed like less of a threat.

The American Revolution was fought in many areas of the colonies. One important area was along the western frontier, or land west of the Appalachian Mountains. The British and some of their Native American allies had raided American settlements. Mohawk chief Joseph Brant led brutal attacks in southwestern New York and northern Pennsylvania.

Henry Hamilton was another British leader on the western frontier. He had a terrible nickname: the "hair buyer." Hamilton paid Native Americans for the scalps of American settlers.

A Patriot named George Rogers Clark wanted to end the attacks on western settlers. Clark was a lieutenant colonel in the Virginia militia. He set out to help in the West. He and a small force captured the British post of Kaskaskia, in what is now Illinois. Clark then decided to capture the British town of Vincennes, in what is now Indiana.

Henry Hamilton recaptured Vincennes in December of 1778. Clark did not give up, though. He staged a surprise attack on Vincennes in February 1779, during a very cold winter. The British surrendered.

Think Critically

1. Explain Why did more Native Americans side with the British than the Patriots?

_____

_____

_____

_____

2. Summarize Describe one event in the Revolutionary War in the West.

_____

_____

_____

_____

_____

_____

Take the Challenge

3. Work with a partner and prepare an interview with one of the people involved in the American Revolution in the West. Do some research and prepare questions and answers. Perform the interview for the class.

This is the letter George Rogers Clark wrote to the British General Hamilton demanding Hamilton surrender Vincennes.

Think Critically

4. Explain What did Americans do to combat the blockade?

_____

_____

_____

_____

Show Your Skill

5. Identify Cause and Effect What was the effect of privateers on the American war effort?

_____

_____

_____

Mark the Text

6. Underline the sentences that tell what John Paul Jones did.

The War at Sea

The war was also fought at sea. The United States did not have a strong navy. Congress called for the building of 13 warships, but only two ever sailed to sea.

Great Britain had a very powerful navy. Its many ships blocked American ports and harbors. This prevented ships from entering or leaving. This worked to control people and supplies that came in and out. This is known as a **blockade.**

Something had to be done to break the blockade. So Congress allowed another solution. It gave special permission to about 2,000 privately owned merchant ships to have weapons attached. The ships could then capture enemy ships in order to take their cargo. These armed merchant ships were called **privateers.** They played a significant role in the American Revolution because they captured more British ships than the American navy.

A very famous battle at sea occurred during the American Revolution. This took place in 1779 off the coast of Great Britain. This battle was between a British ship called the *Serapis* and an American ship called the *Bonhomme Richard*. The captain of the American ship was John Paul Jones. The ships fought for hours. Eventually, the British captain asked Jones if he wanted to surrender. Jones would not surrender, and his response is a well-known quote: "I have not yet begun to fight." John Paul Jones was victorious against the *Serapis*, which he and his crew captured. The victory was the first time an American ship had captured a British ship in British waters.

The warships *Bonhomme Richard* and *Serapis* meet in one of the most famous naval battles of the war. American naval officer, John Paul Jones, led the crew of the *Bonhomme Richard* to victory.

Fighting in the South

It seemed like the British had more advantages in the American Revolution. The British came to realize that they would not be able to win as quickly as they once had thought. They came up with a new strategy. They wanted to win the South.

Early on, the American forces won some important battles in the South. The Patriots beat the Loyalist forces in Wilmington, North Carolina. They also kept the British from capturing Charles Town, which is now called Charleston, South Carolina. Even though these were small battles, they had a big impact.

The British had some successes in the South as well. They took the city of Savannah, Georgia. In 1780 they also captured Charles Town. Thousands of troops were taken prisoner by the British. This was the worst American defeat of the war. The British success would not last, however.

The British believed they would have a lot of Loyalist support in the South. They also wanted to use their naval power to help them win in the South. The British did not get the Loyalist support they hoped for. They also had to deal with a type of fighting they were not used to. Patriot forces would attack the British by surprise, and then disappear again. This is known as hit-and-run tactics. Francis Marion, also known as the "Swamp Fox," was a successful Patriot leader in the South. He was quick and smart, and he could hide from the British easily in the eastern South Carolina swamps.

Other countries were also keeping Great Britain distracted in the South. In 1779, Spain declared war on Great Britain. At that time, Louisiana had a Spanish governor named Bernardo de Gálvez. He helped the Patriots a great deal. He did this by giving them money and allowing them to use the Port of New Orleans. He also shipped tons of supplies and ammunition up the Mississippi River. Gálvez also fought the British in the South. This fighting with Spain weakened the British in their fight against the Patriots.

In the South, the British had a huge victory at Camden, South Carolina. General Cornwallis led the British troops, and General Horatio Gates led the Patriot forces. The battle was a disaster for the Patriots. Even though Gates had more men, the British army surrounded Gates's men and caused 2,000 casualties. Only 324 British were lost.

Some Patriot victories were on the way. Some settlers were neutral, meaning they did not want to take sides. The British told these local people that they must support them. The British said if the locals did not help them, they would hang their leaders and destroy their land. This angered the Americans who lived in the mountains of the South. They formed a militia.

7. Explain Why was Francis Marion called the "Swamp Fox"?

_____

_____

_____

_____

_____

Mark the Text

8. Underline at least two ways Bernardo de Gálvez helped the Americans.

Show Your Skill

9. Identify Cause and Effect What was one effect of the British threatening to hang leaders of Southern communities and destroy their land?

_____

_____

_____

_____

10. Identify Cause and Effect
What effect did the Patriot victory at Kings Mountain have?

_____

_____

_____

_____

_____

_____

11. Infer Why did General Cornwallis give up the fight in the Carolinas and go to Virginia?

_____

_____

_____

_____

_____

_____

About 2,000 Patriots came together from nearby colonies. They fought a Loyalist force at Kings Mountain. The Patriots surrounded the Loyalist forces and killed or captured all of the Loyalist forces. This won the battle and more support from Southern settlers.

More victories followed. Nathanael Greene became the commander of the Continental Army in the South. He decided to split his troops into two sections to fight General Cornwallis on different fronts. One part of the army had success against the British at Cowpens, South Carolina. The other part of the army helped in raids with Francis Marion.

Later in 1781, the two sections came back together. They met Cornwallis's army in what is now Greensboro, North Carolina. Even though the Patriots did not win, the British sustained great losses. General Cornwallis decided to give up the fight in the Carolinas.

Cornwallis and his troops went north into Virginia. As they went, they carried out raids. Cornwallis set up camp with his men at Yorktown on the Virginia coast. Both Marquis de Lafayette and Anthony Wayne went south into Virginia to push Cornwallis back. The battle for the South was entering its final phase.

Key Battles in the South	
Battles	**Outcomes**
Savannah, Georgia (1778)	British forces under General Clinton take the city and occupy it and most of the state.
Charles Town (1780)	British take thousands of prisoners at Charles Town after Patriot forces surrender.
Eastern South Carolina (1780)	Guerilla Patriot forces under Francis Marion prove difficult for British forces to contain.
Camden, South Carolina (August 1780)	Patriot commander General Horatio Gates suffers disastrous defeat to the British.
Kings Mountain, North Carolina (October 1780)	American militia forces kill or capture all British and Loyalist troops.
Greensboro, North Carolina (March 1781)	Patriot forces retreat, but British troops suffer great losses in the fight. Cornwallis gives up on the Carolinas.

 NGSSS Check Choose one of these people and briefly tell how he was involved in the American Revolution: Joseph Brant, George Rogers Clark, John Paul Jones, Francis Marion, or General Charles Cornwallis. SS.8.A.3.6

_____

_____

THE FINAL YEARS

NGSSS

SS.8.A.3.3 Recognize the contributions of the Founding Fathers (John Adams, Sam Adams, Benjamin Franklin, John Hancock, Alexander Hamilton, Thomas Jefferson, James Madison, George Mason, and George Washington) during American Revolutionary efforts.

SS.8.A.3.4 Examine the contributions of influential groups to both the American and British war efforts during the American Revolutionary War and their effects on the outcome of the war.

SS.8.A.3.6 Examine the causes, course, and consequences of the American Revolution.

Essential Question
Why does conflict develop?

Guiding Questions
1. What events occurred in the victory at Yorktown?
2. What helped the Patriots win independence?

Terms to Know

siege
attempt to force surrender by blocking the movement of people and goods into or out of a place

ratify
to approve officially

ambush
an attack in which the attacker hides and surprises the enemy

Where in the World?
Victory at Yorktown

When Did It Happen?

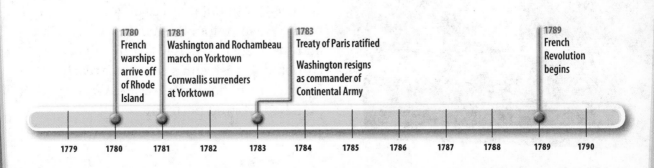

1780
French warships arrive off of Rhode Island

1781
Washington and Rochambeau march on Yorktown

Cornwallis surrenders at Yorktown

1783
Treaty of Paris ratified

Washington resigns as commander of Continental Army

1789
French Revolution begins

1779 1780 1781 1782 1783 1784 1785 1786 1787 1788 1789 1790

PHOTO: idp eastern USA collection/Alamy

Copyright © by The McGraw-Hill Companies, Inc.

Think Critically

1. Describe Explain how General Cornwallis was trapped on the Yorktown Peninsula.

_____

_____

_____

_____

_____

Mark the Text

2. Underline the sentence that tells how General Washington changed his strategy.

Take the Challenge

3. Draw a map that shows Cornwallis and the forces that surrounded him at Yorktown.

Victory at Yorktown

While battles were going on in the South, General Washington stayed with his troops in New York. In July of 1780, the French arrived to help the Americans. French warships appeared off of Rhode Island. They carried thousands of French troops who were led by Comte de Rochambeau. They joined General Washington in New York and waited for a second French fleet to arrive.

General Washington had a plan. He wanted to attack an army base in New York commanded by British General Clinton. A second fleet of French ships was expected. The attack would happen when that force arrived.

General Washington and Comte de Rochambeau waited a long time. The second French fleet never arrived in the North. Instead, Washington received news that the fleet would arrive at Chesapeake Bay. They could help fight General Cornwallis, who was camped on the Yorktown Peninsula.

Cornwallis was in a dangerous position. There was only one direction on land for escape. This had been blocked by Marquis de Lafayette and Anthony Wayne. Now the second French fleet would block escape by water as well.

General Washington changed his plan to attack General Clinton in New York. He and Rochambeau would take their troops down to Virginia to fight against Cornwallis. This strategy, or plan of action, was kept a secret. Washington and Rochambeau moved quickly. Not even their soldiers knew where they were going. Washington did not want anyone to know the Continental Army's next move. He hoped it would trick General Clinton so he would not have time to send help to General Cornwallis.

The plan worked. The French and American troops left New York. They marched 200 miles (322 km) in just over two weeks. General Clinton did not realize they were gone until it was too late.

The Continental forces at Yorktown were ready. Washington, Rochambeau, Lafayette, and the French fleet had Cornwallis cornered. British ships could not reach Cornwallis to help him escape. Washington's plan had worked perfectly.

Tourists can visit the battlefield at Yorktown today and see French mortar guns such as these.

At the end of September 1781, the Americans began a **siege.** This means that the Patriots hoped to force Cornwallis to surrender by keeping the British blocked off from supplies and communication. Cornwallis was not ready to give up yet, however. Though surrounded by 14,000 American and French army and naval forces, he still had 8,000 British and Hessian troops. On October 9, Patriot forces attacked. The British were low on supplies. Many of their men were sick or wounded. On October 14, an aide to General Washington named Alexander Hamilton captured important British defenses. General Cornwallis could see that he could not win. He surrendered.

The Patriots won the Battle of Yorktown. At the surrender ceremony, the French band played the song "Yankee Doodle." The British had once used the song to make fun of the Americans. Now the Americans had the last laugh. In response, the British band played a song, too. It was a children's tune called "The World Turned Upside Down."

Independence Achieved

Yorktown was not the last battle of the American Revolution. The British still held important cities such as Savannah, Charles Town, and New York. Yet Yorktown made the British realize that the fight was finished. The war was too costly to pursue, or continue.

Both sides sent representatives to France to work out a peace agreement. Benjamin Franklin, John Adams, and John Jay represented the United States. The first draft of the Treaty of Paris was **ratified,** or approved, by Congress. The final agreement was signed in September 1783.

4. Identify Cause and Effect
List three factors that contributed to the British loss at Yorktown.

_____

_____

_____

_____

_____

_____

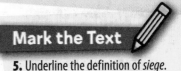

Mark the Text

5. Underline the definition of *siege.*

George Washington enters New York as a hero in 1783.

_____

_____

_____

_____

_____

_____

7. Draw Conclusions
How did France and Spain help the Americans win the war?

_____

_____

_____

_____

_____

8. Infer Why did Washington take action to end the conspiracy in Newburgh?

_____

_____

_____

_____

_____

_____

The treaty was a success for the Patriots. Great Britain would recognize the United States as an independent nation. Other agreements were made as well. The British would withdraw all of their troops from the United States. Americans would also be able to fish off of certain areas of Canada. The British also received benefits. British merchants would be able to collect money owed to them by Americans. Congress also promised to ask the governments of each state to return property taken from Loyalists.

Agreements Between the United States and Great Britain	
United States	Great Britain
Recognized as independent nation	British merchants could collect debts from Americans
British agree to withdraw troops	Promised that Congress would advise state governments to return Loyalist property
Americans granted permission to fish off of Canada	Prisoners of war released

Some time passed between the end of the war and the signing of the treaty. The Continental Army was kept active during this time. They stayed in Newburgh, New York. The soldiers wanted to get paid. They were angry because they felt they were owed money. Some thought that if they were not paid, they should use force against Congress. General Washington stepped in to settle the dispute. He understood such a threat was very serious to the new nation. He asked the soldiers to be patient. He also asked Congress to meet the soldiers' demands because they were justified. Congress agreed. General Washington showed his superior leadership.

When the last of the British troops left New York City in November 1783, Washington decided to resign, or formally give up his position. He wanted to retire, go home to Virginia, and live a quiet life with his family. His retirement did not last very long. He was called to serve the young country in yet a different way.

How did the Americans defeat powerful Great Britain? Even though the British were strong, the Americans had advantages. They fought on their own land for a cause they believed in. They knew the land and how to use it to hide and surprise the enemy. The British, on the other hand, fought a war far from home. Their troops and supplies had to be shipped in. They also had a hard time controlling the Americans even when they captured major cities.

The Americans also had help from many others. The French supplied soldiers and naval support as well as money. The Spanish gave aid when they attacked Britain. Individuals from around the world came to help the Americans fight and build their defenses.

Most of all, the British could not fight against the power of independence. Americans fought hard and with determination because they believed in what they were fighting for. They wanted to protect their land, their families, and their freedom.

Think Critically

9. **Defend** What do you think was the single most important reason why Britain was defeated? State your choice and provide an example to defend your choice.

Fighting on own land

Using guerilla warfare tactics

Reasons the United States Won

Help from other nations

Spirit and determination to win independence

Help from other individuals

This spirit spread to other places in the world as well. Shortly after the American Revolution, French rebels fought for freedom. They fought for the ideals of "Liberty, Equality, and Fraternity." These ideas also took root in the French colony of Saint Domingue, which is now Haiti. Led by a man named Toussaint Louverture, enslaved Africans fought for their freedom. In 1804, Saint Domingue became the second nation in the Americas to win its freedom.

NGSSS Check List two elements that helped the Patriots win the war. SS.8.A.3.4

ESSENTIAL QUESTION *Why does conflict develop?*

Reflect on What It Means . . .

During the American Revolution, the colonists had to make serious decisions about what they believed was right. They had to decide what they valued more: freedom and independence, or loyalty and tradition.

To Me, My Community and the World

Think about the words freedom and independence. What do these words mean to you? In your community and the world, what makes people free and independent? Then think about the ideas of loyalty and tradition. What does it mean to be loyal to another person, to a group, or to an institution? Use the space below to help you reflect on what these ideas mean.

Freedom and Independence	Loyalty and Tradition

TAKE THE CHALLENGE

What means more to you — the freedom to make your own decisions independently, or your loyalty to your family, school, government, and/or religious institutions and the traditions you share? There is no right answer to this question. Both are important. Write a short speech to explain which virtue you personally consider to be more important, and why. Present your speech to the class or to a small group of your classmates.

A MORE PERFECT UNION

NGSSS

SS.8.A.3.9 Evaluate the structure, strengths, and weaknesses of the Articles of Confederation and its aspects that led to the Constitutional Convention.

ESSENTIAL QUESTIONS *Why do people form governments? How do new ideas change the way people live? How do governments change?*

During the years that the new country was governed by the Articles of Confederation, James Madison studied the history and politics of other countries. His studies led him to believe that a confederated league of states could never give a government the strength that it needed to govern well.

PHOTO: Corbis Art/CORBIS

Copyright © by The McGraw-Hill Companies, Inc.

" . . . it is expedient that on the second Monday in May next a convention of delegates who shall have been appointed by the several States be held at Philadelphia for the sole and express purpose of revising the Articles of Confederation . . . "

—CONTINENTAL CONGRESS, FEBRUARY 21, 1787

sole and express purpose

What might the term *sole and express purpose* mean here?

_____

_____

_____

_____

DBQ BREAKING IT DOWN

Why do you think that the Continental Congress felt that holding a constitutional convention was the best way to make the government stronger?

_____

_____

_____

What powers can you think of that would make a government stronger? List examples below.

_____

_____

_____

McGraw-Hill
networks™
There's More Online!

THE ARTICLES OF CONFEDERATION

NGSSS

SS.8.A.3.9 Evaluate the structure, strengths, and weaknesses of the Articles of Confederation and its aspects that led to the Constitutional Convention.

Essential Question

Why do people form governments?

Guiding Questions

1. What kind of government was created by the Articles of Confederation?
2. What process allowed new states to join the union?
3. In what ways was the Confederation government weak?

Terms to Know

bicameral
having two separate lawmaking chambers

republic
a government in which citizens rule through elected representatives

ordinance
law

depreciated
fell in value

Where in the World?

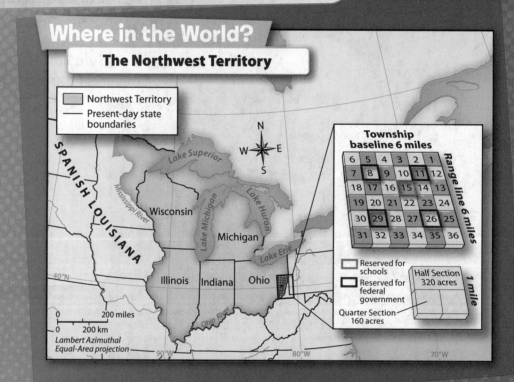

The Northwest Territory

- Northwest Territory
- Present-day state boundaries

SPANISH LOUISIANA

Lake Superior

Mississippi River

Wisconsin

Lake Michigan

Lake Huron

Michigan

Lake Erie

40°N

Illinois   Indiana   Ohio

Ohio River

0   200 miles
0   200 km
Lambert Azimuthal
Equal-Area projection

90°W   80°W   70°W

Township baseline 6 miles

6	5	4	3	2	1
7	8	9	10	11	12
18	17	16	15	14	13
19	20	21	22	23	24
30	29	28	27	26	25
31	32	33	34	35	36

Range line 6 miles

☐ Reserved for schools
■ Reserved for federal government

Half Section 320 acres
1 mile
Quarter Section 160 acres

When Did It Happen?

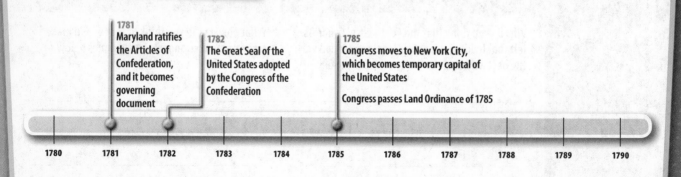

1781
Maryland ratifies the Articles of Confederation, and it becomes governing document

1782
The Great Seal of the United States adopted by the Congress of the Confederation

1785
Congress moves to New York City, which becomes temporary capital of the United States

Congress passes Land Ordinance of 1785

1780   1781   1782   1783   1784   1785   1786   1787   1788   1789   1790

The Making of a Republic

America was finally free of British rule. In May of 1776, the Continental Congress asked states to organize their governments. Each state adopted a state constitution. A constitution is a plan of government.

After years of British rule, Americans did not want to give too much power to one ruler or ruling body. As a result, the states adopted constitutions that limited the power of the governor. States also divided power between the governor and the legislature. Most states set up two-house, or **bicameral,** legislatures. This meant that the work in the legislature would be divided between two separate groups of lawmakers.

Ways to Limit Power to Govern
1. limit power of governor
2. divide power between governor and legislature
3. establish bicameral legislatures

The Framers wanted to keep power in the hands of the people. Because the powers of the governors were limited, the legislature became the most powerful branch of government.

Americans agreed that they wanted their country to be a **republic.** A republic is a government in which citizens rule through elected representatives. They could not agree, however, on what powers the new republic would have.

At first, most Americans wanted a weak central government. The states would rely on a central government only to wage war and to deal with other countries. In 1777 the Second Continental Congress adopted the Articles of Confederation. The Articles provided for a central government under which the states kept most of their power.

Under the Articles of Confederation, Congress had certain powers, such as the power to manage foreign affairs and issue money. However, under the Articles Congress also did not have some important powers, such as the power to control trade or impose taxes. If Congress needed to raise money or an army, it had to ask state legislatures to lend money or send it troops. The states, however, could refuse a request from Congress.

Mark the Text

1. Underline the meaning of a constitution.

Think Critically

2. **Analyze** What might be one result of state constitutions that limited the power of the governor?

_____

_____

_____

Mark the Text

3. Underline the meaning of a republic.

Think Critically

4. **Evaluate** Do you think that a strong executive, such as a president or governor, is important in a system in which the powers of government are divided? Why or why not?

_____

_____

_____

_____

_____

_____

_____

5. Identify the Main Idea

What were three weaknesses of the Articles of Confederation?

_____

_____

_____

_____

_____

Powers of Congress Under the Articles of Confederation	
Congress had these powers:	Congress did NOT have these powers:
manage foreign affairs	control trade
keep up armed forces	force citizens to join army
borrow money	require taxes
issue money	

Think Critically

6. Infer Why would it be difficult to change the Articles of Confederation?

_____

_____

_____

The central government was also lacking a chief executive. A chief executive is an official, such as a president or a governor, who carries out the laws. Under the plan of the Articles, all states had to approve the Articles and any changes. Each state had one vote.

The states were also divided by whether or not they claimed land in the West. Maryland refused to approve the Articles until other states abandoned, or gave up, their claims to lands west of the Appalachian Mountains.

Finally, the states settled their differences. All 13 states approved the Articles. On March 1, 1781, the Articles of Confederation became the government of the United States of America.

Between 1781 and 1789, under the Articles of Confederation, it became clear that the central government was too weak to handle the problems facing the United States. Congress had limited powers. For example, when Congress wanted to pay the country's debts, it could print money, within limits, but it could not pass taxes to raise the money. Even if Congress had had the power to raise taxes, it would have had to pass a law to impose the taxes. Under the Articles, Congress could not pass a law unless nine states voted for it. Any plan to change the Articles themselves required the approval of all 13 states.

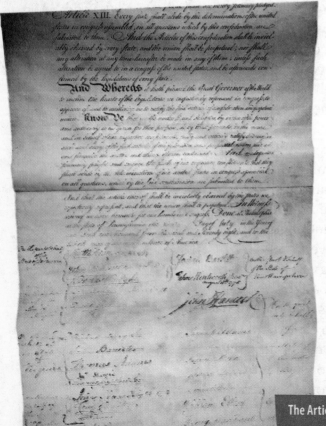

The Articles of Confederation

Policies for Western Lands

The Articles of Confederation did not have any way to add new states. Western settlers wanted to organize their lands as states and join the Union. Congress had to give people a way to form new states.

Mark the Text

7. Underline the way that a western district could apply to become a state.

Western Land

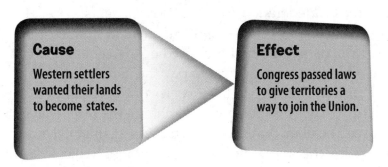

Cause
Western settlers wanted their lands to become states.

Effect
Congress passed laws to give territories a way to join the Union.

Take the Challenge

8. Draw a map of the United States from memory. Shade the area that made up the Northwest Territory.

Show Your Skill

9. **Identify** What were two of the rights promised to settlers by the Northwest Ordinance?

_____

_____

_____

During the 1780s, most states gave up their claims to lands west of the Appalachians. The central government took control of these lands. In 1784 Congress divided the western territory into self-governing districts. When the number of people in a district reached the number of people in the smallest existing state, that district could apply to Congress to become a state.

In 1785 the Confederation Congress passed an **ordinance,** or law, about western lands. This Ordinance of 1785 set up a process to survey and sell the western lands. Land would be sold at a public sale.

In 1787 the Northwest Ordinance created a single Northwest Territory from the lands north of the Ohio River and east of the Mississippi River. The lands were to be divided into three to five smaller territories. When the number of people in a territory reached 60,000, the people could apply for statehood. Each new state would have the same rights as the original 13 states.

The Northwest Ordinance included a bill of rights for the settlers. It promised freedom of religion and trial by jury. The Ordinance also had a clause, or condition added to a document, that stated there could be no slavery in the Northwest Territory.

The Land Act of 1800 was passed to make it easier for people to buy land in the Northwest Territory. For example, the Act made it possible for people to buy land by paying for it a little at a time.

10. Analyze Why did Robert Morris's plan to pay the country's war debts fail?

_____

_____

_____

_____

_____

11. Explain What were some of the problems the young country faced with other nations?

_____

_____

_____

_____

_____

Problems at Home and Abroad

One problem the Confederation government faced was paying its bills. American dollar bills called Continentals did not hold their value. By 1781, Continentals had **depreciated,** or fallen in value. The value fell so far that money was worth almost nothing.

A related problem was that the War for Independence left the Continental Congress with a large debt. Without the power to tax, the Confederation could not pay its debts.

In 1781 Congress created a department of finance led by Robert Morris. Morris had proposed a 5 percent tax on goods brought into the country to help pay the national debt. The plan required a change to the Articles of Confederation that would give Congress the power to charge the tax. Twelve states approved the plan, but Rhode Island was against it. Under the Articles, the single "no" vote was enough to block the plan.

The weaknesses of the new American government also appeared as the United States faced problems with other countries. The British were keeping Americans out of the West Indies and other moneymaking British markets. In the Treaty of Paris of 1783, Britain had promised to pull its army out of the lands east of the Mississippi River. British troops, however, stayed in several important forts in the Great Lakes region.

American relations with Spain were even worse. Spain, which controlled Florida and lands west of the Mississippi River, wanted to stop American growth in its territory. So in 1784, Spain closed the lower Mississippi River to American shipping. Western settlers could no longer use the river for trade.

The Confederation lacked the ability to deal with major problems, such as money and relations with other countries. Americans began to agree that their new country needed a stronger government.

NGSSS Check How did the Articles of Confederation prevent the United States from imposing taxes, issuing money, and managing foreign affairs? SS.8.A.3.9

_____

_____

_____

_____

FORGING A NEW CONSTITUTION

NGSSS

SS.8.A.3.9 Evaluate the structure, strengths, and weaknesses of the Articles of Confederation and its aspects that led to the Constitutional Convention.

SS.8.A.3.10 Examine the course and consequences of the Constitutional Convention (New Jersey Plan, Virginia Plan, Great Compromise, Three-Fifths Compromise, compromises regarding taxation and slave trade, Electoral College, state vs. federal power, empowering a president).

SS.8.A.3.11 Analyze support and opposition (Federalists, Federalist Papers, Anti-Federalists, Bill of Rights) to ratification of the U.S. Constitution.

Essential Question
How do new ideas change the way people live?

Guiding Questions
1. What problems did the government face under the Articles of Confederation?
2. How did leaders reshape the government?
3. What compromises were reached in the new Constitution?

Terms to Know

depression
a period when economic activity slows and unemployment increases

manumission
the freeing of enslaved persons by individual slaveholders

proportional
having the proper size in relation to other objects or items

compromise
an agreement between two or more sides in which each side gives up some of what it wants

When Did It Happen?

1781
Maryland ratifies the Articles of Confederation, which becomes the governing document

1786
Meeting in Maryland to discuss Articles of Confederation

A rebellion begins in Massachusetts led by Daniel Shays

1787
Shays's Rebellion is suppressed

Congress approves meeting in Philadelphia on May 14, 1787, to revise the Articles of Confederation

1788
U.S. Constitution is ratified

1780 1781 1782 1783 1784 1785 1786 1787 1788 1789 1790

What Do You Know?

Directions: Circle the problems you think Congress faced under the Articles of Confederation. When you finish the lesson, come back and circle using a different color.

No leader

Could not raise an army

Limited power

Could not pass laws

Too much power

Could not print money

Could not impose taxes

Lack of state support

The Need for Change

The government under the Articles of Confederation was too weak to deal with the country's problems. After the American Revolution, the United States went through a **depression.** A depression is a period of time when economic activity slows and many people lose their jobs.

Many plantations, or large farms, in the South had been damaged during the war. Rice growers were not able to produce rice crops as large as before the war. They usually sold their rice to other countries. Also, when the British closed the West Indies market to American businesses, trade went down even more.

Reasons for Decrease in Trade in the South
Plantations in the South were damaged during the war
Rice growers in the South were unable to grow as much rice
Britain closed the West Indies market to American businesses

The little money that the government did have went to pay debts, or money owed, to foreign countries. This resulted in a serious shortage of money in the United States.

Economic troubles hit farmers hard. Because they could not sell their goods, they had trouble paying taxes and other debts. When farmers could not pay what they owed, state officials took over farmers' lands. They also threw many farmers in jail. Farmers grew angrier over this treatment.

Farmers in Massachusetts were especially angry. In 1787 former Continental Army captain Daniel Shays led a group of angry farmers toward the federal arsenal in Springfield, Massachusetts. The farmers wanted to take the guns and bullets. The state militia ordered the farmers to stop. The farmers did not stop. The militia fired and killed four farmers. Shays and his followers

Shays's Rebellion is named after Daniel Shays who was a veteran of the American Revolution.

ran away. The rebellion was over, but it frightened many Americans. They thought that the government could not handle unrest and prevent violence.

Shays's Rebellion of 1787

Shays led 1,000 farmers to federal arsenal for guns. → State militia ordered farmers to stop. → State militia shot four farmers. → Farmers fled.

The American Revolution called attention to the clash between the American ideal of freedom and the practice of slavery. Several states in the North passed laws that gradually ended slavery in those states. However, free African Americans were not allowed to go to many public places and few states gave them the right to vote. The children of most free blacks could not go to school with white children.

In the states south of Pennsylvania, slavery was more widespread. The plantation system depended very much on slave labor. Many white Southerners were afraid that their economic system would die without slavery.

After the American Revolution, however, a growing number of slaveholders began to free enslaved people. Virginia passed a law that encouraged **manumission,** the freeing of individual enslaved persons. The number of free African Americans grew in that state.

In spite of these trends, slavery remained a key part of life in Southern states. The end of slavery in the North divided the new country on the powerful issue of whether some people should be allowed to keep other people enslaved.

North
American Revolution led to gradual end of slavery in the North.

The American Revolution and Slavery

South
Economy in the South continued to depend heavily on slave labor.

3. Analyze Why would farmers in Massachusetts want to rebel in 1786 and 1787?

_____

_____

_____

_____

4. Explain In what ways were free African Americans not treated equally?

_____

_____

_____

_____

_____

_____

Show Your Skill

5. Identify the Main Idea
Use the word *manumission* in a sentence to tell what happened in Virginia after the American Revolution.

_____

_____

_____

6. Explain Why was it important for the American people to trust the work of the delegates at the Constitutional Convention?

_____

_____

_____

_____

_____

_____

_____

The Constitutional Convention

The American Revolution had not created a united country. Some leaders liked strong, independent state governments. Other leaders wanted a strong national government. They called for changes in the Articles of Confederation. Two of these leaders were James Madison and Alexander Hamilton.

James Madison was a Virginia farmer. Alexander Hamilton was a lawyer from New York. In September of 1786, Hamilton called for a convention in Philadelphia to talk about trade issues. He also suggested that people at the convention should talk about how to change the Articles of Confederation.

The convention began in May 1787. Many of the 55 delegates were well educated. Native Americans, African Americans, and women did not take part in the convention.

The presence of George Washington and Benjamin Franklin helped ensure that people could trust the convention's work. Trust was important, because the convention did not just change the Articles of Confederation. It produced an entirely new constitution.

Two men from Philadelphia also had key roles. James Wilson did important work on the details of the Constitution, and Gouverneur Morris wrote the final draft. James Madison, who supported a strong national government, kept a record of the convention's work. Madison is often called the "Father of the Constitution" because he wrote the basic plan of government that the convention approved. The delegates chose George Washington to lead the meetings.

Delegates met in Philadelphia for five months in order to discuss and then draft a new plan of government.

Edmund Randolph of Virginia opened the convention with a surprise. He proposed the Virginia Plan that called for a strong national government. The plan created a government with three branches: a two-house legislature, a chief executive chosen by the legislature, and a court system.

The legislature would have the power to set taxes and to manage trade as well as veto, or reject, state laws. Voters would elect members of the lower house of the legislature. The members of the lower house would then choose members of the upper house. Under Madison's plan, the number of members in both houses would be **proportional,** or based on the number of people in each state. Proportional representation would give states with large populations many more delegates than states with the smallest number of people.

Delegates from the small states were against Madison's plan. They wanted all states to be represented equally. They supported a plan by William Paterson of New Jersey. This plan changed the Articles of Confederation, which was all the convention had the power to do.

Under the New Jersey Plan, Congress could set taxes and manage trade. These were powers it did not have under the Articles of Confederation. Congress would elect a weak executive branch made up of more than one person. The New Jersey Plan kept the Confederation's one-house legislature, with one vote for each state.

Show Your Skill

7. **Infer** Virginia was a large state. Why would the state want proportional representation?

_____

_____

_____

8. **Compare and Contrast** How did the number of representatives in the New Jersey Plan differ from the proportional representation in the Virginia Plan?

_____

_____

_____

Take the Challenge

9. Write a newspaper editorial from the perspective of a supporter of the New Jersey Plan. In it, explain why you oppose the Virginia Plan.

Virginia Plan and New Jersey Plan

Virginia Plan

Legislative Branch
- Two houses
- Membership proportional to state's population

Executive Branch
- Chosen by legislature
- Limited power
- Could veto, or reject, legislation

Judicial Branch
- Would serve for life
- Could veto legislation

New Jersey Plan

Legislative Branch
- One house
- Equal representation from all states

Executive Branch
- Chosen by Congress
- Would serve one term

Judicial Branch
- Appointed by executive branch
- Would serve for life

10. Evaluate Why were the compromises on the two issues related to slavery important?

_____

_____

_____

_____

_____

_____

Agreeing to Compromise

On June 19, 1787, the states voted to work toward a new constitution based on the Virginia Plan. However, they had to deal with the difficult issue of representation that divided the large and small states.

Roger Sherman of Connecticut suggested what would later be called the Great Compromise. A **compromise** is an agreement between two or more sides in which each side gives up some of what it wants. Sherman's compromise proposed a two-house legislature. In the upper house—the Senate—each state would have two members. That is, the states would be equal in representation. In the lower house—the House of Representatives—the number of seats for each state would vary based on the state's population.

The delegates also compromised on how to count enslaved people. Southern states wanted to count enslaved persons as part of their population. Northern states objected. The solution was to count each enslaved person as three-fifths of a free person. Every five enslaved persons would equal three free persons. This was called the Three-Fifths Compromise.

The Northern states wanted to ban slavery all across the country. Southern states stated that the slavery was needed for their economy. Northerners agreed to keep the new Congress from doing anything about the slave trade until 1808.

George Mason of Virginia proposed a bill of rights, a listing of key rights and freedoms, to be part of the Constitution. However, most delegates thought the Constitution included enough protection of people's rights. Mason's proposal was defeated.

On September 17, 1787, the delegates gathered to sign the Constitution they had created. The approved draft of the Constitution was then sent to the states for approval. The new Constitution would go into effect with the approval of nine states.

NGSSS Check What were two important compromises the delegates made about representation from each state? SS.8.A.3.10

_____

_____

_____

_____

_____

A NEW PLAN OF GOVERNMENT

NGSSS

SS.8.A.3.10 Examine the course and consequences of the Constitutional Convention (New Jersey Plan, Virginia Plan, Great Compromise, Three-Fifths Compromise, compromises regarding taxation and slave trade, Electoral College, state vs. federal power, empowering a president).

SS.8.A.3.11 Analyze support and opposition (Federalists, Federalist Papers, Anti-Federalists, Bill of Rights).

Essential Question

How do governments change?

Guiding Questions

1. From where did the Framers of the Constitution borrow their ideas about government?
2. How does the Constitution limit the power of the government?
3. How was the Constitution ratified?

Terms to Know

federalism
sharing power between the federal and state governments

legislative branch
lawmaking branch of government

executive branch
branch of government that executes, or carries out, the law and is headed by the president

Electoral College
special group of electors chosen to vote for president and vice president

judicial branch
the branch of government that includes the courts that settle disputes and questions of law

checks and balances
a system by which each branch of government limits the power of other branches

amendment
a change, correction, or improvement added to a document

When Did It Happen?

1781
Maryland ratifies the Articles of Confederation, which becomes the governing document

1786
Meeting in Maryland to discuss Articles of Confederation

1787
Congress approves meeting in Philadelphia on May 14, 1787, to revise the Articles of Confederation

The United States introduces dollar currency

1788
U.S. Constitution is ratified

1780 1781 1782 1783 1784 1785 1786 1787 1788 1789 1790

What Do You Know?

Directions: Draw a diagram to show the three branches of the U.S. government. List what you think the responsibilities of each branch are. When you complete the lesson, come back and adjust your diagram as needed.

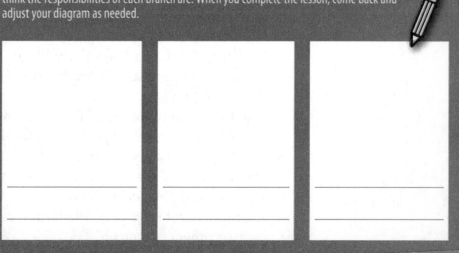

Mark the Text

1. Underline some of the sources, or starting places, of many ideas in the Constitution.

Think Critically

2. Compare In general, what principle of government did Locke and Montesquieu have in common?

_____

_____

_____

_____

_____

The Constitution's Sources

The delegates in Philadelphia produced a new constitution. To help them, they studied and talked about many political ideas from the past. They wanted to avoid the mistakes of past societies. Many ideas in the Constitution came from European political groups and writers.

The Framers of the Constitution knew the political system of Britain. They valued the individual rights that were part of the British system. Although the Americans broke away from British rule, they respected many British traditions. Traditions are cultural ideas and practices held for a long time.

The English Magna Carta placed limits on the power of the country's ruler. The king or queen had to depend on the lawmaking body to pay for wars and the royal government. In the same way, American colonial assemblies controlled their colonies' funds and had some control over colonial governors.

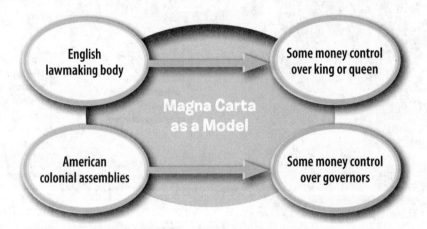

The English Bill of Rights of 1689 provided another model for Americans. Many Americans felt that the Constitution also needed a bill of rights.

The Framers of the Constitution believed in the ideas about the nature of people and government put forth by European writers. They were familiar with the work of John Locke and Baron de Montesquieu (mahn•tuhs•KYOO).

The English writer Locke believed that all people have natural rights. He stated that these rights include the rights to life, liberty, and property. Locke also wrote that government is based on an agreement, or contract, between the people and the ruler. The Framers saw the Constitution as a contract between the American people and their government. The contract protected people's natural rights by limiting government power.

The French writer Montesquieu wrote that the powers of government should be separated and balanced against each other. The Framers of the Constitution carefully spelled out and divided the powers of government.

Under the Articles of Confederation, the states had held most powers. Under the new Constitution, the states gave up some powers to the federal, or national, government. **Federalism,** or sharing power between the federal and state governments, is a key feature of the United States government.

Under the Constitution, the federal government gained powers to tax, manage trade, control the currency, raise an army, and declare war. It could also pass laws that were "necessary and proper" to carry out its powers.

The Constitution, however, left some important powers to the states. The states kept the power to control trade inside their borders. They also had the power to set up local governments and schools and to set marriage and divorce laws.

The Constitution also allows for some powers to be shared between the federal and state governments. Both federal and state governments have the power to tax and direct criminal justice.

The Constitution and the laws that Congress passed were to be the supreme, or highest, law of the land. Any disagreement between the federal government and the states was to be settled by the federal courts and based on the Constitution.

Show Your Skill

3. **Identify the Main Idea**
   What is the most important thing to know about the principle of federalism?

   _____

   _____

   _____

   _____

   _____

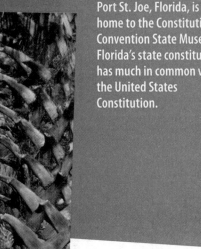

Port St. Joe, Florida, is home to the Constitutional Convention State Museum. Florida's state constitution has much in common with the United States Constitution.

Think Critically

5. **Summarize** Briefly explain the arguments for and against having a strong executive.

_____

_____

_____

_____

_____

_____

_____

Take the Challenge

6. On a separate piece of paper, draw a diagram to show how the Electoral College works.

Government Structure

The Framers of the Constitution used Montesquieu's idea of a division of powers. They divided the federal government into three branches—legislative, executive, and judicial. The first three articles, or parts, of the Constitution describe each branch's powers and tasks.

Article I of the Constitution declares Congress to be the **legislative branch** of the government. Congress is made up of the House of Representatives and the Senate. As a result of the Great Compromise between large and small states, each state's representation in the House is in proportion to its population. Representation in the Senate is equal. There are two senators for each state. The powers of Congress include collecting taxes, coining money, and controlling trade. Congress also has the power to declare war and "raise and support armies." Finally, it has the power to pass all laws needed to do its work.

Memories of rule by the British king made some delegates think that the United States should not have a powerful executive, or ruler. Others thought that the Articles of Confederation failed, in part, because it lacked an executive branch. They argued that a strong executive would limit the power of Congress.

Article II of the Constitution set up the **executive branch,** headed by the president, to carry out the nation's laws and policies. The president serves as head of the armed forces and conducts relations with foreign countries. A special group called the **Electoral College** elects the president and vice president. The Electoral College is made up of electors, who are chosen by the voters of each state. Every state has the same number of electors as it has senators and representatives in Congress. The president and vice president serve four-year terms.

Article III deals with the **judicial branch,** or court system. The nation's judicial power resides, or rests, in the Supreme Court and other federal courts that hear cases dealing with the Constitution, federal laws, and problems between states.

The Framers built in a system of **checks and balances.** Each branch has ways to check, or limit, the power of the others. In this way, no single branch can have control over the government.

Debate and Adoption

Before the Constitution could go into effect, nine states had to ratify, or approve, the document. Supporters of the new Constitution were called Federalists. James Madison, Alexander Hamilton, and John Jay wrote a set of essays to explain and defend the Constitution. These essays were called the Federalist Papers.

Those who opposed the Constitution were called Anti-Federalists. Anti-Federalists argued that a strong national government would take away freedoms Americans had fought for in the American Revolution. They warned that the government would ignore the will of the states and favor the wealthy over the common people. Anti-Federalists wanted local government that was controlled more closely by the people.

Mark the Text

7. Identify Circle the purpose of the Federalist Papers.

Think Critically

8. Contrast How were the views of the Anti-Federalists different than the views of the Federalists?

_____

_____

_____

_____

_____

_____

Anti-Federalist Points Against the Constitution
A strong national government would take away freedoms Americans fought for.
The government would ignore the will of the states.
The government would favor wealthy people.

By June 21, 1788, the ninth state—New Hampshire—ratified the Constitution. That meant the new government could go into effect. However, without the support of the two largest states—New York and Virginia—the new government could not succeed. Virginia ratified the Constitution after being promised that it would include a bill of rights amendment. An **amendment** is something added to a document. The Bill of Rights was added in 1791.

In July 1788, New York finally ratified the Constitution, followed by North Carolina and Rhode Island. The American people celebrated their new government.

NGSSS Check What effect did the Federalist Papers and the addition of the Bill of Rights have on the ratification of the U.S. Constitution? SS.8.A.3.11

_____

_____

_____

_____

ESSENTIAL QUESTION *Why do people form governments?*

Reflect on What It Means . . .

People form governments and establish rules for many reasons. Governments help provide protection from outside threats, establish order within the society, and provide help to those in need.

To My Community and the World

Governments in free societies need to hear from the people. Look in newspapers, magazines, or research online to learn ways that people in your community make their voices heard. Use the diagram below to record similarities and differences in the ways people express their opinions to government.

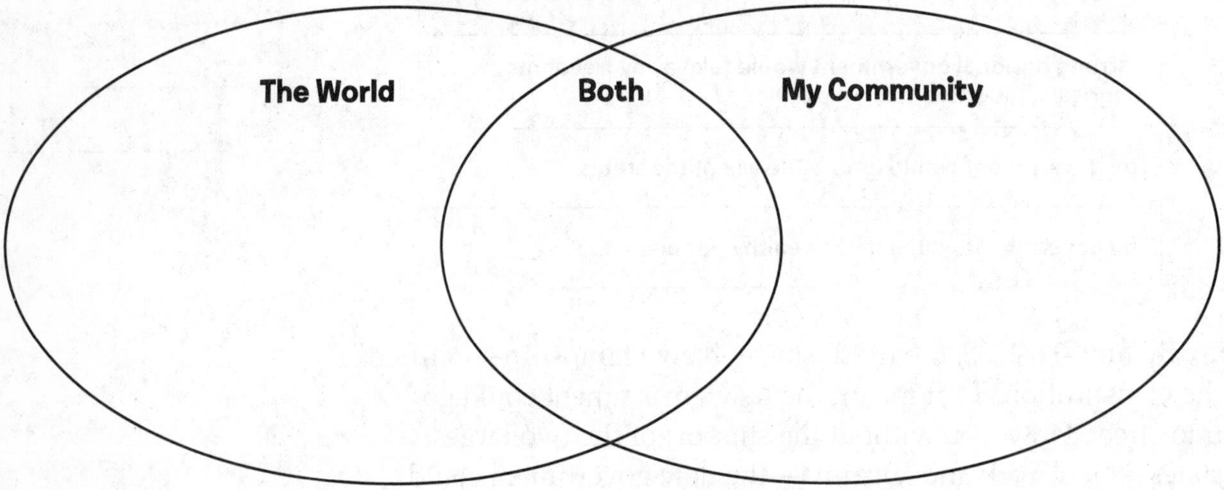

The World   Both   My Community

To Me

Choose an issue that matters to you. Write a cheer or chant below that shows support for, or urges action by, the government.

TAKE THE CHALLENGE

Create a sign that shows support for an issue that matters to you.
Remember to make it clear and colorful to grab people's attention.

CHAPTER 8

THE CONSTITUTION

NGSSS

SS.8.C.1.5 Apply the rights and principles contained in the Constitution and Bill of Rights to the lives of citizens today.

ESSENTIAL QUESTIONS *Why do people form governments? How do new ideas change the way people live?*

According to the Constitution, no one, not even the President of the United States, is above the law. In 1974 Congress was called upon to determine whether a sitting president, Richard Nixon, should be impeached (removed from office for committing a crime). U.S. Representative Barbara Jordan testified before the House Judiciary Committee on July 25, saying

"... when that document was completed on the seventeenth of September in 1787, I was not included in that "We, the people.""

BARBARA JORDAN

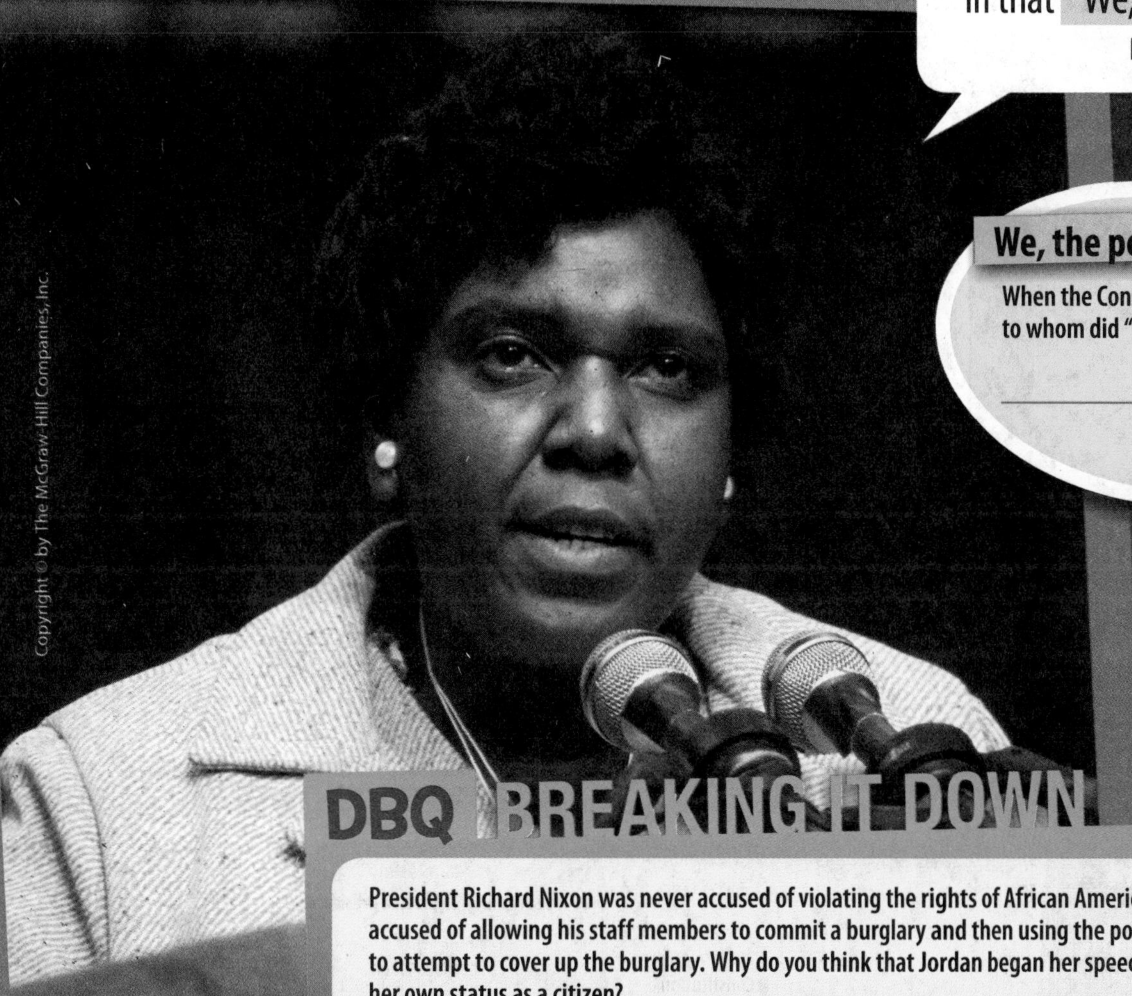

We, the people

When the Constitution was written, to whom did "the people" refer?

____

DBQ BREAKING IT DOWN

President Richard Nixon was never accused of violating the rights of African Americans. He was accused of allowing his staff members to commit a burglary and then using the power of his office to attempt to cover up the burglary. Why do you think that Jordan began her speech by talking about her own status as a citizen?

____

____

____

____

McGraw-Hill networks™ *There's More Online!*

PHOTO: Bernard Gotfryd/Premium Archive/Getty Images

PRINCIPLES OF THE CONSTITUTION

NGSSS

SS.8.C.1.5 Apply the rights and principles contained in the Constitution and Bill of Rights to the lives of citizens today.

SS.8.C.1.6 Evaluate how amendments to the Constitution have expanded voting rights from our nation's early history to present day.

SS.8.C.2.1 Evaluate and compare the essential ideals and principles of American constitutional government expressed in primary sources from the colonial period to Reconstruction.

Essential Question
Why do people form governments?

Guiding Questions
1. What basic principles of government are set forth by the Constitution?
2. How is the Constitution able to change over time?

Terms to Know

popular sovereignty
a form of government where citizens are in control

limited government
a government where no people or groups will get special treatment

enumerated powers
government powers that belong to the federal government alone

reserved powers
government powers that are retained by the states

concurrent powers
government powers that belong to both the federal and state governments

separation of powers
the creation of different parts of government to make sure no one branch has too much power

implied powers
congressional powers that are not specifically stated in the Constitution

Where in the World?

Constitutional Convention

New York

Pennsylvania

Philadelphia

New Jersey

Maryland

Delaware

ATLANTIC OCEAN

N W E S

When Did It Happen?

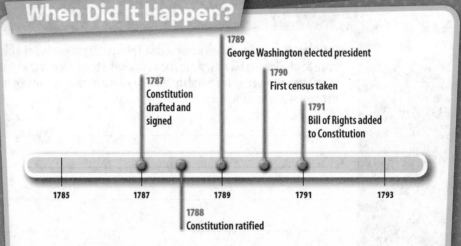

1789
George Washington elected president

1787
Constitution drafted and signed

1790
First census taken

1791
Bill of Rights added to Constitution

1785   1787   1789   1791   1793

1788
Constitution ratified

Our Constitution

The United States Constitution is a document that was made to create our government. The Constitution opens with the words "We the People." Those words, "we the people," are the basic idea of our government—that the people have the right to govern themselves. The idea that people control the powers of government is known as **popular sovereignty.**

The United States Constitution

The introduction to the Constitution, known as the Preamble, is an example of "we the people" exercising that power to create a new government. The government under the Constitution is a democracy, in which we the people participate in the government by voting and electing our leaders.

The Constitution contains seven basic principles that shape the way in which the new government will work. One principle is called republicanism. A republic is a system of government in which the people rule by choosing or electing their representatives. Under the Constitution, citizens in the United States elect the leaders and other government officials. Those officials—our elected representatives—then exercise the powers of government for us. They are the ones who make and carry out our laws.

The Founders knew it was important to limit the power of the government. The Constitution outlines a **limited government,** which means that no person or group will get special treatment from the government or in court. The Constitution makes sure no one is above the law.

3. Contrast What are the differences between enumerated, reserved, and concurrent powers?

_____

_____

_____

_____

_____

_____

_____

4. Explain How does the system of checks and balances work?

_____

_____

_____

_____

_____

5. Evaluate Why do you think the separation of powers and checks and balances are important?

_____

_____

_____

_____

_____

_____

_____

When the Constitution was written, there were still 13 states. Each state wanted to keep its own laws and customs. In order to do this, the Constitution divided power between the state governments and a national government. This is called federalism.

The Constitution names certain powers that belong to the federal government. These are called **enumerated powers.** Enumerated powers include the powers to coin, or print, money, regulate interstate commerce and foreign trade, maintain the armed forces, and create federal courts.

All powers not given to the federal government are kept by the states. Powers held by the states are called **reserved powers.** Reserved powers are used only by the states.

Sometimes, the federal government and the states share a power. These shared powers are called **concurrent powers.** _Concurrent_ means "happening at the same time." However, sometimes there is a conflict between a federal law and a state law. The Constitution makes federal law the "supreme Law of the Land." In the event of a conflict, federal law will win over state law.

Powers of Government

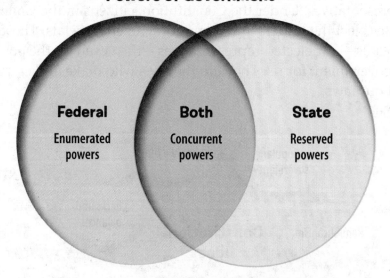

Federal	Both	State
Enumerated powers	Concurrent powers	Reserved powers

The Constitution also includes protections to make certain that no person or group gains too much power. One protection is the **separation of powers.** This refers to the way the Constitution divides powers among three branches of government. These branches are legislative, executive, and judicial. Each branch has a different role.

Another constitutional protection comes from a system of checks and balances. This refers to the way in which each branch can prevent the other branches from becoming too powerful. Each branch is given certain powers that can limit the other branches.

The Constitution also protects individual rights. These rights are the basic freedoms that we enjoy every day. The Bill of Rights, which is the first 10 amendments to the Constitution, lists many of these important freedoms. These include:

- Freedom of religion
- Freedom of speech
- The right to bear arms
- The right to a speedy and public trial
- Freedom from unreasonable search and seizure
- Freedom from cruel and unusual punishment.

Amending the Constitution

The Constitution can be amended, or changed. One part of the Constitution describes the process for amending the document. As a result, the Constitution can be updated as time passes and society changes.

It takes two steps to amend the Constitution. In the first step, Congress or the states—either one—can propose an amendment. In the second step, the states approve, or ratify, the amendment. Three-fourths of the states must approve the amendment in order for it to become part of the Constitution.

Take the Challenge

6. Choose one of the rights protected in the Bill of Rights. Draw a four-part cartoon strip about what your community would be like if that right did not exist.

Show Your Skill

7. **Draw Conclusions** The Constitution has been amended 27 times in over 200 years. What does that tell you about the process?

_____

_____

_____

_____

Amending the Constitution

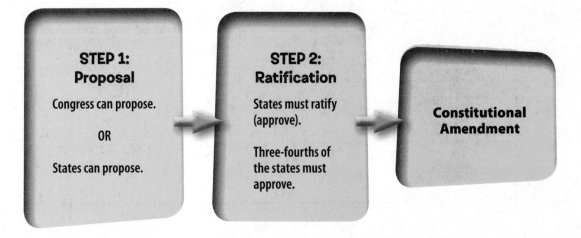

STEP 1: Proposal

Congress can propose.

OR

States can propose.

STEP 2: Ratification

States must ratify (approve).

Three-fourths of the states must approve.

Constitutional Amendment

There have been many important amendments. Some of them have expanded the right to vote. For example, the Fifteenth Amendment sought to ensure the right of African American men to vote. Later, the Nineteenth Amendment gave women the right to vote. The Twenty-sixth Amendment changed the voting age to 18.

8. Classify Information What two clauses form the basis for the implied powers of Congress?

_____

_____

_____

_____

9. Chart Complete the chart to explain the implied powers of Congress.

The Constitution can also change in another way. For example, two major clauses, or sections, of the Constitution seem to give Congress broad powers to act. These are the "elastic clause" and the "commerce clause." Congress has interpreted, or understood, these clauses as giving them the power to pass a wide variety of laws.

The elastic clause states that Congress may "make all Laws which shall be necessary and proper" to carry out the powers of the federal government. The commerce clause allows Congress to "regulate Commerce with foreign Nations, and among the several States." Congress and the courts have interpreted these two clauses to give Congress some broad **implied powers.** As a result, Congress may act in ways that seem to change the Constitution even when the powers are not stated in the Constitution.

Implied Powers of Congress	
Elastic Clause	**Commerce Clause**

NGSSS Check The Constitution and the Bill of Rights were written over 200 years ago. How do they protect your rights today? SS.8.C.1.5

_____

_____

GOVERNMENT AND THE PEOPLE

NGSSS

SS.8.C.1.1 Identify the constitutional provisions for establishing citizenship.

SS.8.C.1.5 Apply the rights and principles contained in the Constitution and Bill of Rights to the lives of citizens today.

SS.8.C.2.1 Evaluate and compare the essential ideals and principles of American constitutional government expressed in primary sources from the colonial period to Reconstruction.

Essential Question
How do new ideas change the way people live?

Guiding Questions
1. What are the three branches of government?
2. What are the rights and elements of participation of American citizens?

Terms to Know

judicial review
allows the Supreme Court to look at the actions of the other two branches and decide if the Constitution allows those actions

due process
rule the government must follow before it takes action against a citizen

equal protection
the right of all people to be treated equally under the law

naturalization
a process for people born in other countries to become American citizens

Where in the World?

District of Columbia

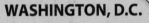

MARYLAND

WASHINGTON, D.C.

White House

U.S. Supreme Court

U.S. Capitol

VIRGINIA

Potomac R.

Potomac R.

N
W E
S

When Did It Happen?

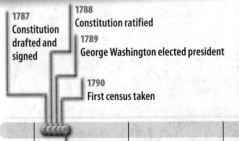

1787 Constitution drafted and signed

1788 Constitution ratified

1789 George Washington elected president

1790 First census taken

1791 Bill of Rights added to Constitution

1865 Thirteenth Amendment added to Constitution

1868 Fourteenth Amendment added to Constitution

1870 Fifteenth Amendment added to Constitution

1785   1800   1815   1830   1845   1860   1875

networks™ Read Chapter 8 Lesson 2 in your textbook or online.

Show Your Skill

1. Compare and Contrast How are the number of representatives a state has in the Senate and House of Representatives determined?

_____

_____

_____

_____

_____

_____

Think Critically

2. Evaluate Every House member must run for reelection every two years. How might this affect a person's performance as a representative?

_____

_____

_____

_____

_____

_____

The Federal Government

The federal government is divided into three branches. This ensures a separation of powers. The three branches are the legislative, executive, and judicial branches.

Article I of the Constitution sets up the legislative branch. The legislative branch is called Congress. Congress is made up of two houses. They are the House of Representatives and the Senate.

Congress makes laws for the nation. Congress also has the power to increase or decrease taxes, approve spending money, create government programs, and declare war.

The House of Representatives is the larger house of Congress. The number of representatives that a state has is proportional to its population. *Proportional* means that the number of representatives from each state depends on the number of people in that state. States that have more people have more representatives in the House. Today, the House has 435 voting members and six nonvoting delegates. Representatives are elected for a term of two years. Every two years, all 435 House seats are up for election at the same time.

The Senate has fewer members. Each state is represented equally with two senators. This makes a total of 100 senators. Senators are elected for a term of six years. Every two years, there are elections for the Senate. Only one-third of the seats are up for election at a time. This is to avoid large changes and disruption in the Senate.

The Senate and House of Representatives meet in the United States Capitol in Washington, D.C.

In order for a bill to become a law, both houses must agree on the bill. After that, the bill goes to the president to be signed. If the president approves, the bill becomes a law.

Article II of the Constitution sets up the executive branch. The president is the leader of this branch, which also includes the vice president and the cabinet. The main job of the executive branch is to carry out laws passed by Congress.

The president has other duties as well, such as dealing with foreign policy. The president is also the commander in chief of the armed forces.

Article III of the Constitution sets up the judicial branch. It creates the U.S. Supreme Court. Under Article III, Congress has created federal district courts and federal appeals courts. The Supreme Court is the final legal authority in the judicial branch. The Court has an important power called **judicial review.** This allows the Supreme Court to look at the actions of the other two branches and decide if those actions and laws meet Constitutional requirements. The Supreme Court has nine justices.

Mark the Text

3. **Chart** Complete the chart about the three branches of government.

Think Critically

4. **Contrast** All three branches of government have something to do with laws. Describe what each branch does related to laws.

_____

_____

_____

_____

Separation of Powers in the U.S. Constitution

Constitution, Article I	Constitution, Article II	Constitution, Article III
Defines: legislative branch	Defines: executive branch	Defines: judicial branch
Headed by:	Headed by:	Headed by:
_____	_____	_____
_____	_____	_____
Made up of:	Made up of:	Made up of:
_____	_____	_____
_____	_____	_____
_____	_____	_____

Think Critically

5. Compare In what ways are due process and equal treatment similar?

_____

_____

_____

_____

_____

Mark the Text ✏

6. Chart Complete the chart to explain the categories of rights.

What It Means to Be a Citizen

A citizen is guaranteed certain rights and freedoms. However, citizens also have duties and responsibilities. Our rights fall into three main categories:

- The right to be protected from unfair government actions
- The right to be treated equally under the law
- The right to enjoy basic freedoms

Due process is a right guaranteed by the Fifth Amendment. The amendment states that no one shall "be deprived of life, liberty, or property, without due process of law." This means that the government must follow certain rules before it tries to take a right away from a citizen. For example, a person accused of a crime has the right to a trial before his freedom is taken away.

Equal protection is a right guaranteed by the Fourteenth Amendment. Equal protection means that all people—of any race, religion, or other group—must receive the same treatment under the law. All people are equal under the law.

Many basic freedoms are described in the Bill of Rights. These include freedom of speech and the press, freedom of religion, and the right to petition the government. This right gives people the freedom to complain or ask the government for help without worrying about being punished for doing so.

Our rights and freedoms do have some limits. Laws may limit one person's freedoms when it is important to respect the rights of others.

Categories of Rights
Due process means the government must _____.
Equal protection means that all people are _____.
Examples of basic freedoms are _____.

People may not say things that are untrue to ruin another person's reputation. This is called defamation, and it is not protected under the First Amendment. These limits must be applied equally to everyone.

A citizen is a person who owes loyalty to a country and receives its protection. There are several ways to become an American citizen. One way is to be born on American soil. Another is to have a parent who is a citizen. People born in other countries can become citizens by following a process called **naturalization.**

Citizenship comes with duties and responsibilities. A duty is something you must do. Duties include paying taxes, following laws, and sitting on a jury when called. A responsibility is something you should do, but it is not required. It is a matter of choice. If citizens do not take care of their responsibilities, however, the quality of their government will decrease.

A Citizen's	
Duties	**Responsibilities**
Obey the law	Vote
Pay taxes	Take part in government
Sit on a jury when called	Respect the rights of others

NGSSS Check Explain three ways a person can become a United States citizen. SS.8.C.1.1

_____

_____

_____

_____

Explain the principle of equal protection and give an example of it in the lives of citizens today. SS.8.C.1.5

_____

_____

_____

7. Explain What is a naturalized citizen?

_____

_____

_____

_____

8. Contrast What is the difference between a duty and a responsibility?

_____

_____

_____

_____

_____

Take the Challenge

9. There is a test that a person takes to become a naturalized citizen. Research some of the possible test questions. Write down some of the questions and see how many you can answer correctly.

ESSENTIAL QUESTION *Why do people form governments?*

Reflect on What It Means . . .

Governments make it possible for people to have their rights protected by the rule of law—basic principles of fair and lawful conduct and action. One way to represent those principles is to write them down in a constitution. But it is also possible to use visual symbols to represent lawful principles.

A coat of arms is a shield that has symbols on it. The symbols stand for certain principles. The United States does not have a coat of arms. Using the space below, design a coat of arms for the United States. Think about the principles that are in the Constitution, and use symbols to represent those principles. Add labels to explain each symbol and what it means.

To the World, My Community, and Me

How does the rule of law affect our country's involvement in the rest of the world? How does your community relate to the rule of law?

◆ In your coat of arms, include a symbol that represents international fairness and justice.

◆ Add at least one symbol that represents an individual right that is protected by the rule of law.

TAKE THE CHALLENGE

Make a slideshow presentation out of your coat of arms, including a slide for each symbol. Present your slideshow to your class, explaining each symbol and what it represents orally as you present each image visually.

THE FEDERALIST ERA

NGSSS

SS.8.A.3.12 Examine the influences of George Washington's presidency in the formation of the new nation.

SS.8.A.3.13 Explain major domestic and international economic, military, political, and socio-cultural events of John Adams's presidency.

ESSENTIAL QUESTIONS *What are the characteristics of a leader? How does conflict develop? How do governments change?*

Abigail Adams wrote this letter to her husband, John Adams, in 1797, just after he was elected president. She wrote from their home in Quincy, Massachusetts.

PHOTO: Stock Montage/Getty Images

Copyright © by The McGraw-Hill Companies, Inc.

> " Quincy Febry 8 1797 . . .
> My feelings are not those of pride, or ostentation upon the occasion. They are solemnized by a sense of the obligations, the important Trusts and Numerous Duties connected with it, that you may be enabled to discharge them with Honour to yourself, with justice and impartiality to your Country, and with satisfaction to this great people . . . "

ostentation

What context clues are given that help you know the definition of *ostentation*?

_____

_____

_____

DBQ BREAKING IT DOWN

In the space below, write your own letter to a newly elected president, imagining that an election has just taken place and that the new president has not yet entered the office. Give the new president your advice on how to be a good leader.

_____

_____

_____

McGraw-Hill
netw⊙rks™
There's More Online!

THE FIRST PRESIDENT

NGSSS

SS.8.A.3.12 Examine the influences of George Washington's presidency in the formation of the new nation.

Essential Question
What are the characteristics of a leader?

Guiding Questions
1. What decisions did President Washington and the new Congress have to make about the new government?
2. How did the economy develop under the guidance of Alexander Hamilton?

Terms to Know

precedent
something done that becomes an example for others to follow

cabinet
a group of advisers for the president

bond
a paper note that is a promise to repay borrowed money at some point in the future—plus some additional amount of money, called interest

Where in the World?

The United States: 1790

Disputed between Northwest Territory and Rupert's Land (Great Britain)

Disputed between Massachusetts and Colony of New Brunswick (Great Britain)

Rupert's Land (Great Britain)

PACIFIC OCEAN

UNCLAIMED TERRITORY

Louisiana (Spain)

Disputed between New York and Vermont

Mass.

40°N

N.H.
Mass.
New York
R.I.
Conn.

Claimed by Connecticut

Penn.

N.J.
Del.
Md.

Northwest Territory

New Spain (Spain)

Virginia

ATLANTIC OCEAN

Unorganized Territory

North Carolina

South Carolina

0   400 miles
0   400 km

30°N
120°W

Georgia

Lambert Azimuthal Equal-Area projection

States
Territories
Other countries
Disputed areas

West Florida (Spain)

Disputed between United States and West Florida

East Florida (Spain)

Gulf of Mexico

100°W   90°W   80°W   70°W

When Did It Happen?

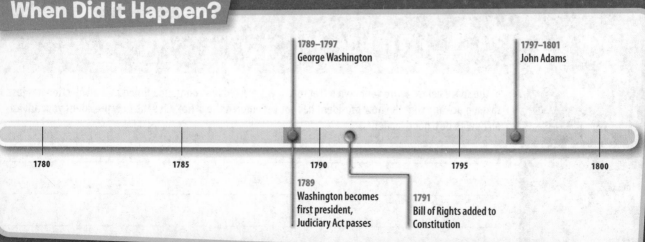

1789–1797
George Washington

1797–1801
John Adams

1780   1785   1790   1795   1800

1789
Washington becomes first president, Judiciary Act passes

1791
Bill of Rights added to Constitution

Washington Takes Office

George Washington was the first president of the United States. He knew that the **precedents,** or traditions, he established would be important. They would shape the future of the country and the government. With Congress, Washington created departments within the executive branch. Washington and Congress also set up the court system. Congress added the Bill of Rights to the Constitution.

The executive branch began with three departments and two offices. This was called the president's **cabinet.**

The Judiciary Act of 1789 created a federal court system. It had district courts at the lowest level, courts of appeal at the middle level, and the Supreme Court, which was at the top of the court system. It would be the final authority on many issues. State courts and laws remained intact. However, the federal courts had the power to reverse state decisions.

The first ten amendments, or changes, to the Constitution are known as the Bill of Rights. They limit the powers of government. They also protect individual liberties.

Department or Office	Head	Function
State Department	Thomas Jefferson	Managed foreign relations
Department of the Treasury	Alexander Hamilton	Handled financial matters
Department of War	Henry Knox	Provided for the nation's defense
Attorney General	Edmund Randolph	Handled legal affairs
Postmaster General	Benjamin Franklin	Managed postal system

George Washington was inaugurated as president in 1789.

Think Critically

1. **Explain** Why do you think it was important to set up a federal court system?

_____

_____

_____

_____

Mark the Text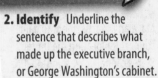

2. **Identify** Underline the sentence that describes what made up the executive branch, or George Washington's cabinet.

Think Critically

3. **Summarize** What were three important actions taken by President Washington and Congress?

_____

_____

_____

The New Economy

The new United States faced serious financial problems. The national debt—the amount of money owed by the nation's government—was growing. Alexander Hamilton was secretary of the treasury. He worked to solve the nation's financial problems.

4. Analyze Why do you think Alexander Hamilton wanted to pay back the bonds from the confederation government?

_____

_____

_____

_____

_____

Show Your Skill

5. Draw Conclusions Why did southern states oppose Hamilton's plan to pay off state war debts?

_____

_____

_____

_____

Take the Challenge

6. Make an advertisement to gain support for locating the United States capital in Washington, D.C.

During the Revolutionary War, the confederation government had borrowed a large amount of money. It had issued bonds. These are paper notes promising to pay back money in a certain length of time. Hamilton argued that the United States should pay back money borrowed from other countries. He also wanted to pay back individual American citizens. Hamilton believed that the national government should also pay the war debts of the states.

Some people opposed Hamilton's plan. Many bondholders were worried that they would never be paid back. In order to get some money for their bonds, they had sold their bonds to speculators for less than the bonds were worth. Speculators hoped to make money later if the government finally paid back the bonds. The original bondholders were concerned that speculators would get rich and the bondholders would get nothing. Southern states also complained about the plan to pay state war debts. They had built up much less debt than the Northern states. They argued that the plan would make them pay more than their share.

Hamilton worked out a compromise with Southern leaders. If they voted for his plan, he would support locating the new nation's capital in the South. A new district called Washington, D.C., would be created between Virginia and Maryland.

To help build a strong national economy, Hamilton asked Congress to create a national bank. It would issue a single type of money for use in all states. Some people opposed the idea, but Washington agreed with Hamilton. A national bank called the Bank of the United States was created.

Hamilton also proposed a tariff that would help protect American products. A **tariff** is a tax on goods bought from foreign countries. It makes products from other nations more expensive than ones made at home. This protective tariff would help American companies compete against foreign companies.

Hamilton's Actions

- Paid back bonds
- Created Bank of the United States
- Introduced a protective tariff to help U.S. companies
- Supported locating the nation's capital in the South

NGSSS Check Identify two ways that George Washington used the office of president to shape the formation of the new nation. SS.8.A.3.12

_____

_____

LESSON

2 EARLY CHALLENGES

Essential Question
Why does conflict develop?

Guiding Questions
1. What challenges on the frontier did the new government face?
2. Why did President Washington want to remain neutral in foreign conflicts?

Terms to Know

impressment
the practice of seizing people and forcing them into government service; in this case it was Great Britain forcing American crews into the British navy.

What Do You Know?

Reflect on what you have already learned and look forward to what you are about to read. Make predictions in response to the questions below. Check your answers after you read the lesson.

Why might the new government of the United States face challenges on the frontier?

Why might President Washington want to stay out of conflicts between foreign nations?

When Did It Happen?

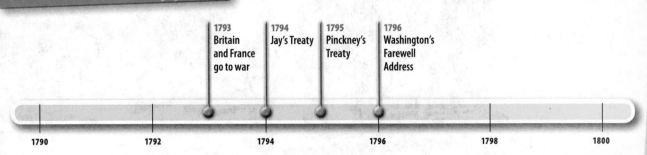

| 1793 Britain and France go to war | 1794 Jay's Treaty | 1795 Pinckney's Treaty | 1796 Washington's Farewell Address |

1790   1792   1794   1796   1798   1800

Show Your Skill

1. **Classify Information** What three European countries were involved in American affairs?

_____

_____

Mark the Text

2. Underline the sentence that describes the impact of the U.S. government's actions during the Whiskey Rebellion.

Show Your Skill

3. **Draw Conclusions** How did settlers moving west react to the treaties signed by Native Americans?

_____

_____

_____

_____

Trouble in the New Nation

The new government faced many challenges, or demanding situations. In western Pennsylvania farmers objected to a tax on whiskey. An armed mob attacked tax collectors. They burned down buildings. This armed protest was called the Whiskey Rebellion. It worried government leaders. President Washington and his advisers decided to crush the challenge using the army. This action sent a message to people: The government would use force when necessary to maintain, or keep, order.

In the Northwest Territory, Native Americans resisted American settlers who were moving west. Washington signed treaties with the Native Americans. He hoped to keep the Native Americans free of British or Spanish influence. American settlers ignored the treaties. They moved into lands promised to the Native Americans. Fighting broke out. Washington sent General Arthur St. Clair to restore order, but St. Clair was defeated.

Angry citizens capture tax collectors during the Whiskey Rebellion after the new federal government was formed.

Britain and France wanted to involve the United States in their own conflicts. The British were afraid that the United States would take sides with France. They asked Native Americans to attack American settlements west of the Appalachian Mountains. Washington sent an army under Anthony Wayne. The army defeated the Native Americans at the Battle of Fallen Timbers. The Native Americans signed the Treaty of Greenville, agreeing to give up most of the land in what is now Ohio.

Take the Challenge

4. Draw a mental map of the United States, and label four areas where the United States faced conflicts.

Conflicts		
Where?	**Who?**	**What happened?**
Western Pennsylvania	Farmers and others	Whiskey Rebellion crushed by Washington
Northwest Territory	Arthur St. Clair	Defeated by Native Americans
West of Appalachian mountains	British	Asked Native Americans to attack American settlers
Ohio	Anthony Wayne	Defeated Native Americans at the Battle of Fallen Timbers; Native Americans signed Treaty of Greenville

Problems with Europe

Britain and France went to war in 1793. Some Americans sided with France and others supported Britain. Washington hoped that the United States could maintain its neutrality. That means not taking sides in a conflict.

The French tried to get American volunteers to attack British ships. In response, President Washington issued a Proclamation of Neutrality. It prohibited American citizens from fighting in the war. It also barred French and British warships from American ports. The British captured American ships that traded with the French. They forced the American crews into the British navy. This practice was called **impressment.** It angered the Americans.

Mark the Text

5. Circle two agreements that the United States made with foreign countries.

Think Critically

6. **Cause and Effect** What was the result of Pinckney's Treaty?

_____

_____

_____

_____

_____

Washington sent John Jay to work out a peaceful solution with Britain. Jay proposed a treaty. In the terms of Jay's Treaty, the British would agree to withdraw from American soil. The treaty did not deal with the problems of impressment, however. It also did not deal with British interference with American trade. Jay's Treaty was unpopular, but the Senate approved it.

Spanish leaders feared that the United States and Great Britain would work together against them in North America. Thomas Pinckney went to Spain to settle the differences between the United States and Spain. In 1795 he proposed a treaty that said Americans could travel on the Mississippi River. Pinckney's Treaty also gave Americans the right to trade in New Orleans.

Jay's Treaty
- British agreed to leave American soil
- Did not deal with impressment
- Did not deal with British interfering with American trade
- Unpopular

Pinckney's Treaty
- Between Spain and the United States
- Gave Americans right to travel the Mississippi River
- Gave Americans right to trade at New Orleans

Washington decided to retire and not run for a third term. In his farewell address to the nation, Washington said, "It is our true policy to steer clear of permanent alliances with any portion of the foreign world. . . ." In his last speech, he warned the country not to get involved in foreign problems. He also warned against creating political parties.

NGSSS Check How did Washington influence the new nation's foreign policy? SS.8.A.3.12

_____

_____

_____

_____

THE FIRST POLITICAL PARTIES

NGSSS

SS.8.A.3.13 Explain major domestic and international economic, military, political, and socio-cultural events of John Adams's presidency.

Essential Question
How do governments change?

Guiding Questions
1. How did different opinions lead to the first political parties?
2. What important events occurred during the presidency of John Adams?

Terms to Know

partisan
one who favors one party or faction

caucus
a meeting of members of a political party to choose candidates for upcoming elections

aliens
people living in a country who are not citizens of that country

sedition
activities aimed at weakening the established government by inciting resistance or rebellion

nullify
to legally overturn

states' rights
the idea that states should have all powers that the Constitution does not give to the federal government or forbid to the states

When Did It Happen?

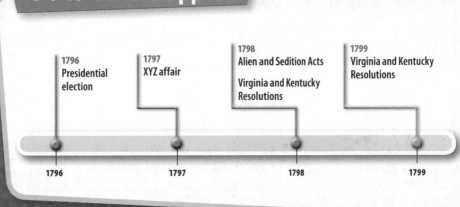

1796 Presidential election

1797 XYZ affair

1798 Alien and Sedition Acts
Virginia and Kentucky Resolutions

1799 Virginia and Kentucky Resolutions

1796   1797   1798   1799

What Do You Know?

Directions: Before you read the lesson, circle if you think the United States had good or poor relationships with each of these countries when George Washington left office. Revisit your answers after you complete this lesson.

Before Reading the Lesson		After Reading the Lesson
Good Poor	France	Good Poor
Good Poor	Spain	Good Poor
Good Poor	Britain	Good Poor

1. Underline the sentences that describe two opinions about political parties. Which opinion do you agree with? Why?

_____

_____

_____

2. **Classify Information** Name the first two political parties and the leader of each. What are the two major political parties in Florida today?

_____

_____

_____

_____

_____

_____

Opposing Parties

President Washington warned against political parties. He feared that political parties would divide the nation. Others thought that it was natural for people to disagree about issues. By 1796 Americans were beginning to separate into opposing groups.

In Washington's cabinet, Alexander Hamilton and Thomas Jefferson often took opposing sides. They disagreed about economic policy and foreign relations. They disagreed about how much power the federal government should have. They also disagreed on how to interpret the Constitution. Even Washington was **partisan**—favoring one side of an issue. While Washington believed he stood above politics, he usually supported Hamilton's positions. The two political parties that formed were called Federalists and Republicans.

Federalists	Republicans
Headed by Alexander Hamilton	Headed by Thomas Jefferson
Supported government by representatives	Feared strong central government controlled by only a few people
Believed government had broad powers implied by the Constitution	Believed government only had powers specifically mentioned in the Constitution

Jefferson and Hamilton were both in Washington's cabinet. They disagreed on many things, but Washington sought the advice of each of them.

In 1796 there was a presidential election. Before the election, the two parties held meetings called **caucuses.** At the caucuses, members of Congress and other leaders chose their parties' candidates for office.

The Federalists nominated John Adams for president. The Republicans chose Thomas Jefferson. This was the first time candidates identified themselves as members of political parties.

Adams received 71 electoral votes to win the election. Jefferson finished second with 68 votes. Under the Constitution at that time, the person with the second-highest number of electoral votes became vice president. Jefferson thus became the new vice president. The new government in 1797 had a Federalist president and a Republican vice president.

Think Critically

3. **Explain** Who were the people that President Adams referred to as X, Y, and Z?

_____

_____

_____

_____

John Adams as President

When Adams became president, France and the United States were still in conflict. The French thought that Jay's Treaty allowed Americans to help the British. The French seized American ships that carried goods to Britain.

In 1797 Adams sent a team to Paris to try to end the dispute. The French foreign minister refused to meet with the Americans. Instead, he sent three agents. They demanded a bribe from America. They also demanded a loan for France. When Adams heard about the meetings, he was angry. He called the three French agents "X, Y, and Z." Adams urged Congress to prepare for war. The incident became known as the XYZ affair.

President John Adams was the second president of the United States. He faced challenges in foreign affairs not long after taking office.

4. Draw Conclusions Why were the Alien and Sedition Acts passed?

_____

_____

_____

_____

5. Write a request to your teacher about a school or classroom rule you think should be nullified.

People were angry with France. Americans became more suspicious of **aliens.** Aliens are immigrants living in a country who are not citizens of that country. Federalists passed strict laws to protect the nation's security. In 1798 they passed a group of measures known as the Alien and Sedition Acts. **Sedition** refers to activities that weaken the government. The Alien Act allowed the president to put aliens in prison. He could also send them out of the country if he thought they were dangerous.

The Virginia and Kentucky Resolutions were passed in 1798 and 1799. They claimed that the Alien and Sedition Acts violated the Constitution. States should not put them into action. The Kentucky Resolution also suggested that states might **nullify,** or legally overturn, federal laws that they thought violated the Constitution.

The resolutions supported the idea of **states' rights.** This idea says that the powers of the federal government should be limited. Its powers should be only those clearly given to it by the Constitution. The states should have all other powers except those clearly forbidden by the Constitution. The issue of states' rights would remain important in the future.

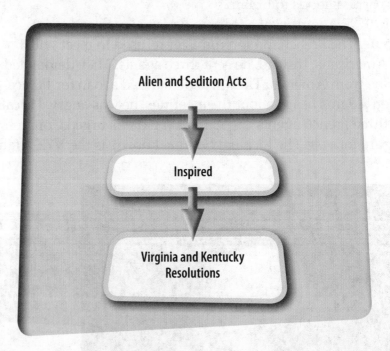

Alien and Sedition Acts

↓

Inspired

↓

Virginia and Kentucky Resolutions

 NGSSS Check Identify one important domestic and one international event that took place during the presidency of John Adams, and explain your choices. SS.8.A.3.13

_____

_____

_____

_____

ESSENTIAL QUESTION *What are the characteristics of a leader?*

Reflect on What It Means . . .

Leaders are always in demand in business, politics, and in many other areas of life. But people sometimes wonder what it takes to be a leader. You will use words and images to summarize the characteristics of leaders close to home and across the world.

To My Community and the World

In the space below, put together an inspirational collage of examples of good leaders. Try to find quotations from or about these leaders to include in your collage. Your quotations should show what traits make each man or woman an especially good leader. Include leaders from your local community and state, leaders from other parts of the United States, and leaders from around the world.

Keep Going! ➤➤

To Me

Based on the examples of the leaders you have chosen, write a saying or slogan for yourself that will inspire you to be a leader in your daily life. Write why that saying or slogan has meaning for you.

TAKE THE CHALLENGE

As a class, create a "Leadership Quote of the Day" display board and post it in your classroom. Each person should be responsible for finding a quote for the display board.

THE JEFFERSON ERA

NGSSS

SS.8.A.3.14 Explain major domestic and international economic, military, political, and socio-cultural events of Thomas Jefferson's presidency.

SS.8.A.4.1 Examine the causes, course, and consequences of United States westward expansion and its growing diplomatic assertiveness (War of 1812, Convention of 1818, Adams-Onis Treaty, Missouri Compromise, Monroe Doctrine, Trail of Tears, Texas annexation, Manifest Destiny, Oregon Territory, Mexican American War/Mexican Cession, California Gold Rush, Compromise of 1850, Kansas Nebraska Act, Gadsden Purchase).

ESSENTIAL QUESTIONS *How do governments change? How does geography influence the way people live? Why does conflict develop?*

William Clark and Meriwether Lewis did not travel alone to the Pacific coast. They had a guide, a Shoshone woman named Sacagawea. In their journal entries, Lewis and Clark wrote of Sacagawea's assistance.

"... the point of a high plain to our right [is a]... hill she says her nation calls the beaver's head from a conceived resemblance of it's [its] figure to the head of that animal. She assures us that we shall either find her people on this river or on the river immediately west of it's [its] source; which from it's [its] present size cannot be very distant."

MERIWETHER LEWIS

conceived resemblance

Using context clues, tell what is meant by *conceived resemblance*.

_____

_____

DBQ BREAKING IT DOWN

Lewis and Clark needed to meet with the Shoshone because they hoped to buy horses to help carry their stores for the rest of the journey to the Pacific.

What might you infer about relations between the Shoshone and the United States at the time of the Lewis and Clark expedition?

_____

McGraw-Hill
networks™
There's More Online!

PHOTO: Bettmann/Corbis

LESSON

1

A NEW PARTY IN POWER

NGSSS

SS.8.A.3.14 Explain major domestic and international economic, military, political, and socio-cultural events of Thomas Jefferson's presidency.

SS.8.A.4.13 Explain the consequences of landmark Supreme Court decisions (*McCulloch v. Maryland* [1819], *Gibbons v. Ogden* [1824], *Cherokee Nation v. Georgia* [1831], and *Worcester v. Georgia* [1832]) significant to this era of American history.

Essential Question
How do governments change?

Guiding Questions
1. What did the election of 1800 show about the nature of politics?
2. What did Jefferson want to accomplish during his presidency?

Terms to Know

customs duties
taxes that are collected on goods that are imported

jurisdiction
the power of right to interpret and apply a law

Where in the World?

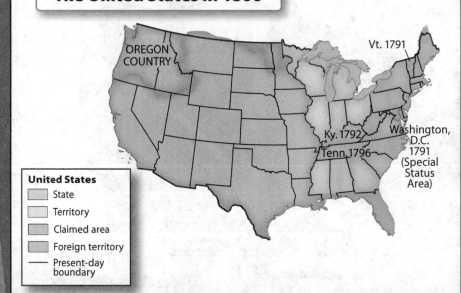

The United States in 1800

OREGON COUNTRY

Vt. 1791

Ky. 1792

Tenn. 1796

Washington, D.C. 1791 (Special Status Area)

United States
- State
- Territory
- Claimed area
- Foreign territory
- Present-day boundary

When Did It Happen?

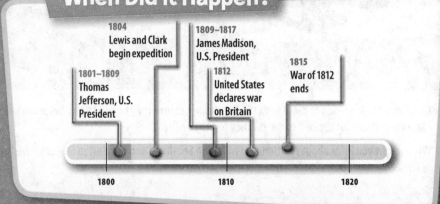

1804 Lewis and Clark begin expedition

1809–1817 James Madison, U.S. President

1801–1809 Thomas Jefferson, U.S. President

1812 United States declares war on Britain

1815 War of 1812 ends

1800   1810   1820

The Election of 1800

In the election of 1800, Federalists supported President Adams to be elected for another term. The Republicans nominated Thomas Jefferson for president.

Party	President	Vice President
Federalists	John Adams	Charles Pinckney
Republicans	Thomas Jefferson	Aaron Burr

Election campaigns of that time were different from the political campaigns we see today. Adams and Jefferson did not travel around the country to try to get votes. Instead, the candidates wrote to citizens and newspaper editors to try to persuade people to vote for them. Both sides worked hard to win the election.

Elections were different at this time as well.

The Election Process in 1800	
1.	People choose electors. Electors are the people who actually elect the president.
2.	Electors vote for two people. They do not say which vote is for president and which is for vice president.
3.	The person with the most votes becomes president. The person with the next highest number of votes becomes vice president.
4.	The House of Representatives votes if there is a tie.

In 1800, there was a tie. Jefferson and Burr received the same number of votes. The House of Representatives voted 35 times. Each time the vote was a tie. The next time they voted, one person changed his vote. Jefferson won.

In 1803, Congress changed the Constitution. The change is called the Twelfth Amendment. Each elector has one vote for president and one for vice president.

Jefferson became president in 1801. The ceremony that made him president is called an inauguration. Jefferson wore plain clothes. He walked to the Senate. There he took the oath of office.

Jefferson also gave a speech called the inaugural address. Jefferson said that he wanted to limit the power and size of the federal government. He thought states should have more power. His ideas were like French ideas called *laissez-faire*. That term means "let the people do as they choose without the government getting in the way."

Mark the Text

1. Underline the presidential candidates in 1800. Circle the vice presidential candidates.

Analyzing

2. The Twelfth Amendment changes how the president is elected. Summarize the change.

_____

_____

_____

Think Critically

3. **Contrast** How do political campaigns in 1800 and today differ?

_____

_____

_____

_____

Mark the Text

4. Underline the meaning of *laissez-faire*.

Mark the Text

5. Underline two ways the government collected money when Jefferson was president.

Jefferson as President

The new president had strong ideas about government. He wanted to make the country great. To do this, he put new policies in place. They included:

- lowering the national debt.
- cutting military spending.
- having only a few hundred government workers.
- getting rid of most federal taxes.

Under Jefferson, the U.S. government raised revenue, or money, from **customs duties** (taxes on imported goods). The government also made money from selling land in the West.

Before Jefferson, John Adams was president. Under Adams, there were many changes in the court system. President Adams appointed, or chose, hundreds of new judges. These appointments kept Jefferson from making new judges; therefore, the Federalists controlled the courts.

Men could not become judges until they got official papers, known as commissions. Some of the judges Adams appointed did not receive their papers before Jefferson became president. Jefferson told Secretary of State James Madison not to deliver them.

William Marbury was appointed by President Adams but never received his official papers. He wanted the job as judge so he took his case to the U.S. Supreme Court. The case was *Marbury v. Madison*. The court took the side of Madison and did not force him to deliver the papers.

As a result of this case, the U.S. Supreme Court established new principles for itself. Chief Justice John Marshall wrote the opinion.

John Marshall was the Chief Justice of the Supreme Court for over 30 years. He played a large role in establishing the authority of the national government. He helped cement the important position of the Supreme Court.

He named three principles of judicial review. Principles are basic ideas. Marshall said:

1. The Constitution is the supreme, or highest, law.

2. If the Constitution states one thing and another law states something else, the Constitution takes precedence.

3. The judicial branch (courts) can say laws are unconstitutional.

The court could say that acts of the President or Congress were unconstitutional.

Other important court cases affected the power of the Supreme Court. This chart shows three cases and the effect of each case.

Case	Effect
McCulloch v. Maryland	Congress can do more than the Constitution specifically says it can do. Actions by the states are not allowed to overrule federal laws.
Gibbons v. Ogden	Federal law takes priority over state law in cases of commerce and transportation between states.
Worcester v. Georgia	States cannot make rules about Native Americans. Only the federal government can do this.

 NGSSS Check List two changes Jefferson made during his presidency. SS.8.A.3.14

_____

_____

_____

What was the general result of rulings by the Supreme Court when John Marshall was Chief Justice?

_____

_____

6. Interpret information Explain the principles of judicial review.

_____

_____

_____

_____

7. Generalize What was the general effect of the rulings of the court in *Ogden v. Gibbons* and *Worcester v. Georgia*?

_____

_____

_____

Think Critically

8. Conclude Do you think Jefferson was pleased with the decisions in *Ogden v. Gibbons* and *Worcester v. Georgia*? Why or why not?

_____

_____

_____

_____

_____

Take the Challenge

9. You have been hired to help Thomas Jefferson run for reelection. Write a campaign ad that highlights some of his accomplishments as president.

LESSON

2

NGSSS

SS.8.A.3.14 Explain major domestic and international economic, military, political, and socio-cultural events of Thomas Jefferson's presidency.

THE LOUISIANA PURCHASE

Essential Question
How does geography influence the way people live?

Guiding Questions
1. How did Spain and France play a role in Americans moving west?
2. How did the Louisiana Purchase open an area of settlement?

Terms to Know

secede
break away from a country or group

Where in the World?

The Louisiana Purchase

OREGON COUNTRY

Vt. 1791

LOUISIANA PURCHASE 1803

Ohio 1803

Ky. 1792

Tenn. 1796

Washington, D.C. 1791 (Special Status Area)

United States
- State
- Territory
- Claimed area
- Foreign territory
- Present-day boundary

When Did It Happen?

1801–1809
Thomas Jefferson, U.S. President

1802
Spain stops the United States from trading in New Orleans

1803
The United States buys the Louisiana Territory from France

1804
Lewis and Clark start expedition

Hamilton and Burr duel

1805
Pike starts expedition

1800   1801   1802   1803   1804   1805

netw⊕rks Read Chapter 10 Lesson 2 in your textbook or online.

Westward Ho!

The Mississippi River was the western boundary of the United States in 1800. The area west of the river was called the Louisiana Territory. The Louisiana Territory went west to the Rocky Mountains. It went south to New Orleans. It did not have a clear border to the north.

Show Your Skill

1. **Interpret Map** On the map, color and label the Louisiana Territory.

Mark the Text

2. Circle two things that settlers needed. Underline why they needed these things.

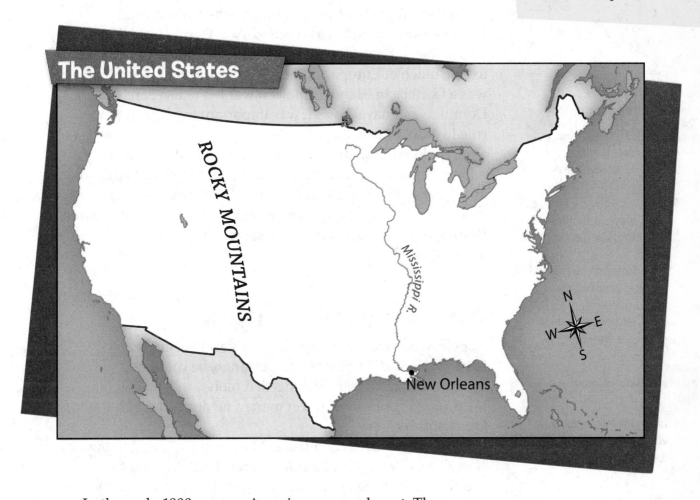

The United States

ROCKY MOUNTAINS

Mississippi R.

New Orleans

N W E S

In the early 1800s, many Americans moved west. They were called pioneers. They wanted land and adventure. Many pioneers were farmers. Travel was very difficult. Settlers used **Conestoga wagons** to carry the things they owned. Two important possessions were rifles and axes. They used rifles for protection and hunting animals for food. They used axes to cut paths through forests for their wagons.

Many pioneers settled along rivers that flowed into the Mississippi River. They started farms. The farmers shipped their crops to markets using the rivers. They shipped many goods down the Mississippi River to New Orleans. From New Orleans, the goods traveled to East Coast markets.

_____

_____

_____

_____

_____

_____

Think Critically

4. Sequence Number each of the following statements in the order they happened.

_____ Napoleon sent troops to take back Santo Domingo.

_____ Toussaint-Louverture led a revolt in Santo Domingo.

_____ The French were driven out of Santo Domingo.

Show Your Skill

5. Interpret Information Why was Napoleon willing to sell Louisiana?

_____

_____

_____

_____

_____

_____

Spain controlled the area west of the Mississippi, including New Orleans. Spain allowed Americans to travel on the Mississippi and trade in New Orleans. Farmers needed to be able to ship and trade goods there.

In 1802 Spain suddenly stopped letting settlers trade in New Orleans. President Jefferson learned that France and Spain had a secret agreement. France was going to gain control of the Louisiana Territory. This agreement was a big problem for the United States. French control of the Mississippi River would cause problems for U.S. trade. President Jefferson sent Robert Livingston to France to represent the U.S. government. Jefferson told Livingston to buy New Orleans and West Florida from France.

Napoleon Bonaparte was the leader of France. He wanted to rule much of Europe and North America. Santo Domingo was a Caribbean island. Napoleon wanted to use Santo Domingo as a naval base. It was important to his plan to rule in North America.

Napoleon's plan did not work. An enslaved African named Toussaint-Louverture led a revolt of enslaved Africans and other workers in Santa Domingo. They won and claimed independence. In 1802, Napoleon sent troops to take back Santo Domingo. They failed. By 1804, the French had been forced out of Santo Domingo.

An Expanding Nation

Napoleon needed Santo Domingo to start his empire in North America. Without Santo Domingo, he could not control Louisiana. Napoleon needed money to help pay for his war against Britain. To get money, he decided to sell the Louisiana Territory.

Robert Livingston and James Monroe were trying to buy New Orleans and West Florida. A French official said they could buy all of the Louisiana Territory. Livingston and Monroe were surprised. They also worried that they did not have the authority, or power, to make that decision.

In spite of their worry, Livingston and Monroe decided it was too good an opportunity to pass up. They agreed to pay $15 million dollars to buy the land.

Even Jefferson was not sure he had the authority to buy the Louisiana Territory. The Constitution did not say anything about buying new land. The Constitution said he could make treaties. Jefferson decided his right to make treaties allowed him to buy the land. The Senate approved the purchase in October 1803. The new land doubled the size of the United States.

Having this new territory was good because it provided a great amount of new land for farmers. It also protected shipping on the Mississippi River.

Americans did not know much about the new territory. Jefferson wanted to learn more about it. Congress agreed to send a group to explore the new land.

The group had several goals. They were supposed to

- collect information about the land
- learn about plants and animals
- suggest sites for forts
- find a northwest passage, or a water route across North America.

A northwest passage would make travel to Asia faster and less expensive.

Jefferson chose Meriwether Lewis to lead the group. Lewis's co-leader was William Clark. Both men were interested in science and had done business with Native Americans.

The group led by Lewis and Clark was called the Lewis and Clark expedition. The expedition included river men, gun makers, carpenters, scouts, a cook, and Native American-French interpreters. A Shoshone woman, Sacagawea, joined the group as a guide. An African American named York was also a member of the team that headed into the unknown.

The group left St. Louis in spring 1804. They traveled about 4,000 miles to the Pacific. The trip took 18 months. They returned in 1806. They brought back a lot of information about the people, plants, animals, and geography of the West. What they found encouraged people to want to move westward.

Mark the Text

6. Underline two reasons the United States wanted the Louisiana Territory.

Take the Challenge

7. You are leading an expedition to an unexplored part of the world. What skills would you look for when forming a team? You can take ten skilled people with you. List the ten skills you would look for on your team.

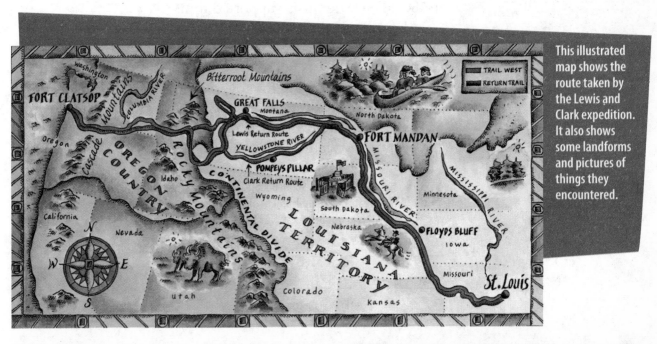

This illustrated map shows the route taken by the Lewis and Clark expedition. It also shows some landforms and pictures of things they encountered.

Aaron Burr challenged Alexander Hamilton to a duel.

PHOTO: Bettman/Corbis

Think Critically

8. Explain Why were the Federalists worried about expansion into the West?

_____

_____

_____

_____

_____

Other people also explored the West. Zebulon Pike led two expeditions. He brought back information about the Great Plains and the Rocky Mountains. He mapped part of the Rio Grande. He also explored land that is now part of southern Texas.

Federalists in the northeast worried about the country growing in the West. They were afraid they would lose power. One group of Federalists planned to **secede,** or leave, the nation.

These Federalists decided they needed New York in order to be successful. They asked Aaron Burr to help them. The Republicans were unhappy with Burr because he did not pull out of the election of 1800. He ran for governor of New York in 1804. The Federalists supported him.

Alexander Hamilton did not trust Aaron Burr. He heard about the plan to secede. He said Burr was plotting treason. He thought Burr was going to betray the United States.

Burr lost the election for governor. He blamed Hamilton for his loss. To get even, Burr challenged Hamilton to a duel. Burr shot Hamilton, and Hamilton died the next day. Burr ran away so he would not be arrested.

 NGSSS Check Some people believe that the Louisiana Purchase was the greatest accomplishment of Jefferson's presidency. Give several reasons why this might be so. SS.8.A.3.14

_____

_____

_____

LESSON 3

A TIME OF CONFLICT

SS.8.A.3.14 Explain major domestic and international economic, military, political, and socio-cultural events of Thomas Jefferson's presidency.

SS.8.A.4.1 Examine the causes, course, and consequences of United States westward expansion and its growing diplomatic assertiveness (War of 1812, Convention of 1818, Adams-Onis Treaty, Missouri Compromise, Monroe Doctrine, Trail of Tears, Texas annexation, Manifest Destiny, Oregon Territory, Mexican American War/Mexican Cession, California Gold Rush, Compromise of 1850, Kansas Nebraska Act, Gadsden Purchase).

Essential Question

Why does conflict develop?

Guiding Questions

1. How did the United States become involved in a conflict with Tripoli?
2. What issues challenged James Madison during his presidency?

Terms to Know

tribute
money paid to a leader or state for protection

neutral rights
privileges or freedoms given to countries that don't take sides in a war

embargo
blocking of trade with another country

nationalism
loyalty or dedication to one's country

Where in the World?

Trouble in the Northern Hemisphere

BRITAIN

CANADA

FRANCE

UNITED STATES

When Did It Happen?

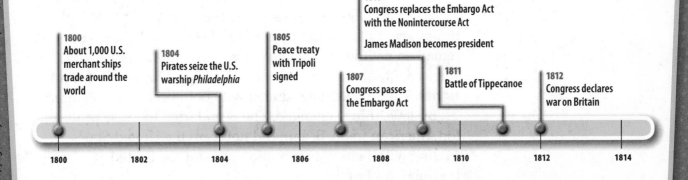

1800
About 1,000 U.S. merchant ships trade around the world

1804
Pirates seize the U.S. warship *Philadelphia*

1805
Peace treaty with Tripoli signed

1807
Congress passes the Embargo Act

1809
Congress replaces the Embargo Act with the Nonintercourse Act

James Madison becomes president

1811
Battle of Tippecanoe

1812
Congress declares war on Britain

1800   1802   1804   1806   1808   1810   1812   1814

Show Your Skill

1. Identify Cause and Effect
What caused many British and French ships to stay home in the mid-1790s? What did this mean to American shipping?

_____

_____

_____

_____

_____

_____

Mark the Text

2. Underline the meaning of the word *tribute*. Underline the sentence that tells why countries paid tribute.

Think Critically

3. Sequence Use the time line to put events in the war with Tripoli in the right order as you read.

American Ships on the High Seas

U.S. shipping grew in the late 1700s. People sailed to China and other parts of the world. They hoped to make a lot of money.

In the mid-1790s, France and Britain were at war. French and British merchant ships stayed home. They were afraid of being captured. This meant American merchants had less competition.

Sailing was dangerous, though. Pirates from the Barbary Coast attacked ships. One place on the Barbary Coast was called Tripoli, which demanded **tribute.** Tribute is money people pay for protection. Many countries paid tribute. It was less expensive than going to war with the pirates.

The United States paid tribute to Tripoli. In 1801 Tripoli asked the United States for more tribute. Jefferson refused to pay, so Tripoli declared war on the United States. Then Jefferson sent ships to blockade Tripoli. The ships kept other ships from getting to or leaving Tripoli.

Pirates took control of the United States war ship *Philadelphia* in 1804. They took the ship to Tripoli Harbor. They put the sailors in jail. American Stephen Decatur led a small group into the harbor. He burned the *Philadelphia* so the pirates could not use the ship.

Tripoli agreed to stop asking for tribute. The war ended in 1805. The United States kept paying tribute to other Barbary Coast states until 1816.

War With Tripoli

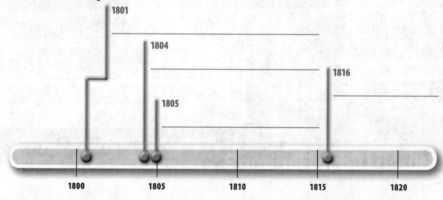

Thomas Jefferson was reelected president in 1804. At that time, Great Britain and France were at war. The United States remained neutral. It did not take sides in the war. American ships could sail the seas and not take sides. This is called **neutral rights.** The United States traded with both Britain and France.

By 1805, things changed. The war started to cause problems for American trade. Britain did not want the United States trading with France. France did not want the United States trading with Britain.

Tension between the United States and Britain increased following an attack by a British warship on the American ship, the *Chesapeake*.

Britain used ships to block the French coast. It said it would search all ships that traded with France. France said it would take and search all ships trading with Britain.

The British needed sailors for the war. Many sailors had deserted, or left their ships, because life in the British navy was so terrible. British ships began to stop American ships. They were looking for British sailors who had deserted. They made these sailors come back to British ships. They also took American sailors and forced them to serve on British ships. Forcing people to serve in the navy is called impressment.

In June 1807, the British warship *Leopard* stopped the American ship *Chesapeake*. The *Leopard's* captain wanted to search the *Chesapeake*. The captain would not let him. The British ship shot at the American ship. It was damaged, and three American sailors died. Americans were very angry about the attack. Many wanted war with Britain. President Jefferson did not want war.

After the attack on the *Chesapeake,* President Jefferson took action. He asked Congress to pass the Embargo Act. Congress passed the **embargo** in December 1807. An embargo is a trade ban. The Embargo Act stated that the United States would not trade with any other countries.

The Embargo Act was a failure. Britain bought goods from other countries, and American trade suffered. Congress stopped the Embargo Act in 1809. They replaced it with the Nonintercourse Act. The Nonintercourse Act did not allow trade with Britain or France. People did not like this act, and it also was a failure.

Think Critically

4. Summarize Briefly describe what happened between the *Leopard* and the *Chesapeake*.

_____

_____

_____

_____

_____

_____

Show Your Skill

5. Compare and Contrast Use the chart to identify ways the Embargo Act and the Nonintercourse Act were similar and ways they were different.

	Embargo Act	Nonintercourse Act
Similarities		
Differences		

Jefferson did not run for a third term. In 1808, the candidates were James Madison for the Republicans and Charles Pinckney for the Federalists.

People were angry about the embargo. Federalists hoped this anger would make people vote for Pinckney. However, Madison easily won the election.

War at Home and Abroad

When James Madison became president, he faced three big problems:

- The economy was not good because of the embargo, and people were angry.
- Britain kept stopping American ships.
- In the western United States, tension was growing with Native Americans.

Britain and France limited trade with the United States. In 1810 Congress said it would allow the United States to trade with the country that lifted its trade ban. Napoleon said he would allow open trade with the United States.

Even though trade started again, the French kept taking American ships. The French sold the ships and kept the money. The United States was about to go to war. Was the enemy Britain or France? Madison thought Britain was more dangerous to the United States.

Madison's problems were not only with other countries. There were also problems in the western United States. White settlers wanted more land. The land they wanted had been given to Native Americans in treaties, or agreements. Tensions grew.

Native Americans tried two things:

- They talked to the British in Canada about working together.
- They joined together with other Native American groups.

Tecumseh was a Shawnee chief who thought Native Americans needed to work together. He got different Native American groups to form a confederacy, or united group. They would work together to protect their land rights.

Tecumseh also wanted Native Americans to work with the British. He thought that together they could stop settlers from moving into Native American lands.

Tecumseh's brother was known as the Prophet. He founded Prophetstown in Indiana. It was located near the Tippecanoe and Wabash Rivers.

William Henry Harrison was governor of the Indiana Territory. He was worried about the power of Tecumseh and the Prophet. He was afraid they would join forces with the British.

Tecumseh went to get others to join his confederacy. While he was away, Harrison attacked Prophetstown. This was called the Battle of Tippecanoe. The Prophet's forces fought for more than two hours. Then they fled.

Americans claimed the Battle of Tippecanoe as a great victory. This was also bad news for the Americans, though. The American victory caused Tecumseh to join forces with the British.

Many young Republicans wanted Madison to be more aggressive against Britain. This group was called the War Hawks. They believed the United States would gain from war with Britain. They wanted the United States to be more powerful. Many Americans liked the War Hawks' **nationalism,** or loyalty to their country.

There were two groups in the War Hawks:

- Southern Republicans who wanted Florida
- Western Republicans who wanted lands in southern Canada

The Federalists in the Northeast were against war.

On June 1, 1812, Madison asked Congress to declare war on Britain.

In the meantime, the British had decided to stop searching American ships. The news of this change took too long to get to the United States, though. By the time American leaders learned of the change, it was too late. The United States had already declared war on Britain.

 NGSSS Check Madison faced several challenges as president. Complete the table below with details about foreign and domestic challenges he faced. SS.8.A.4.1

Foreign Challenges	Domestic Challenges

Mark the Text

10. Underline a negative result of the victory at Tippecanoe for the Americans.

Show Your Skill

11. **Identify Cause and Effect** What were three causes that led to war with Britain?

_____

_____

_____

_____

_____

Think Critically

12. **Infer** Why might the War Hawks be interested in getting Florida from Spain?

_____

_____

_____

Take the Challenge

13. Write a to-do list for President Madison. List the top five problems he needed to solve during his presidency. Put them in order with the most important problem at the top of the list.

NGSSS

SS.8.A.4.1 Examine the causes, course, and consequences of United States westward expansion and its growing diplomatic assertiveness (War of 1812, Convention of 1818, Adams-Onis Treaty, Missouri Compromise, Monroe Doctrine, Trail of Tears, Texas annexation, Manifest Destiny, Oregon Territory, Mexican American War/Mexican Cession, California Gold Rush, Compromise of 1850, Kansas Nebraska Act, Gadsden Purchase).

Essential Question
Why does conflict develop?

Guiding Questions
1. In what ways was the United States unprepared for war with Britain?
2. Why were Americans instilled with national pride after the battle of New Orleans?

Terms to Know

frigate
fast, medium-sized warship

Where in the World?

The War of 1812

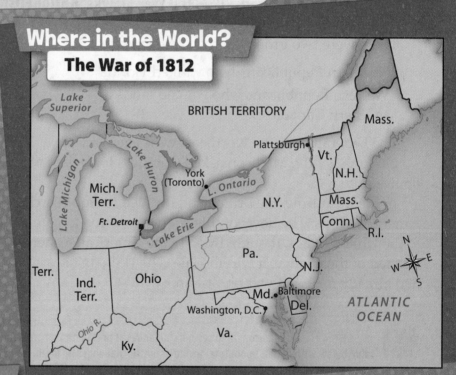

When Did It Happen?

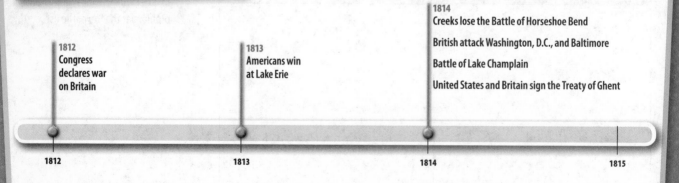

1812
Congress declares war on Britain

1813
Americans win at Lake Erie

1814
Creeks lose the Battle of Horseshoe Bend

British attack Washington, D.C., and Baltimore

Battle of Lake Champlain

United States and Britain sign the Treaty of Ghent

1812   1813   1814   1815

Defeats and Victories

The United States was not prepared for war. The United States had fewer than 7,000 soldiers, and many of the experienced leaders were too old to fight. Public opinion was not in favor of the war. The Americans also misjudged the strength of Britain and the Native Americans.

The war began in July 1812. Two forces tried to invade Canada:

- General William Hull led the American army from Detroit to Canada. They met Tecumseh and his forces. Hull surrendered Detroit.
- General William Henry Harrison also tried to invade Canada. He also did not succeed.

Harrison thought the United States would not succeed in Canada while the British controlled Lake Erie.

The United States had three of the fastest **frigates** in the world. Frigates are a kind of warship. The frigate *Constitution* destroyed two British ships early in the war. Armed private ships captured many British ships. This raised American spirits.

Oliver Hazard Perry led a fleet of American ships on Lake Erie. The big battle was on September 10, 1813. Perry and his ships destroyed the British fleet.

Americans now controlled Lake Erie. The British and Native Americans tried to pull back from the Detroit area. Harrison and his troops cut them off. They fought the Battle of the Thames. Tecumseh was killed in this battle.

The Americans also attacked York, in Canada. They burned government buildings there. The British still held control of Canada, but the United States had won several victories.

Before the Battle of the Thames, Tecumseh had talked to the Creeks in the Mississippi Territory. He wanted them to join his confederation. When he died, the confederation did not take place.

In March 1814, Andrew Jackson attacked the Creeks. He and his forces killed more than 550 Creek in the Battle of Horseshoe Bend. After this defeat, the Creeks gave up most of their land.

<table>
<tr><th colspan="2">Key Victories</th></tr>
<tr><th>Battle</th><th>Outcome</th></tr>
<tr><td>Battle for Lake Erie</td><td>U.S. destroys British fleet and wins control of Lake Erie</td></tr>
<tr><td>Battle of the Thames</td><td>U.S. defeats British and Native Americans; Tecumseh is killed.</td></tr>
<tr><td>Battle of Horseshoe Bend</td><td>Troops led by Andrew Jackson attacked Creeks and gained most of their land</td></tr>
</table>

Mark the Text

1. What is a *frigate?* Underline the definition.

Think Critically

2. **Infer** What was one strength the United States had going into the war?

Show Your Skill

3. Why was the success at Lake Erie so important?

4. **Identify Cause and Effect** Why were the British able to send more troops to fight the United States in 1814?

5. Contrast In what ways was what happened in the battle in Baltimore different than what happened when the British attacked Washington, D.C.?

_____

_____

_____

_____

_____

_____

The British Offensive

When the War of 1812 started, the British were still at war with France. In 1814, they won that war. This made it possible for them to send more troops to fight in America.

In August 1814, the British arrived in Washington, D.C. They quickly defeated the American militia. They burned and wrecked much of the city. Americans were surprised the British did not try to hold the city.

Instead they left Washington, D.C., and headed to Baltimore. They attacked Baltimore in September 1814. Baltimore was ready. Fort McHenry is in Baltimore Harbor. It helped defend the city and kept the British out.

Francis Scott Key watched the bombs burst over Fort McHenry on September 13. The next morning he saw the American flag flying over the fort. He was inspired to write a poem that later became known as "The Star-Spangled Banner."

Also in September 1814, General Sir George Prevost led 10,000 British troops into New York. He wanted to capture Plattsburgh, a key city on the shore of Lake Champlain. An American naval force defeated the British fleet on Lake Champlain. The British were afraid the Americans would surround them, so they retreated into Canada.

After the Battle of Lake Champlain, the British decided not to fight with the Americans any more. The war was too expensive, and they felt that there was little to gain from it.

In December 1814, representatives from the United States and Britain signed a peace treaty in Ghent, Belgium. The Treaty of Ghent ended the war. It did not

- change borders
- mention impressment of sailors
- talk about neutral rights.

PHOTO: Tim Sloan/AFP/Getty Images

The flag that flew over Ft. McHenry is one of the greatest treasures of the Smithsonian Institution.

The last battle of the war took place before people in the United States knew about the peace treaty. British troops moved toward New Orleans in December 1814. Andrew Jackson and his troops were ready for them. The American soldiers hid behind cotton bales. The bales protected the soldiers from most of the bullets fired. The British, in their red-and-white uniforms, were easy targets. Hundreds of British soldiers were killed.

The Battle of New Orleans was a clear victory for the Americans. Andrew Jackson became a hero. His fame helped him become president in the election of 1828.

Federalists in New England were against the war from the start. They met in Hartford in December of 1814. A few wanted to secede. Most wanted to stay in the United States. They made a list of changes they wanted made to the Constitution.

August 1814   **December 1814**

Pride in America grew with the success in the war. After the war, many people thought the Federalist complaints were unpatriotic. They lost respect for the Federalists, and the party grew weaker.

As the Federalists grew weaker, the War Hawks grew stronger. The War Hawks took control of the Republican Party. They wanted five things:

- a strong national government
- trade
- more settlement in the west
- an improved economy
- a strong army and navy.

After the war of 1812, Americans had great pride in their country. Other countries had more respect for the United States, too.

 NGSSS Check List some of the effects of the War of 1812. SS.8.A.4.1

_____

_____

_____

Think Critically

6. Sequence Put these events from the end of the War of 1812 onto the time line in order.

A. Americans win the Battle of New Orleans.

B. British decide to end the war.

C. British are defeated in Battle of Lake Champlain.

D. Treaty of Ghent is signed.

E. British try to capture Plattsburgh.

7. Contrast What happened to Federalists and the Republicans after the War of 1812?

_____

_____

_____

_____

Take the Challenge

8. You are a newspaper reporter during the War of 1812. Choose one event and do some additional research. Write a headline and a short news report about the event.

MY REFLECTION

Reflect on What It Means . . .

The Lewis and Clark Expedition came into contact with many Native American groups. They would often give the leader a peace medal that pictured Thomas Jefferson on one side and clasped hands pictured on the other. This was to symbolize that the land was now part of the United States and that the United States hoped for peace.

Below you will draw a coin that uses symbols only to tell about you, your community, and your place in the world. Add callouts or labels off to the side to explain your symbols.

To Me

On one side of the coin, draw two symbols that will introduce you to a new person and tell them something about yourself.

To the Community and the World

On the other side of the coin, draw a symbol that tells about your community. Add another symbol that connects your community to the world.

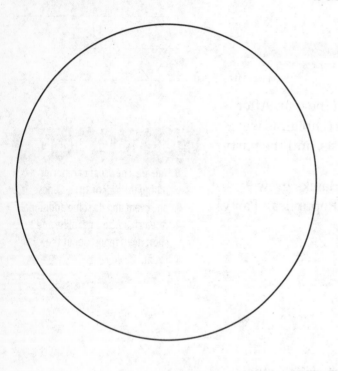

TAKE THE CHALLENGE

The Lewis and Clark Expedition documented many plants and animals that were new to most Americans. Research the writings of William Bartram who did similar work in Florida. Draw a picture of one of those plants or animals and include Bartram's description. Put your picture together with those of other students to make a booklet for your classroom library.

GROWTH AND EXPANSION

NGSSS

SS.8.A.4.17 Examine key events and peoples in Florida history as each impacts this era of American history.

ESSENTIAL QUESTIONS *How does geography influence the way people live? Why does conflict develop?*

Before he became President, John Quincy Adams was Secretary of State. He negotiated the Adams-Onís Treaty with Don Luis de Onís, the Spanish Minister to the United States, in 1819. The treaty was a compromise—the U.S. gave up its claim to Texas, while Spain gave up its own claim to the Northwest Territory.

" His Catholic Majesty [King of Spain] cedes to the United States, in full property and sovereignty, all the territories which belong to him, situated to the eastward of the Mississippi, known by the name of East and West Florida. "

—ADAMS-ONÍS TREATY

cedes

Write a synonym for *cedes*.

_____

sovereignty

What word inside the word *sovereignty* means "to rule"?

_____

DBQ BREAKING IT DOWN

The treaty gives information about the location of the land being given up by Spain. What words are in that description?

_____

_____

_____

On a separate piece of paper, draw a small map from memory that shows the location of the land being described.

**McGraw-Hill
networks**
There's More Online!

LESSON 1
A GROWING ECONOMY

NGSSS

SS.8.A.4.6 Identify technological improvements (inventions/inventors) that contributed to industrial growth.

SS.8.A.4.7 Explain the causes, course, and consequences (industrial growth, subsequent effect on children and women) of New England's textile industry.

SS.8.A.4.10 Analyze the impact of technological advancements on the agricultural economy and slave labor.

Essential Question

How does geography influence the way people live?

Guiding Questions

1. How did new technology affect the way things were made?
2. Why did agriculture remain the leading occupation of Americans in the 1800s?
3. How did the growth of factories and trade affect cities?

Terms to Know

cotton gin
a machine that removed the seeds from cotton very quickly

interchangeable parts
a part to a machine that can be replaced by another identical part

patent
legal rights to an invention and its profits

capitalism
a type of economy where people and companies control production

capital
money

free enterprise
a type of economy where people are free to buy, sell and produce whatever they want

Where in the World?

The Growth of Industrial Cities

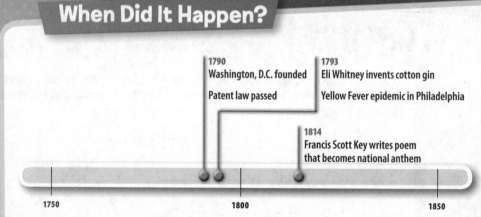

When Did It Happen?

1790
Washington, D.C. founded

Patent law passed

1793
Eli Whitney invents cotton gin

Yellow Fever epidemic in Philadelphia

1814
Francis Scott Key writes poem that becomes national anthem

1750   1800   1850

Industrial Growth

Most Americans lived and worked on farms in colonial times. People used their hands and simple tools to make goods. They built household items, furniture and farm equipment.

In the mid-1700s, the way goods were made began to change. The changes began in Great Britain. The British began using new machines. For example, they used a new machine to make cloth. This machine spun thread. They built textile mills along rivers. The water from the river powered their machines. People stopped working in their homes. They moved to cities to work in the mills and earn money. This big change in how things were made is known as the Industrial Revolution.

The Industrial Revolution reached the United States around 1800. The changes began in New England. The region's poor soil made farming hard. People looked for other kinds of work. New England had rivers and streams for waterpower to run machinery in new factories. The area had many ports that could ship goods.

Technology was an important part of the Industrial Revolution. The invention of new machines changed the way people made goods and did work. In 1793 Eli Whitney invented the **cotton gin.** This machine removed seeds from cotton fiber. Whitney also invented **interchangeable parts.** These were identical machine parts that could be put together quickly to make a complete product. This made it easier to produce many goods quickly. It also lowered the price of the goods.

In 1790 Congress passed a **patent** law. This law protected the rights of inventors. A patent makes an inventor the only person with legal rights to the invention and the only person who can receive profits from it. However, there was no protection for British inventions. Samuel Slater memorized the design of machines used in the factory where he worked in Britain. He used the design for a cotton mill in the United States. He copied the British machines that made cotton thread.

Francis Cabot Lowell made Slater's idea even better. All the steps of cloth making were done under one roof in Lowell's textile plant. A system in which all manufacturing steps are brought together in one place is called a factory system.

Think Critically

1. Analyze How did interchangeable parts help the growing economy?

_____

_____

_____

2. Explain What is a patent?

_____

_____

_____

_____

This is a model of Eli Whitney's cotton gin.

Think Critically

3. Explain How do business owners use capital in a free enterprise system?

_____

_____

_____

Show Your Skill

4. Identify Cause and Effect Why did the number of slaves grow quickly between 1790 and 1810?

_____

_____

Industrial growth needs an economic system that allows competition with little government interference. **Capitalism** is the economic system of the United States. Under this system, people put their **capital,** or money, into a business. They hope the business will make a profit. The American economy is also called **free enterprise.**

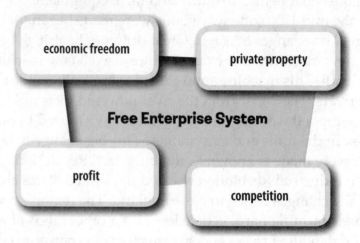

economic freedom

private property

Free Enterprise System

profit

competition

Agriculture Grows

Many people went to work in factories, but agriculture was still the main economic activity in the United States in the 1800s. In the Northeast, farms were small so families could still do all the work.

The growth of textile industries in New England and Europe led to increased cotton production in the South. The cotton gin made it faster and easier to clean cotton fiber. Greater cotton production also led to a need for more slaves. In 1790 there were 700,000 enslaved Africans in the United States. By 1810, there were 1.2 million.

Farming also grew in the West. Southerners who wanted new land moved west to grow cotton. Some farmers in the West also raised pork and cash crops such as corn and wheat.

In this picture, cotton is being formed in bales for easier transport.

Cities like Cincinnati grew because of their location on important water routes.

Economic Independence

Small investors began to finance new businesses. They invested their money in the hope of making profits. Large businesses called corporations began to develop. They are companies owned by many people. The corporations made it possible to sell stock, or shares of ownership in a company.

The growth of factories and trade led to the growth of cities. Many cities developed near rivers because factories could use water to power their machines. They could also get their goods to markets more easily. Older cities, such as New York and Boston, grew as centers of shipping and trade. In the West, towns, such as Cincinnati and Pittsburgh, benefited from their location on major rivers. These towns grew rapidly as farmers shipped their products by water.

Cities at that time had no sewers to carry away waste. Diseases like cholera sometimes killed many people. Many buildings were made of wood, and few cities had fire departments. Fires spread quickly.

The good things cities had to offer generally outweighed the bad things. Cities had a variety of jobs to choose from. They also had places where people could enjoy free time, like libraries, museums, and shops.

 NGSSS Check How did improvements in technology contribute to changes in society during the Industrial Revolution? SS.8.A.4.6

_____

_____

_____

Show Your Skill

5. Identify Cause and Effect
How did New England's physical geography help the growth of industries?

_____

_____

_____

_____

_____

6. What was a problem found in big cities?

_____

_____

_____

_____

Take the Challenge

7. Make a poster to convince more workers to move to a big city during the 1800s. Point out at least three features that would make the city attractive to someone looking for a new place to live and work.

2 MOVING WEST

NGSSS

SS.8.A.4.5 Explain the causes, course, and consequences of the 19th century transportation revolution on the growth of the nation's economy.

SS.8.A.4.6 Identify technological improvements (inventions/inventors) that contributed to industrial growth.

SS.8.A.4.8 Describe the influence of individuals on social and political developments of this era in American History.

Essential Question

How does geography influence the way people live?

Guiding Questions

1. What helped increase the movement of people and goods?
2. Why did Americans tend to settle near rivers?

Terms to Know

census
the official count of the population

turnpike
a road on which tolls are collected

canal
an artificial waterway

lock
separate compartment in which water levels rise and fall in order to raise or lower boats to higher or lower levels of a canal

When Did It Happen?

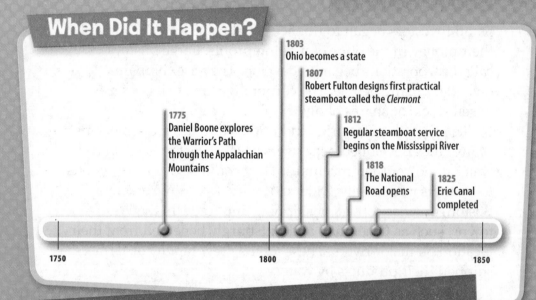

1775 Daniel Boone explores the Warrior's Path through the Appalachian Mountains

1803 Ohio becomes a state

1807 Robert Fulton designs first practical steamboat called the *Clermont*

1812 Regular steamboat service begins on the Mississippi River

1818 The National Road opens

1825 Erie Canal completed

1750   1800   1850

What Do You Know?

Directions: In the first column, decide if you think the statement is true or false based on what you know before you read the lesson. After this lesson, complete the last column.

Before the Lesson			After the Lesson	
True	False	The Wilderness Road cut a path through the Rocky Mountains.	True	False
True	False	Water travel was more comfortable than travel on land routes.	True	False
True	False	Locks are used to raise and lower water levels in canals.	True	False
True	False	The population of the western states declined dramatically in the early 1800s.	True	False

Headed West

In 1790 the first **census** was taken. A census is an official count of the population. The census revealed that nearly 4 million people lived in the United States at the time. Most Americans lived east of the Appalachian Mountains. That pattern soon changed. More settlers headed west.

Daniel Boone was one of the early western pioneers. He explored a Native American trail through the Appalachian Mountains called the Warrior's Path. He expanded the path and called it the Wilderness Road. More than 100,000 people traveled it between 1775 and 1790.

Daniel Boone leads settlers on the Wilderness Road. The sunlight in the painting is designed to show the hopeful nature of the journey.

Traveling west was not easy. The United States needed roads to move people and goods inland. Some companies built **turnpikes,** or toll roads. The tolls travelers paid to use the roads helped pay for building them. In 1803 Ohio asked the federal government to build a national road to connect it to the East. Construction on the National Road started in 1811. The first section opened in 1818.

Traveling by wagon and horse on roads was rough and bumpy. It was also time consuming. Traveling on the rivers was quicker and more comfortable. It was also easier to carry large loads of farm goods on boats and barges than in wagons. However, river travel had two problems. First, most large rivers in the northeast region flowed north to south. Most people and goods headed east to west. Second, traveling upstream against the river current was hard and slow.

Show Your Skill

1. Generalize Where in the country did most people in the United States live in 1790?

_____

_____

Think Critically

2. Infer How do you think the National Road affected the population of Ohio?

_____

_____

_____

_____

Travel by Land	Travel by River
• Roads were rough and bumpy. • Traveling on roads was slow. • It was hard to carry large loads of farm goods.	• Travel was more comfortable. • More goods could be carried on a boat. • Rivers could not move people east to west. • Traveling against the river current was hard and slow.

Think Critically

3. Explain How are locks and canals related?

_____

_____

_____

_____

Mark the Text

4. Underline how the Erie Canal improved water transportation.

Show Your Skill

5. Identify Cause and Effect
How did improved transportation affect the economy and the growth of cities?

_____

_____

_____

_____

_____

Robert Fulton developed the *Clermont*, a steamboat with a powerful engine. In 1807 the *Clermont* traveled up the Hudson River from New York to the city of Albany in record time. It took only 32 hours to make the trip. Using only sails, the trip would have taken four days.

The use of steamboats changed river travel. Steamboats made transportation much easier and more comfortable. Shipping goods by steamboat became cheaper and faster. Steamboats also helped river cities, like St. Louis and Cincinnati, grow. By 1850, there were 700 steamboats in operation in the United States.

Steamboats improved river transportation. But they depended on existing rivers, most of which flowed north to south. Steamboats could not link the eastern and western parts of the country. De Witt Clinton and other officials made a plan to link New York City with the Great Lakes area. They would build a **canal** across the state of New York. A canal is an artificial waterway.

Thousands of workers, mostly Irish immigrants, worked on building the Erie Canal. They built a series of **locks** along the canal. Locks are separate compartments used to raise or lower water levels. Boats could be raised or lowered at places where the elevation changed. The Erie Canal finally opened in 1825. Clinton used the canal to make the first trip from Buffalo, New York, to Albany, New York, and then down the Hudson River to New York City.

At first, the Erie Canal did not allow steamboats. Their powerful engines could damage the canal. But, in the 1840s, canals were made stronger to allow steamboats to travel on them. Many other canals were built. By 1850, the United States had more than 3,600 miles (5,794 km) of canals. Canals lowered the cost of shipping goods. They also helped towns and cities along their routes grow larger.

Here you see the New York State Thruway passing over the Erie Canal. Both are important for transportation and our economy today.

The Move West Continues

By 1820 more than 2 million people lived west of the Appalachian Mountains. New western states were created. The population in the new states grew quickly. Ohio had only 45,000 settlers in 1800. By 1820, it had 581,000 residents.

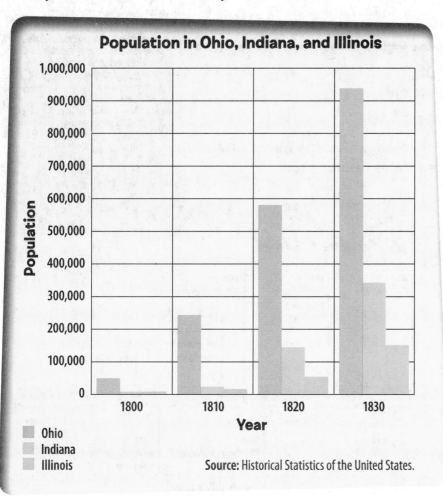

Population in Ohio, Indiana, and Illinois

■ Ohio
■ Indiana
■ Illinois

Source: Historical Statistics of the United States.

Pioneers moved to the West to find a better life. Most pioneer families settled along the big rivers so they could more easily ship their crops and goods to markets. Canals allowed people to live farther away from rivers. People usually settled with others from their home communities. Western families often gathered for social events, such as sports and sewing parties.

 NGSSS Check List 3 problems with land travel during this period. SS.8.A.4.5

6. Interpret Graphs Describe the change in the population of Illinois between 1800 and 1830.

7. Summarize How did rivers and canals affect where settlers chose to live?

8. Draw a line down the center of a piece of drawing paper. On one side of the page, draw and label images showing life in the United States in 1800. On the other side of the page, draw and label images showing life in the United States in 1820.

NGSSS

SS.8.A.4.1 Examine the causes, course, and consequences of United States westward expansion and its growing diplomatic assertiveness.

SS.8.A.4.2 Describe the debate surrounding the spread of slavery into western territories and Florida.

SS.8.A.4.17 Examine key events and peoples in Florida history as each impacts this era of American history.

SS.8.A.4.18 Examine the experiences and perspectives of different ethnic, national, and religious groups in Florida, explaining their contributions to Florida's and America's society and culture during the Territorial Period.

LESSON

3 UNITY AND SECTIONALISM

Essential Question
Why does conflict develop?

Guiding Questions
1. How did the country change after the War of 1812?
2. How did the United States define its role in the Americas?

Terms to Know

American System
a program that aimed to help the country's economy and increase the power of the federal government

monopoly
a market where there is only one provider

interstate commerce
trade between or among states

sectionalism
rivalry based on the special interest of different areas

When Did It Happen?

1810		1820		1830

1812 War of 1812

1816 James Monroe elected as President

1820 Missouri Compromise passed

1821 Mexico gains independence from Spain

1825 Erie Canal completed

1819 *McCullough* v. *Maryland* court case

The Adams-Onís treaty gives the U.S. control over Florida

1824 *Gibbons* v. *Ogden* court case

What Do You Know?

Directions: Look at the terms and the time line on this page. Use that information to write two questions you have about the information you may find in this lesson. After you have finished the lesson, come back and see if you can answer the questions.

_____

_____

_____

_____

National Unity

A feeling of national unity was present in the United States after the War of 1812. The intense, or very strong, divisions that once split the nation seemed to be gone. James Monroe easily won the election of 1816. A Boston newspaper called these years the Era of Good Feelings. President James Monroe was a symbol of these good feelings. He urged the federal government to encourage the growth of trade and industry.

Henry Clay of Kentucky was a leader in the House of Representatives. He was known as "The Great Compromiser" because he was good at resolving arguments. Clay proposed the American System. This program called for higher tariffs and internal improvements, or improvements within the country, such as roads, bridges and canals. It also proposed a new national bank. Not all leaders agreed with Clay's proposal.

The charter for the first Bank of the United States ended in 1811. Then in 1816, President Madison signed a bill that created the Second Bank of the United States. When the first bank had closed, many state banks acted unwisely. They made too many loans. This created a rise in the price of goods. The Second Bank of the United States restored order to the money supply in the country. It helped American businesses grow.

Cause		Effect
The state banks made too many loans.	→	The price of goods went up.
The Second Bank of America restored order to the money supply.	→	American businesses grew.

After the War of 1812, many people purchased goods from British factories. The British goods were of higher quality and cost less. American manufacturers called for high tariffs to protect America's growing industries. The Republicans passed a protective tariff in 1816. Merchants had to pay a tariff on imported goods. The price of imported goods rose. This encouraged people to buy American-made goods. Southerners were angry about the tariffs. They felt the tariffs protected the Northern manufacturers. The Southerners felt forced to pay higher prices.

Think Critically

1. Generalize What was the general mood of the country after the War of 1812?

_____

_____

_____

Show Your Skill

2. Identify Cause and Effect What caused the need to create a Second Bank of the United States in 1816?

_____

_____

_____

_____

Mark the Text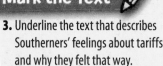

3. Underline the text that describes Southerners' feelings about tariffs and why they felt that way.

John C. Calhoun spoke for the South.

Henry Clay spoke for the West.

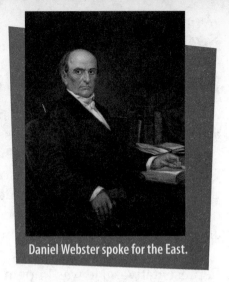

Daniel Webster spoke for the East.

PHOTO: (l) Stock Montage/Archive Photos/Getty Images; (c) Stock Montage/Archive Photos/Getty Images; (l) Stock Montage/Archive Photos/Getty Images

By 1820 the Era of Good Feelings ended because of regional differences. Most Americans felt loyal to the region where they lived. They thought of themselves as living in the North, South, or West. This loyalty to a region is called **sectionalism.** Geography, economics, and history contributed to sectional differences.

Each section of the country had a voice in Congress in the early 1800s. Henry Clay represented the West. John C. Calhoun of South Carolina spoke for the South. Daniel Webster of Massachusetts spoke for the North. Each leader tried to protect the interests of his section of the country.

The Supreme Court made decisions involving sectionalism. In *McCulloch* v. *Maryland,* the Court ruled that the national government's interest comes before state interests. In *Gibbons* v. *Ogden,* the Court ruled that states could not pass laws that would interfere with federal power over **interstate commerce** or trade between states. In this case, the state of New York had granted a **monopoly** to a steamship operator running ships between New Jersey and New York. A monopoly is sole control over an industry. The Supreme Court said that only Congress had the power to make this law. People who supported states' rights did not agree with the Court's rulings.

Henry Clay tried to resolve sectional conflicts. In 1819, there was a clash between the North and the South. Missouri wanted to enter the Union as a slave state. The government disagreed. Clay came up with a plan to solve this disagreement over slavery. The Missouri Compromise called for Missouri to be admitted as a slave state. Another new state, Maine, would be a free state. This meant that there would still be an equal number of slave and free states. Neither side could change the laws governing slavery.

The Missouri Compromise also dealt with slavery in the rest of the Louisiana Territory. The land south of Missouri could allow slavery, and the land north of it could not.

Think Critically

4. Explain What did the Supreme Court decide about monopolies?

_____

_____

_____

_____

Show Your Skill

5. Draw Conclusions How was the Missouri Compromise a compromise?

_____

_____

_____

_____

_____

_____

Foreign Affairs

The Louisiana Purchase in 1803 doubled the size of the nation. However, there were questions about the territory's boundary. Some Americans believed the purchase included West Florida. Spain continued to control this region after the purchase. Escaped slaves fled to Florida since the United States did not have the authority to arrest them there. Some Native Americans moved to West Florida also.

In 1810 and 1813, Americans simply added parts of West Florida to Louisiana and Mississippi. Spain took no action because it was involved in a war with France. General Andrew Jackson invaded Spanish East Florida. He took over St. Marks and Pensacola. The Adams-Onís Treaty was signed in 1819. In the treaty, the United States gained East Florida, and Spain gave up its claims to West Florida. At the same time, Spain was losing power in Mexico. In 1821 Mexico finally gained its independence.

Simón Bolívar won independence from Spain for the present-day countries of Venezuela, Colombia, Panama, Bolivia, and Ecuador. José de San Martín won freedom from Spain for Chile and Peru. By 1824, Spain had lost control of most of South America.

In 1822 several European countries talked about a plan to help Spain take back its American colonies. President Monroe did not want more European involvement in North America. In 1823 he issued the Monroe Doctrine. It said that European powers could no longer set up colonies in North America and South America.

 NGSSS Check List three areas where Spain lost power during the early 1800s.
SS.8.A.2

_____

_____

_____

PHOTO: Andre Jenny/Alamy

Copyright © by The McGraw-Hill Companies, Inc.

Show Your Skill

6. Identify Cause and Effect
What was the result of the Adams-Onís Treaty?

_____

_____

_____

Mark the Text

7. Underline the names of two leaders who helped Latin American countries gain independence from Spain.

Think Critically

8. Explain Why did President Monroe issue the Monroe Doctrine?

_____

_____

_____

_____

Take the Challenge

9. On a piece of drawing paper, draw a map of Florida from memory. Label cities that were once in West Florida and ones that were once in East Florida.

CHAPTER 11 MY REFLECTIONS

ESSENTIAL QUESTION *How does geography influence the way people live?*

Reflect on What It Means . . .

In this chapter, you learned about growth in the U.S. economy, new settlements west of the Mississippi, and changes in the U.S. following the War of 1812.

Make a connection between what you learned and the world today!

Use this graphic organizer to describe the effects of growth and expansion.

Invention of Cotton Gin
OR
Factory System

Growth and Expansion

Pioneers Begin to Settle The West

Spain Cedes Florida to the U.S.

TAKE THE CHALLENGE

As a class, make a three-dimensional topographic map representing the United States during the early 1800s. You may want to use a piece of wood as your base, and put modeling clay on top, shaping mountains and rivers out of clay. Add railroads and canals that began to be used during the early 1800s. Add markers to represent well-established towns, and other markers to show areas where pioneers were beginning to settle and areas that were governed by Native American nations or by Spanish authorities in Mexico. You may also want to add labels that explain the historical significance of certain locations.

CHAPTER 12

THE JACKSON ERA

NGSSS

SS.8.A.4.17 Examine key events and peoples in Florida history as each impacts this era of American history.

SS.8.A.4.18 Examine the experiences and perspectives of different ethnic, national, and religious groups in Florida, explaining their contributions to Florida's and America's society and culture during the Territorial Period.

ESSENTIAL QUESTIONS *What are the characteristics of a leader? What are the consequences when cultures interact? How do governments change?*

Just before the Battle of Ouithlacoochee in 1835, Brigadier General Duncan Lamont Clinch sent messages to Seminole leader Osceola, telling Osceola that it was useless to resist and that the Seminole should surrender. Read this excerpt from Osceola's reply:

> "You have guns, and so do we; You have powder and lead and so do we; You have men and so do we; Your men will fight, and so will ours until the last drop of the Seminoles' blood has moistened the dust of his hunting grounds."
>
> OSCEOLA

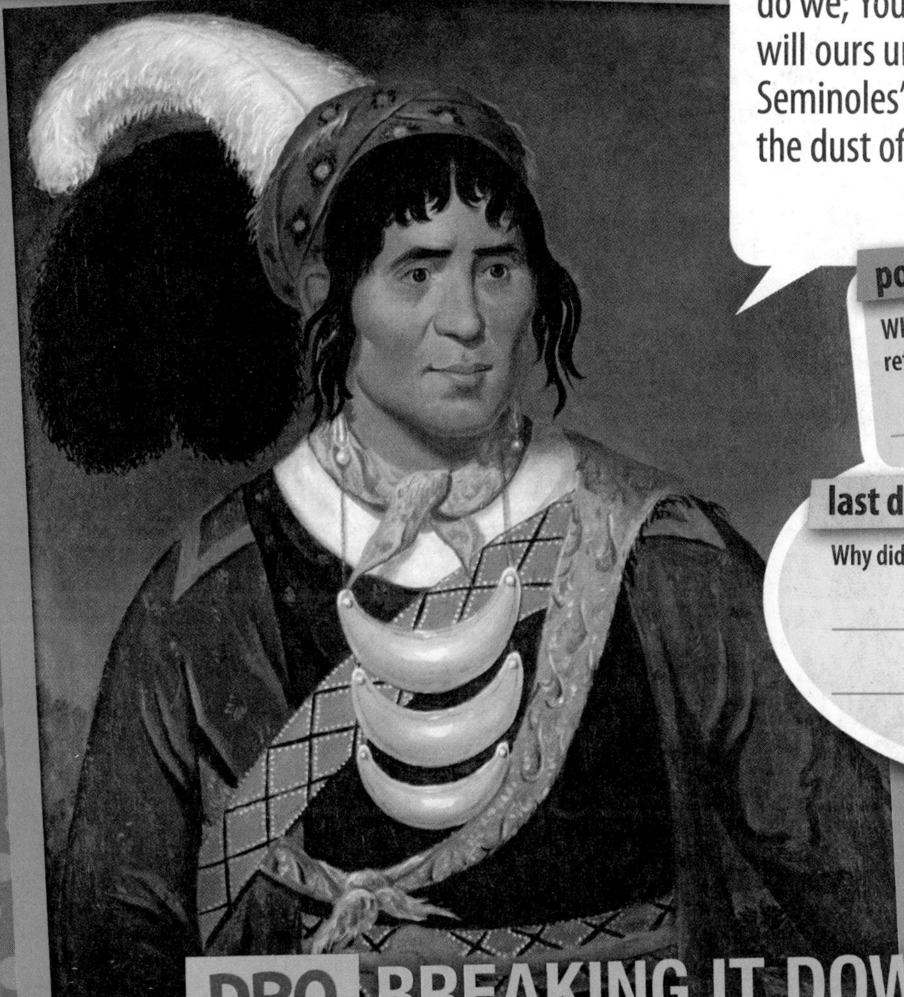

powder and lead

What does Osceola mean when he refers to *powder* and *lead*?

____

last drop

Why did Osceola use this term?

____

____

DBQ BREAKING IT DOWN

What characteristics of leadership does Osceola show in his letter?

____

____

____

McGraw-Hill networks™ *There's More Online!*

NGSSS
SS.8.A.4.16 Identify key ideas and influences of Jacksonian democracy.

Terms to Know

favorite son
a candidate for national office who has support mostly from his home state

plurality
the largest number of something, but less than a majority

majority
greater than half of the total number of something

mudslinging
a method in election campaigns that uses gossip and lies to make an opponent look bad

bureaucracy
a system of government in which specialized tasks are carried out by unelected or appointed officials

spoils system
practice of handing out government jobs to supporters; replacing government employees with the winning candidate's supporters

nominating convention
a meeting in which representative members of a political party choose candidates to run for important elected offices

Essential Question
What are the characteristics of a leader?

Guiding Questions
1. What new ways of campaigning appeared during the elections of 1824 and 1828?
2. How did Andrew Jackson make the American political system more democratic?
3. How did a fight over tariffs become a debate about states' rights versus federal rights?

When Did It Happen?

1821
Spain officially transfers Florida to the United States

1823
Monroe Doctrine is issued

1825
John Quincy Adams becomes president

1829
Andrew Jackson becomes president

1820   1825   1830

What Do You Know?

Directions: In the first column, circle "True" if you think the statement is true or circle "False" if you think it is false based on what you know before you read the lesson. After this lesson, complete the last column.

Before the Lesson			After the Lesson	
True	False	A favorite son candidate is the oldest in the family.	True	False
True	False	Andrew Jackson was a military hero.	True	False
True	False	The person who wins the most votes from the people is always elected president.	True	False
True	False	Being critical of another candidate running for office is a new practice.	True	False

New Parties Emerge

From the earliest days of the United States, there were political factions. Political factions quickly became political parties. These parties backed candidates and set policies. As the new federal government began to take shape, the parties and their views changed. Between 1816 and 1824, there was only one major political party—the Democratic-Republicans.

For the election of 1824, there were four candidates for president. The candidates were all members of the same party. However, they had different ideas about the government. Party leaders supported one of these candidates, William Crawford. The other three candidates were **favorite sons.** These candidates got most of their support from their home states. Each of these candidates favored the interests of his state.

John Quincy Adams of Massachusetts was the son of a former president. Most of his support came from merchants and businesspeople in the Northeast. Henry Clay of Kentucky was Speaker of the House. He had the support of his state, which was on the frontier. Andrew Jackson of Tennessee was a war hero, so he was already known and popular. He had come from a poor family. Jackson became an able leader and wanted ordinary people to have a voice in politics. He was backed by his home state of Tennessee.

The vote was split among the four candidates. Jackson won a **plurality,** or more votes than any of the other candidates. However, no candidate had a **majority,** or more than half, of the electoral votes. The Constitution provided the rules for such a result. It said that if a candidate does not win a majority of the electoral votes, the House of Representatives must decide. The representatives in the House voted and selected John Quincy Adams.

Presidential Candidates, 1824		
Candidate	**Political Party**	**Main Base of Support**
William Crawford	Democratic-Republican	
	Democratic-Republican	People in the Northeast, especially merchants
Henry Clay	Democratic-Republican	People in Kentucky and in the West (on the frontier)
Andrew Jackson		People in Tennessee and in the West, and people who felt like they were being left out of politics

Think Critically

1. Summarize Who won the election of 1824, and how was the winner determined?

2. Infer What did Crawford's failure to win the 1824 election say about the party's strength?

Mark the Text

3. Chart Complete the missing elements on the chart.

Mark the Text

4. Complete the chart by filling in the missing information.

Think Critically

5. Explain What were some campaign methods used in the election of 1828?

_____

_____

_____

Show Your Skill

6. Make Inferences What changes that were taking place in the country contributed to Jackson's victory?

_____

_____

_____

_____

_____

_____

_____

7. Make a Connection What campaign practices of the 1828 election are still used today?

_____

_____

_____

Like many people in the Northeast, Adams believed in a strong federal government. In the growing country, though, many disagreed, especially people on the frontier. By the next presidential election in 1828, the Democratic-Republican Party had split into two separate parties. The National Republicans backed Adams. National Republicans wanted a strong central government. The Democrats supported Jackson and supported states' rights.

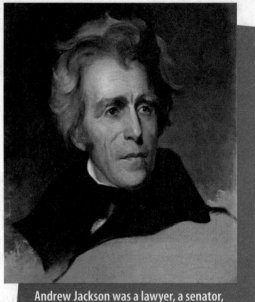

Andrew Jackson was a lawyer, a senator, and a war hero before becoming president.

In the election of 1828, Jackson faced Adams. Jackson was a man of the frontier. Adams was a man whose father was one of the original Founders of the nation. Their views were very different and so were their supporters.

The National Republicans wanted a strong federal government and a national bank. They thought the bank would help the economy. The National Republicans were more likely to be wealthy than the Democrats. Many of the Democrats were workers, farmers, or immigrants.

Election of 1828		
	Democrats	**National Republicans**
Idea of government		
National bank	opposed national bank	supported national bank
Base of support	workers, farmers, immigrants	wealthy voters, merchants
Candidate		

The campaign grew ugly. Both parties used **mudslinging** to gain voter support. The parties and candidates threw insults at the other side to muddy or dirty the opposing candidate's name. The candidates also came up with new slogans so voters would remember them. Candidates handed out printed flyers. They held rallies and barbeques to try to win voters' support. Jackson's popularity gave him an easy victory in the 1828 election.

Jackson as President

Jackson believed that a larger group of white men should get the benefits of American democracy. This idea was generally favored by the states. By 1828, most states had made the voting process more democratic. Owning property was no longer required in order to be allowed to vote. This allowed more people to become voters. Originally, state legislators voted for electors, and the electors voted for the president. By 1828, many states had changed their constitutions. State legislators would not vote for the electors anymore. Voters would vote directly for the presidential electors in their states.

Jackson also thought that part of the federal government had become undemocratic. Many of the workers were not elected officials. They were part of a **bureaucracy.** Jackson thought other people should have a chance to work for the government. He used what became known as the **spoils system.** He fired many of the workers and replaced them with people who had supported his election.

Other changes also began to allow more people to take part in their government. Usually, candidates for office were chosen at a party caucus—a meeting of top party officials. The caucus system was replaced by **nominating conventions.** At these special state meetings, elected representatives voted for the party's candidate.

The Tariff Debate

Americans were also split about their views about taxes, or tariffs, on goods from other countries. The merchants in the Northeast wanted higher tariffs. These tariffs would make European goods cost more than the ones made at home. The Southerners did not want higher tariffs. They liked buying cheaper goods from Europe. They were also worried that Europeans might tax the cotton the Southerners sold in Europe, meaning the Southerners would lose business.

Regional Differences of Tariffs		
Region	**Position on Tariffs**	**Reason for Position**
South	Against	
North	For	

Mark the Text

8. Underline two ways that states expanded democracy in the 1820s.

Think Critically

9. **Analyze** How did Jackson treat the federal bureaucracy?

_____

_____

_____

_____

_____

_____

Show Your Skill

10. **Draw Conclusions** How did nominating conventions make government more democratic?

_____

_____

_____

_____

_____

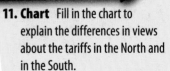

Mark the Text

11. **Chart** Fill in the chart to explain the differences in views about the tariffs in the North and in the South.

12. Contrast On what three issues did Jackson and Calhoun clash?

_____

_____

_____

13. Infer How did Northeastern factory owners react to a high tariff? Why?

_____

_____

_____

_____

_____

_____

Take the Challenge

14. Work with a partner to reenact a conversation between Jackson and Calhoun about a few of the areas about which they disagreed.

Jackson's vice president, John C. Calhoun, was from South Carolina. Calhoun was a strong supporter of states' rights. His views were very different from those of Jackson. Their differences created some problems between the two men. When Congress passed a bill that raised new tariffs, Calhoun was very angry. He did not think the tariff was in the interest of his state. He believed that a state could and should nullify, or cancel, federal laws that were not good for that state.

When Congress again raised tariffs in 1832, South Carolina passed a new law. The law said that the state would not pay the new tariffs. The state also threatened to secede from, or leave, the United States if the federal government tried to enforce the tariff law.

Jackson believed there were limits to the power of federal government. He did not agree with his vice president, however. He did not believe the states had the right to nullify federal laws or to secede from the Union.

Some laws involve only the state, for example, laws about roads. Jackson did not think the federal government should have a say in these laws. However, Jackson thought the federal government should support projects that helped the entire nation. He believed that the federal government had the right to enact tariff laws because they involved international trade.

In the South, anger over the tariff continued to grow. Jackson tried to calm the storm by working with Congress to lower the tariffs. Yet to make his point about keeping the Union together and strong, he also supported a new bill. The Force Act would allow him to enforce federal laws, with the military if necessary. South Carolina was happy to have the tariffs lowered. Nevertheless, the state nullified the Force Act.

NGSSS Check Explain why Jackson opposed states' rights when it came to states nullifying a federal law and seceding from the United States. SS.8.A.4.16

_____

_____

_____

What factors caused Andrew Jackson to be elected president? SS.8.A.4.16

_____

_____

_____

LESSON 2

CONFLICTS OVER LAND

NGSSS

SS.8.A.4.1 Examine the causes, course, and consequences of United States westward expansion and its growing diplomatic assertiveness.

SS.8.A.4.4 Discuss the impact of westward expansion on cultural practices and migration patterns of Native American and African slave populations.

SS.8.A.4.13 Explain the consequences of landmark Supreme Court decisions (McCulloch v. Maryland [1819], Gibbons v. Odgen [1824], Cherokee Nation v. Georgia [1831], and Worcester v. Georgia [1832]) significant to this era of American history.

SS.8.A.4.16 Identify key ideas and influences of Jacksonian democracy.

SS.8.A.4.17 Examine key events and peoples in Florida history as each impacts this era of American history.

SS.8.A.4.18 Examine the experiences and perspectives of different ethnic, national, and religious groups in Florida, explaining their contributions to Florida's and America's society and culture during the Territorial Period.

Essential Question

What are the consequences when cultures interact?

Guiding Questions

1. Why were Native Americans forced to abandon their land and move west?
2. Why did some Native Americans resist resettlement?

Terms to Know

relocate
to move to another place

Where in the World?

Removal of Native Americans, 1820–1840

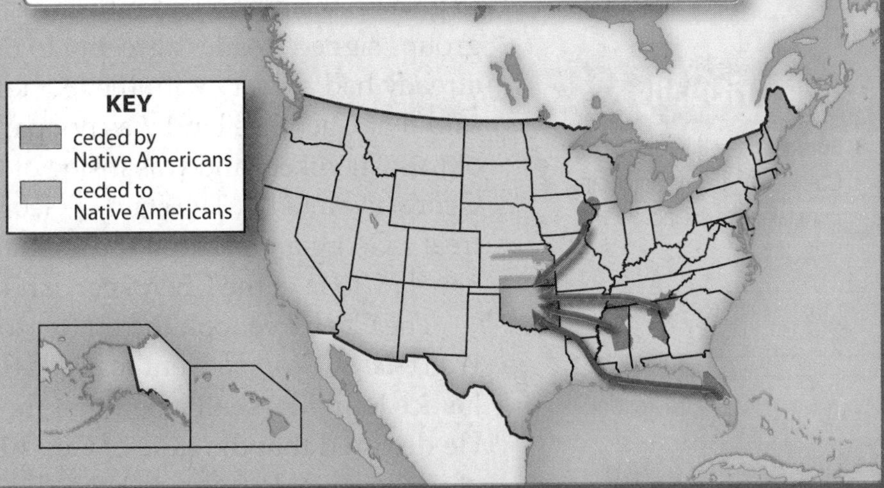

When Did It Happen?

- **1830** Congress passes Indian Removal Act
- **1832** Supreme Court rules in *Worcester* v. *Georgia*
- **1835–1842** Second Seminole War
- **1838** Cherokee removal begins
- **1842** Most eastern Indians have been moved west
- **1855–1858** Third Seminole War

1830 1840 1850 1860

Think Critically

1. Describe Where did most of the "Five Civilized Tribes" live?

_____

_____

_____

_____

Show Your Skill

2. Draw Conclusions Why did some people object to the Treaty of New Echota?

_____

_____

_____

_____

Think Critically

3. Summarize How did the Cherokee try to stop Americans from taking their land?

_____

_____

_____

_____

Removing Native Americans

In the early 1800s, American settlers were expanding both west and south. The growing country had to decide what to do about Native Americans who lived on this land. The Cherokee, Creek, Seminole, Chickasaw, and Choctaw peoples lived in Georgia, Alabama, Mississippi, and Florida. These Native American groups lived in successful farming communities. Their communities were much like many other American communities. As a result, other Americans referred to these groups as the "Five Civilized Tribes."

As settlers moved farther south and west, many people wanted the federal government to force the Five Civilized Tribes to **relocate.** The tribes would be forced to move. Settlers needed more land, and they wanted to take it from Native Americans. President Jackson had once fought the Creek and Seminole people in Georgia and Florida. He agreed that Native Americans should not be allowed to stand in the way of this expansion.

As president, Jackson pushed a bill through Congress that would help the settlers. The Indian Removal Act of 1830 allowed the federal government to pay eastern Native Americans to give up their land and move west. Most Native American groups signed treaties agreeing to do so. However, the Cherokee already had a treaty with the federal government. That treaty said that Cherokee land was not part of the United States. Much of this Cherokee land was inside of the state of Georgia. By 1830, Georgia wanted it. The state of Georgia ignored the Cherokee's treaty. Georgia pressured the federal government to use the new law to take the Cherokee's land.

The Cherokee took the matter to court. The case, called _Worcester_ v. _Georgia_, went to the U.S. Supreme Court. Chief Justice John Marshall ruled that the Cherokee owned the land. He declared that the state of Georgia could not take control of it. President Jackson disagreed with the Court's ruling. He refused to prevent Georgia from forcing the Cherokee to move.

In 1835 the federal government signed a new treaty with a small group of Cherokee. In the Treaty of New Echota, this small group promised that all the Cherokee would move by 1838. However, Cherokee chief John Ross and most of the important Cherokee leaders had not signed this treaty. For this reason, Ross did not think the treaty could be enforced. Some members of Congress agreed. Nonetheless, a majority agreed with President Jackson and the treaty became law.

Most Cherokee did not want to relocate. In 1838 President Van Buren sent the army to enforce the treaty. The army forced the Cherokee off their land and into a new territory west of the Mississippi River. It was called the Indian Territory because Congress had created it to be the new home of many eastern Native Americans. Most of this territory is the present-day state of Oklahoma. The other Five Civilized Tribes and other Native Americans were also forced to move to the Indian Territory.

The Cherokee had to travel from their homes in Georgia to the Indian Territory. Losing their homes and taking this long and difficult journey greatly saddened the Native Americans. Many died waiting for the journey to begin. Many more died along the way. Their journey was later called the Trail of Tears.

Resistance and Removal

Most of the "Five Civilized Tribes" did not want to sell their lands. Osceola, a leader of the Seminoles in Florida, refused to move. Instead, he and his followers decided to stay and fight. This began a long and bloody period of conflict called the Seminole Wars. The Seminoles were skilled at fighting in Florida's swamps and marshlands. Small groups surprised and attacked army troops and then ran away into the swamps. This method of fighting is called guerilla tactics. It was successful, at least for a while. The Seminoles were greatly outnumbered, but they kept the army from a quick victory.

In their fight, Seminoles were joined by Black Seminoles. Black Seminoles were escaped slaves who ran away to Florida. Since Florida was not a state yet, they thought they would be safe there. Some of the runaway slaves built their own homes. Others lived among the Seminole people. When war broke out, Black Seminoles fought alongside the Native Americans. They were afraid that the army might return them to slavery.

Men, women, and children were forced to make the journey that became known as the Trail of Tears. Thousands died on the long trek westward.

Think Critically

4. Contrast How was the Supreme Court's ruling in *Worcester* v. *Georgia* different from what happened?

_____

_____

_____

_____

Mark the Text

5. Underline the sentence that explains the meaning of *guerrilla tactics*.

Show Your Skill

6. Make Inferences Why were Black Seminoles willing to support the Seminole fight to stay in Florida?

_____

_____

_____

_____

7. Summarize What happened to the Seminoles after the fighting ended?

_____

_____

_____

_____

_____

_____

Take the Challenge

8. Research one of the native groups in this lesson. Learn about three of their traditions and share what you learn with the class.

The fighting continued, on and off, for more than 20 years, from 1835 to 1858. Neither side was able to defeat the other. Eventually, most of the Seminoles either died or moved to the Indian Territory. Some, however, remained in Florida, where their descendants still live today.

By the end of the Seminole Wars, very few Native American groups were still living in the eastern United States. Most had been removed to the Indian Territory. They shared the land with other Native American groups already living there. In later years, American settlers would want to expand into the Indian Territory, too. Many of he same problems would be repeated years later.

Osceola was the leader of the Seminoles during the Second Seminole War. He was captured when he arrived for what he had been told would be peace negotiations.

NGSSS Check How did the expansion of the American settlers affect Native American groups? SS.8.A.4.4

_____

_____

Who was Osceola and what was his contribution to history in Florida? SS.8.A.4.17

_____

_____

NGSSS

SS.8.A.4.13 Explain the consequences of landmark Supreme Court decisions (McCulloch v. Maryland [1819], Gibbons v. Odgen [1824], Cherokee Nation v. Georgia [1831], and Worcester v. Georgia [1832]) significant to this era of American history.

SS.8.A.4.16 Identify key ideas and influences of Jacksonian democracy.

SS.8.E.2.2 Explain the economic impact of government policies.

Essential Question
How do governments change?

Guiding Questions
1. What events occurred when President Jackson forced the National Bank to close?
2. What events occurred during the 1840s that led to the weakening of the Whig Party?

Terms to Know

veto
to reject a bill and prevent it from becoming law

When Did It Happen?

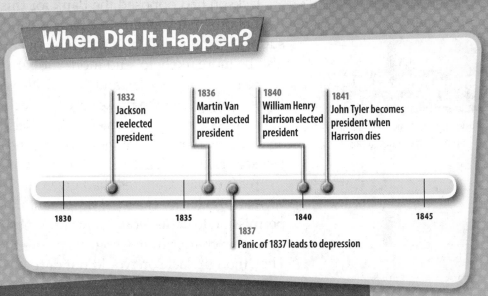

1832
Jackson reelected president

1836
Martin Van Buren elected president

1840
William Henry Harrison elected president

1841
John Tyler becomes president when Harrison dies

1830   1835   1840   1845

1837
Panic of 1837 leads to depression

What Do You Know?

Directions: Look at the guiding questions and the time line. Write two questions you have about the information you think will be in this lesson. After you have finished the lesson, come back and see if you can answer the questions.

Mark the Text

1. Underline the text that describes the role of the Second Bank of the United States.

Think Critically

2. **Explain** Why did Western settlers need it to be easy to get loans from banks?

_____

_____

_____

Mark the Text

3. Underline the definition of a charter.

Show Your Skill

4. **Identify Cause and Effect** What caused the Second Bank of the United States to close?

_____

_____

_____

_____

_____

Jackson's War Against the Bank

Congress created the Second Bank of the United States to hold the federal government's money. Its job was to control the nation's money supply. However, the Bank was not run by government officials. It was run by bankers in the East. Most of these bankers had wealth and a good education.

President Andrew Jackson had neither of these. He was a pioneer from the West. He had worked hard and became president. He did not like the wealthy bankers who ran the Bank. Jackson understood the needs of the settlers in the West. They depended on banks to loan them money to run their farms. However, the Bank's control over smaller private banks was so strict that farmers often had a hard time getting the loans they needed.

Jackson had opposed the Bank for this reason. He thought the nation's many small state banks could manage the money supply. Without the Bank watching over them, they would also be more likely to lend money to farmers.

Senators Henry Clay and Daniel Webster supported the Bank. They wanted to make sure that Jackson did not put it out of business. They also wanted to keep Jackson from being elected again. They thought that most Americans liked the Bank, and if Jackson tried to close it, he would lose votes in the next election.

Years earlier, Congress had given the Bank a charter for 20 years. A charter is a legal document that gives an organization permission to do its work. Clay and Webster helped the Bank get a new charter from Congress before the old charter ran out. They thought Jackson would not dare to **veto** the new charter in an election year. Jackson vetoed it anyway. This meant that the Bank would be forced to go out of business in a few years. Most people supported Jackson's veto. It actually helped him get reelected.

After the election, Jackson took the federal government's money out of the Bank and put it into smaller state banks. When the Bank's charter ended, the Second Bank of the United States closed.

BORN TO COMMAND

OF VETO MEMORY

HAD I BEEN CONSULTED

KING ANDREW the FIRST

In this cartoon, Andrew Jackson is shown as "King Andrew" because some people felt he had expanded the powers of the presidency too far.

Martin Van Buren, Jackson's vice president, ran for president in 1836. Jackson was still very popular. Jackson's support for his vice president helped Van Buren win. Soon after the election, though, the country was in trouble. Jackson's actions toward the Bank had led to an economic panic.

When Jackson took the government's money out of the Bank, it had less money to make loans. It also cracked down on state banks so that they made fewer loans as well. This action hurt farmers and businesses that needed to borrow money. Then the Bank's charter expired and it closed. With no national bank to control them, state banks began printing more banknotes. Federal officials became concerned that these notes had little value. As a result, the federal government decided to require gold and silver as payment for public land. It would not accept the banknotes.

People who had banknotes feared their notes might become worthless. This fear set off an economic panic, the Panic of 1837. Many people lost their jobs and their land. Thousands of businesses had to close.

President Van Buren believed that the government should not do anything to help the nation during the depression. He did, however, work with Congress to create a federal treasury where the federal government would keep its money. The government, not private bankers, would own and run the treasury. Leaders hoped that this new treasury would prevent future panics.

The Whigs in Power

Van Buren ran for reelection in 1840. With the country still in the depths of a depression, the Whigs thought they had a chance to win the presidency. The Whigs ran William Henry Harrison against Van Buren.

Like Andrew Jackson, Harrison was a hero of the War of 1812. His running mate was John Tyler, a planter from Virginia. Their campaign slogan was "Tippecanoe and Tyler Too."

HARRISON
AND
TYLER.
—
OLD KNOX
WILL CHERISH IN MANHOOD
THE DEFENDER OF HER IN-
FANCY.

The log cabin was a popular symbol for the Harrison and Tyler campaign.

Mark the Text

5. Underline the reason that people began to think that their money might become worthless.

Show Your Skill

6. **Determine Cause and Effect** What was the main cause of the Panic of 1837?

_____

_____

Think Critically

7. **Summarize** What was the purpose of the new treasury system?

_____

_____

_____

_____

_____

8. **Explain** Why did the Whigs think they had a chance to win the presidency in 1840?

_____

_____

_____

_____

_____

_____

Show Your Skill

9. Draw Conclusions Why did the Whigs present Harrison as a frontiersman?

_____

_____

_____

_____

Mark the Text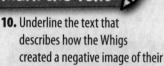

10. Underline the text that describes how the Whigs created a negative image of their opponent, President Van Buren.

Think Critically

11. Analyze Identify two reasons why John Tyler was not a very effective president.

_____

_____

_____

_____

_____

Take the Challenge

12. Harrison was the first president who was not able to complete his term of office. Do some research and learn about the other times when a president has not completed the term to which he was elected.

Harrison had to gain the support of the laborers and farmers who had voted for Jackson. He was wealthy and from Ohio, but his campaign painted him as a simple frontiersman like Jackson. The Democrats responded to this false picture. They said all Harrison was good for was sitting in front of a log cabin and collecting his military pension. The Whigs turned the attack around. They adopted the simple frontier log cabin as the symbol of their campaign.

At the same time, the Whigs painted Van Buren as a wealthy snob with perfume-scented whiskers. They blamed him for the depression and accused him of spending money on fancy furniture for the White House. The Whigs' tactics worked. A record number of voters elected Harrison by a wide margin.

Harrison delivered his long inaugural speech in the bitter cold without a hat or coat. He died of pneumonia 32 days later. He served the shortest term of any president. John Tyler became the first vice president to become president because the elected president died in office.

Tyler had been elected as a Whig. He had once been a Democrat and did not support many Whig policies. Whig Party leaders thought he would attract voters in the South. Webster and Clay believed that they would be able to get Harrison to agree to their plans for the country. Harrison's death spoiled their plan.

Tyler vetoed several Whig bills. His lack of party loyalty outraged many Whigs. Finally, they threw him out of the party. He became a president without a party. Tyler's biggest success was the Webster-Ashburton Treaty, which was signed by the United States and Great Britain. The treaty ended the disagreement over the border between Maine and Canada. It also settled the long U.S.–Canadian border from Maine to Minnesota.

Unfortunately, the Whigs could not agree on goals for their party. They did agree on their opposition to President Tyler, however. The Whigs continued to vote more and more according to sectional ties—North, South, and West—not party ties. It is likely that Whig presidential candidate Henry Clay lost the election of 1844 because of this division. James Polk, a Democrat, was the new president.

 NGSSS Check List two reasons why President Jackson destroyed the Second Bank of the United States. SS.8.A.4.16

_____

_____

_____

MY REFLECTIONS

ESSENTIAL QUESTION *What are the characteristics of a leader?*

Reflect on What It Means . . .

A leader has to be more than just the "boss" of a group. A good leader is respected, admired, and provides clear goals for the group.

Search newspapers, magazines, or news Web sites for examples of leaders in your community and worldwide, or find examples of leaders in your textbook.

To My Community and the World

Pick one leader from your community and one from the world. Fill out the leadership map below, filling in each of the blank boxes with a leadership trait exemplified by the leader you have chosen.

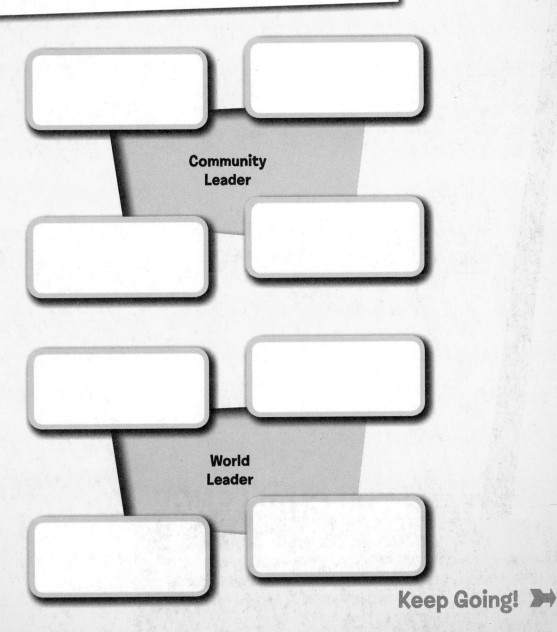

Keep Going! ➤➤

To Me

Pick a leadership trait that you especially admire. Write a paragraph explaining why you admire this trait and how you could develop more of this trait in yourself.

TAKE THE CHALLENGE

If you were starting a new community in a new land, who would you choose to lead it? Choose one leader you admire. Dress up like the leader, and give a short speech to the class related to the accomplishments of the person. The class will vote on which leader should lead the new community.

MANIFEST DESTINY

NGSSS

SS.8.A.4.1 Examine the causes, course, and consequences of United States westward expansion and its growing diplomatic assertiveness (War of 1812, Convention of 1818, Adams-Onis Treaty, Missouri Compromise, Monroe Doctrine, Trail of Tears, Texas annexation, Manifest Destiny, Oregon Territory, Mexican American War/Mexican Cession, California Gold Rush, Compromise of 1850, Kansas Nebraska Act, Gadsden Purchase).

ESSENTIAL QUESTIONS *How does geography influence the way people live? Why does conflict develop? How do new ideas change the way people live?*

Iowa and Florida were both admitted into the Union at the same time, in 1845, so that the balance of free and slave states could remain equal. As a result of the Act of Admission, Floridians elected William D. Moseley, the first state governor of Florida.

PHOTO: Florida Photographic Collection

Copyright © by The McGraw-Hill Companies, Inc.

" Be it enacted, by the Senate and House of Representatives of the United States of America in Congress assembled, That the states of Iowa and Florida be and the same are hereby, declared to be States of the United States of America, and are hereby admitted into the Union on equal footing with the original States in all respects whatsoever. "

AN ACT FOR THE ADMISSION OF THE STATES OF IOWA AND FLORIDA INTO THE UNION

on equal footing

What does the term "on equal footing" mean here?

_____

_____

DBQ BREAKING IT DOWN

When new states joined the country they were given the same rights and powers as states that had been part of the country since the country began. Do you think that is fair? List two reasons why it might be fair and two reasons why it might not be fair.

_____

_____

McGraw-Hill
networks™
There's More Online!

LESSON

1

THE OREGON COUNTRY

NGSSS

SS.8.A.4.1 Examine the causes, course, and consequences of United States westward expansion and its growing diplomatic assertiveness (War of 1812, Convention of 1818, Adams-Onis Treaty, Missouri Compromise, Monroe Doctrine, Trail of Tears, Texas annexation, Manifest Destiny, Oregon Territory, Mexican American War/Mexican Cession, California Gold Rush, Compromise of 1850, Kansas Nebraska Act, Gadsden Purchase).

SS.8.A.4.8 Describe the influence of individuals on social and political developments of this era in American History.

Essential Question
How does geography influence the way people live?

Guiding Questions
1. Why did Americans want to control the Oregon Country?
2. What is Manifest Destiny?

Terms to Know

joint occupation
people from two countries can occupy an area

mountain man
person who lived in the Rocky Mountains and made his living by trapping beaver for the furs

emigrants
people who leave their country

prairie schooner
a wagon with a canvas covering used by pioneers in the mid-1800s to travel West

Manifest Destiny
belief that the United States was destined by God to extend its boundaries to the Pacific Ocean

Where in the World?

Oregon Country

When Did It Happen?

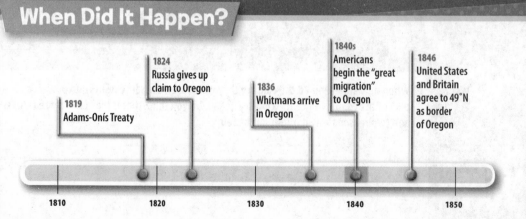

- **1819** Adams-Onís Treaty
- **1824** Russia gives up claim to Oregon
- **1836** Whitmans arrive in Oregon
- **1840s** Americans begin the "great migration" to Oregon
- **1846** United States and Britain agree to 49°N as border of Oregon

1810   1820   1830   1840   1850

Rivalry in the Northwest

The Oregon Country covered much more land than today's state of Oregon. Oregon, Washington, Idaho and parts of Montana and Wyoming were all included in it.

In the early 1800s, four countries claimed the Oregon Country. They were Russia, Spain, Great Britain, and the United States. In 1819, the United States and Spain signed the Adams-Onís Treaty. Spain gave up its claims in the Oregon Country. They agreed that the border of its territory was the northern border of California.

Russia also gave up its claim to land south of Alaska. Britain would not give up its claim. The United States and Great Britain agreed to **joint occupation.** This meant that settlers from both countries could live there.

The first Americans to live in the Oregon Country were fur trappers. These men would trap beaver for their skins. Fur companies bought the skins to sell as furs in the United States and Europe. The fur trappers were called **mountain men.** The mountain men traded with Native Americans. Many adopted Native American ways. They often dressed in the same type of clothes and sometimes had Native American wives.

For years the trappers made their living trading furs. But they trapped so many beaver that there were almost none left. The mountain men had to find other jobs. Some became farmers. Others used their knowledge of the area to guide settlers on the long trip to the Oregon Country. The route they used most often was called the Oregon Trail.

Mark the Text

1. Underline the country that gave up its claims to Oregon in the Adams-Onís Treaty.

Think Critically

2. **Explain** What is *joint occupation?* Which two countries agreed to joint occupation of Oregon?

_____

_____

_____

_____

_____

Show Your Skill

3. **Formulate Questions** What is one question you would ask a mountain man who had been forced to give up trapping furs?

_____

_____

_____

Parts of the original Oregon Trail can still be hiked today. Stone markers like this one can be found at many locations along the trail from Missouri to Oregon.

_____

_____

_____

_____

Mark the Text

5. Graphic Organizer Complete the graphic organizer to explain how each is connected to the "great migration" to the West.

Oregon and Manifest Destiny

Soon Americans heard about the good farmland in Oregon. Many traveled there to settle. Dr. Marcus Whitman and his wife Narcissa went to Oregon in 1836. They built a mission among the Cayuse people. The Cayuse were Native Americans who lived near what is now Walla Walla, Washington. The Whitmans wanted to convert the Cayuse to Christianity. They also wanted to provide medical care.

Settlers traveling to Oregon often stopped to rest at the Whitman's mission. In 1847 the people at the mission began getting measles. Many Cayuse children died. The Cayuse blamed the Whitmans for these deaths. They attacked the mission. They killed the Whitmans and eleven others.

Settlers kept coming to Oregon. Reports of fertile land attracted many of them. Others faced economic hard times in the East. They wanted a fresh start. These pioneers were called **emigrants.** Emigrants are people who leave their home country for another place.

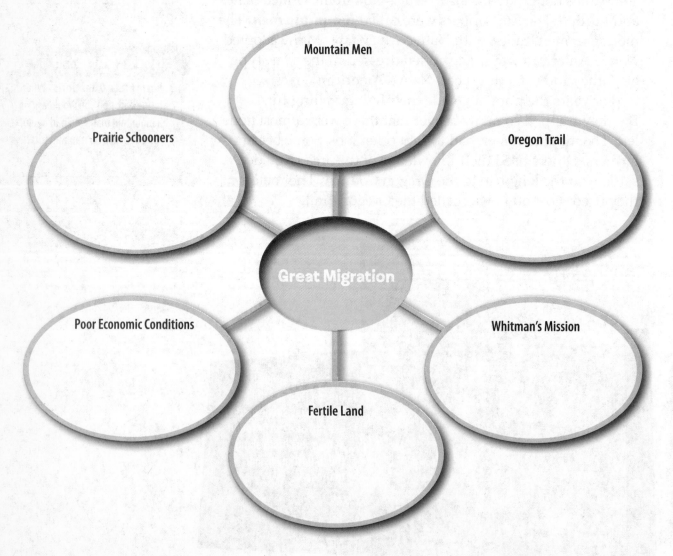

This recreated prairie schooner is near Scotts Bluff, Nebraska. Wagon trains used landmarks such as this bluff for navigation on the journey.

PHOTO: Richard Cummins/CORBIS

To reach Oregon, they had to travel about 2,000 difficult miles. They packed everything they owned in covered wagons. These wagons were called **prairie schooners.** From a distance, they looked like a ship called a schooner. Even though it was a very hard trip, thousands of people started for Oregon. This was called the "great migration." A migration is when many people move to the same place.

In the early 1800s, many Americans thought the nation had a special role to play in the world. Many Americans thought they should spread freedom by settling the whole continent, all the way to the Pacific Ocean. Newspaper editor John O'Sullivan called this mission "**Manifest Destiny.**" The name caught on, and everyone started talking about it.

Some Americans thought the United States should own all of Oregon. James K. Polk ran for president in 1846. He believed in Manifest Destiny. His campaign slogan was "Fifty-four Forty or Fight!" This meant that the United States claimed Oregon to the line on the map of latitude 54° 40'.

The British did not agree to this. The border was finally set at latitude 49°N. James K. Polk won the election because of his support for Manifest Destiny.

NGSSS Check What were the emigrants who moved west hoping to find? SS.8.A.4.8

_____

_____

_____

Show Your Skill

6. **Draw Conclusions** "Manifest Destiny" meant that America had a special mission. What was that mission?

_____

_____

_____

Take the Challenge

7. Draw a prairie schooner on a sheet of drawing paper and label the parts. Make a list of some of the items that would be carried in the prairie schooner.

LESSON

2

STATEHOOD FOR FLORIDA AND TEXAS

NGSSS

SS.8.A.4.1 Examine the causes, course, and consequences of United States westward expansion and its growing diplomatic assertiveness (War of 1812, Convention of 1818, Adams-Onis Treaty, Missouri Compromise, Monroe Doctrine, Trail of Tears, Texas annexation, Manifest Destiny, Oregon Territory, Mexican American War/Mexican Cession, California Gold Rush, Compromise of 1850, Kansas Nebraska Act, Gadsden Purchase).

Essential Question
Why does conflict develop?

Guiding Questions
1. How did Florida become a state?
2. How did Texas become a state?

Terms to Know

Tejano
a Texan of Hispanic, often Mexican, descent

decree
official order

barricade
block off

annex
take control of

Where in the World?

The Southern United States

Texas

Florida

N W E S

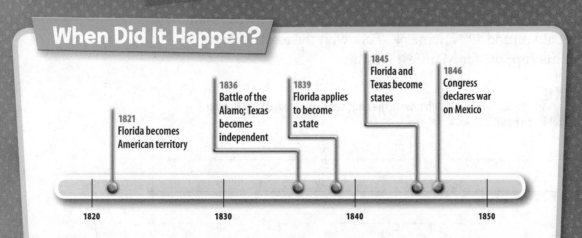

When Did It Happen?

1821 Florida becomes American territory

1836 Battle of the Alamo; Texas becomes independent

1839 Florida applies to become a state

1845 Florida and Texas become states

1846 Congress declares war on Mexico

1820   1830   1840   1850

Florida

Florida belonged to Spain until 1821. In that year, the United States purchased Florida from Spain. Tallahassee was made the capital of the territory in 1824. It was located between two major cities, St. Augustine and Pensacola.

Thousands of new settlers came to Florida from the United States. Many came because of the fertile soil. Among these were planters from Virginia, Georgia, and the Carolinas. The soil at home was worn out from overuse. The planters settled mostly in western and northern Florida. They set up large cotton and tobacco plantations. Small farms and cattle ranches grew up in central Florida.

The population began to grow quickly. By 1837, the population was 48,000. Enslaved people made up about half of the population.

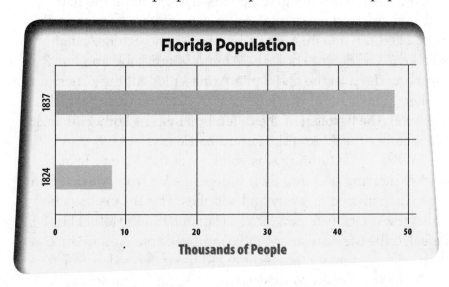

Florida Population

Thousands of People

Voters in Florida wanted to become a state. They chose delegates to write a constitution.

Florida's First Constitution
• Governor elected for four years
• An elected General Assembly, or legislature
• System of public schools
• Slavery allowed

In 1839 the constitution was submitted to the U.S. Congress for approval. The question of allowing slavery created a problem. Congress wanted to keep the number of slave states and the number of free states equal. Admitting Florida as a slave state would upset that balance. Six years later, Iowa joined the Union as a free state and Florida joined as a slave state.

Think Critically

1. Infer Describe Tallahassee's location. Why might it have been chosen for the capital?

_____

_____

_____

_____

_____

Show Your Skill

2. Identify Cause and Effect Why did planters move to Florida from Virginia, Georgia, and the Carolinas?

_____

_____

_____

3. Interpret Graphs State one fact you learned from the graph.

_____

_____

_____

_____

Mark the Text

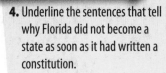

4. Underline the sentences that tell why Florida did not become a state as soon as it had written a constitution.

This flag of Texas reminds us that Texas is sometimes called the "Lone Star State."

Mark the Text

5. Circle the definition of *decree.* Then underline what the Mexicans decreed.

Think Critically

6. **Analyze** Why was Santa Anna important?

_____

_____

Show Your Skill

7. **Compare and Contrast** How were the Battle of the Alamo and the Battle of San Jacinto similar and how were they different?

_____

_____

_____

_____

Take the Challenge

8. Research five details about the Alamo. Write those details as questions and see if your classmates know the answers.

Texas

At this time, Mexico owned Texas. Mexican citizens who lived there were called **Tejanos** (teh•HAH•nohs). Mexico wanted more people to settle in Texas. They encouraged Americans to come and live there. Stephen F. Austin brought hundreds of American families to Texas and became their leader.

Americans did not want to follow the rules that Mexico made for those living in Texas. They would have to learn Spanish and become Catholic. Mexico made a **decree,** or official order, that no more Americans could come to Texas. Austin and Sam Houston tried to reach an agreement with Mexico, but could not. They decided to separate from Mexico and form their own government.

Mexican general Santa Anna marched his army into Texas to stop the Americans. The Mexicans had many more soldiers. Still, the Texans captured the city of San Antonio.

Santa Anna did not give up. His army marched to San Antonio. It found a group of American soldiers **barricaded,** or blocked off, in a mission called the Alamo. Santa Anna attacked. The defenders of the Alamo fought long and hard for many days. In the end Santa Anna killed all the American soldiers. The general was sure that the Texans were beaten. However, the heroism of the defenders inspired other Texans. "Remember the Alamo" became a battle cry.

In 1836 while fighting was going on at the Alamo, Texas leaders met and declared their independence from Mexico. Sam Houston gathered an army and supplies. The Texans launched a surprise attack near San Jacinto (san hah•SIHN•toh). They defeated the Mexican army and captured Santa Anna. Santa Anna signed a treaty that recognized the independence of Texas.

Texas was now a country named the Lone Star Republic. Voters elected Sam Houston as president. He asked the United States to **annex,** or take control of, Texas. Adding Texas as a slave state would upset the balance in Congress. Southerners favored annexing Texas. Northerners opposed the idea of adding a slave state to the Union.

By 1844, the mood of the country had changed. Manifest Destiny had become very popular. James K. Polk was elected president. He strongly supported expanding the country in Oregon and in Texas. In 1845 Texas entered the Union.

NGSSS Check How did Florida and Texas become states, and how was that process different for each? SS.8.A.4.1

_____

_____

PHOTO: Brooke Slezak/Taxi/Getty Images

Copyright © by The McGraw-Hill Companies, Inc.

WAR WITH MEXICO

NGSSS

SS.8.A.4.1 Examine the causes, course, and consequences of United States westward expansion and its growing diplomatic assertiveness (War of 1812, Convention of 1818, Adams-Onis Treaty, Missouri Compromise, Monroe Doctrine, Trail of Tears, Texas annexation, Manifest Destiny, Oregon Territory, Mexican American War/Mexican Cession, California Gold Rush, Compromise of 1850, Kansas Nebraska Act, Gadsden Purchase).

Essential Question
Why does conflict develop?

Guiding Questions
1. How did the Santa Fe Trail benefit the New Mexico Territory?
2. How did the culture of California develop?
3. Why did war break out between the United States and Mexico?

Terms to Know

rancho
ranch, especially the large estates set up by Mexicans in the American West

ranchero
rancher, owner of a rancho

Where in the World?

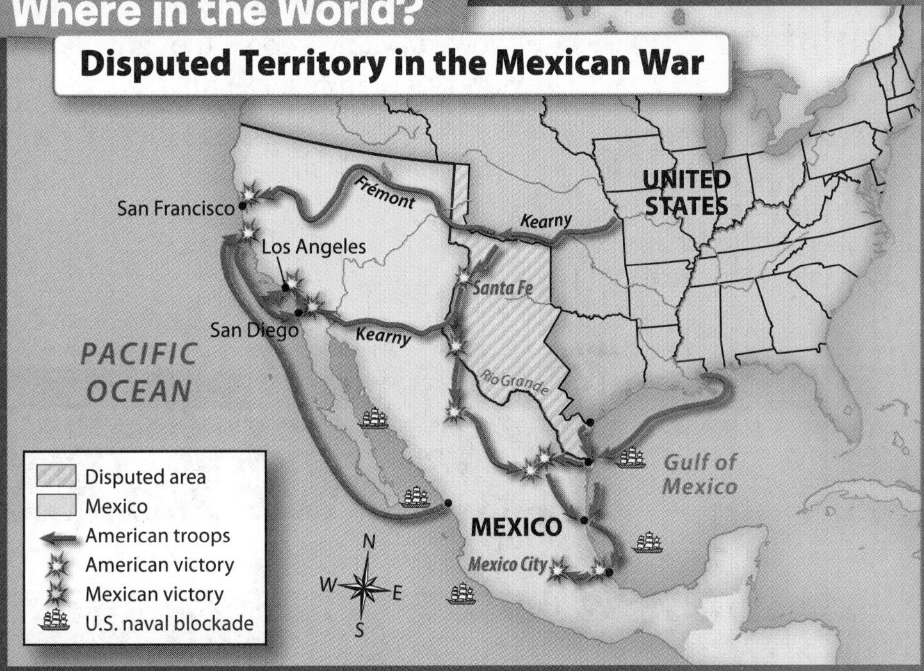

Disputed Territory in the Mexican War

San Francisco
Los Angeles
San Diego
Fremont
Kearny
UNITED STATES
Santa Fe
Kearny
Rio Grande
PACIFIC OCEAN
Gulf of Mexico
MEXICO
Mexico City

Disputed area
Mexico
American troops
American victory
Mexican victory
U.S. naval blockade

N W E S

When Did It Happen?

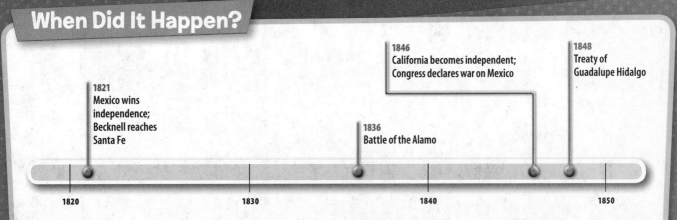

1821
Mexico wins independence; Becknell reaches Santa Fe

1836
Battle of the Alamo

1846
California becomes independent; Congress declares war on Mexico

1848
Treaty of Guadalupe Hidalgo

1820   1830   1840   1850

Mark the Text

1. Underline the states that were a part of the New Mexico Territory.

Think Critically

2. **Sequence** Explorers from what country claimed New Mexico before 1821?

_____

Who claimed it in 1821?

_____

3. **Explain** Why did Mexico allow Americans to settle in New Mexico?

_____

_____

Show Your Skill

4. **Make Inferences** How might the geography of the Santa Fe Trail make it a popular route?

_____

_____

networks Read Chapter 13 Lesson 3 in your textbook or online.

The New Mexico Territory

The New Mexico Territory included all of present-day New Mexico, Arizona, Nevada, Utah, and parts of Colorado and Wyoming. Native Americans had lived in the area for thousands of years. Then Spanish explorers claimed it for Spain. They founded a settlement at Santa Fe. In 1821, Mexico won its independence. New Mexico then became part of Mexico.

The Spanish did not want Americans to live in New Mexico. They were afraid the Americans would take the land away from them. However, the Mexican government welcomed Americans. They hoped more trade would improve the economy.

William Becknell was the first American trader to reach Santa Fe in New Mexico. He brought many goods to sell. The trail he used was mostly flat. It became known as the Santa Fe Trail. Other American traders began to use the trail. Settlers followed. Many people thought New Mexico was part of the country's Manifest Destiny.

In this reenactment of a wagon train journey across the Santa Fe Trail in 2008, some participants traveled over 2,000 miles to recreate a journey some of their ancestors had taken over 160 years earlier.

Parts of some of the original missions built by the Spanish still stand today. This is the Mission San Juan Capistrano in southern California.

California's Spanish Culture

The Spanish were the first Europeans to reach California. In the 1700s, Catholic priests from Spain built missions along the coast. They wanted to convert Native Americans to Christianity. When California became a part of Mexico, Mexican settlers bought mission lands. They turned the land into **ranchos,** or huge estates. The estates were owned by wealthy **rancheros.** Native Americans worked on ranchos. In exchange, they received food and shelter. However, rancheros treated them almost like slaves.

In the 1840s, more Americans came to California. One person who came was John C. Frémont, an army officer. He wrote about how nice the weather was there. He also described the vast natural resources. This attracted even more Americans.

Americans began to talk about adding California to the United States. If California became a state, the western border of the nation would be the Pacific Ocean. Americans would not have to worry about sharing a western border with any other country. Shippers also wanted to build seaports on the Pacific coast. From there they could trade with countries in Asia.

Conflict Begins

President Polk saw both New Mexico and California as part of Manifest Destiny. He offered to buy the land, but Mexico would not sell it. The only other way to get the territory was to find an excuse to go to war with Mexico. He planned a way to get Mexico to start the fighting.

Think Critically

5. Contrast How is a rancho different from a ranchero?

_____

_____

_____

Show Your Skill

6. Identify Cause and Effect How did John C. Frémont contribute to the settling of California?

_____

_____

_____

_____

Take the Challenge

7. You have been asked to recruit settlers to a new place. Write a commercial to get settlers interested in moving. What will you tell them to spark their interest?

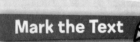
Mexico and the United States disagreed about where the border was between Texas and Mexico. The United States said it was the Rio Grande, the river to the south. Mexico said the border was the Nueces (nu•AY•sehs) River. It was 150 miles farther north.

Polk sent General Zachary Taylor to march his army into the area between the two rivers. He hoped that Mexican soldiers would fire first. They did. Congress then voted in favor of a war with Mexico. Polk had three goals to win the war.

U.S. Goals
1. Drive Mexican forces out of Texas
2. Take control of New Mexico and California
3. Capture Mexico City

General Taylor accomplished the first goal in Texas. General Stephen Kearney led American troops in New Mexico. They captured Santa Fe.

Meanwhile, General John C. Frémont was leading a revolt against Mexico in California. Frémont won. The rebels declared independence. They named California the Bear Flag Republic. After that, American navy ships sailed into the ports of San Francisco and San Diego. These were two cities on the coast of California. The navy claimed California for the United States.

Mexico did not give up, however. Finally, General Winfield Scott and his troops captured Mexico City. Then the Mexicans stopped fighting. The treaty, or agreement, that ended the war was called the Treaty of Guadalupe Hidalgo. Mexico gave up California and the New Mexico Territory. It also agreed that the Rio Grande was the border between Mexico and Texas. The United States paid Mexico $15 million dollars for the land. The dream of Manifest Destiny was now complete.

	Role in the Mexican War
President Polk	
Zachary Taylor	
Stephen Kearney	
John C. Frémont	
Winfield Scott	

 NGSSS Check List three results of the Mexican War. SS.8.A.4.1

_____

_____

_____

NGSSS

SS.8.A.4.1 Examine the causes, course, and consequences of United States westward expansion and its growing diplomatic assertiveness (War of 1812, Convention of 1818, Adams-Onis Treaty, Missouri Compromise, Monroe Doctrine, Trail of Tears, Texas annexation, Manifest Destiny, Oregon Territory, Mexican American War/Mexican Cession, California Gold Rush, Compromise of 1850, Kansas Nebraska Act, Gadsden Purchase).

Essential Question

How do new ideas change the way people live?

Guiding Questions

1. How did the discovery of gold help California?
2. Why did the Mormons settle in Utah?

Terms to Know

forty-niner
fortune-seeker who came to California during the Gold Rush in 1849

boomtown
a fast-growing community

vigilante
person who acts as police, judge, and jury without formal legal authority

Where in the World?

California During the Gold Rush

- PACIFIC OCEAN
- COAST RANGES
- California
- Sacramento R.
- American R.
- SIERRA NEVADA
- Sacramento
- San Francisco
- Sutter's Mill
- San Joaquin R.
- Utah Territory

When Did It Happen?

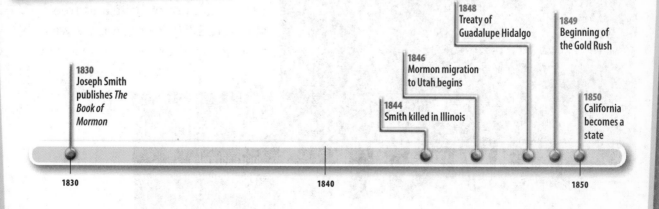

1830 Joseph Smith publishes *The Book of Mormon*

1844 Smith killed in Illinois

1846 Mormon migration to Utah begins

1848 Treaty of Guadalupe Hidalgo

1849 Beginning of the Gold Rush

1850 California becomes a state

1830   1840   1850

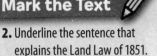

Think Critically

1. Explain Why were miners called forty-niners?

_____

_____

Mark the Text

2. Underline the sentence that explains the Land Law of 1851. Circle who often lost land because of this law.

Show Your Skill

3. Identify Cause and Effect What caused life in a boomtown to be so hard? What was one effect of the hard life?

_____

_____

Take the Challenge

4. Strike it rich! Come up with a business idea that you think would be successful in California in 1849. Make a poster to advertise your business.

networks Read Chapter 13 Lesson 4 in your textbook or online.

California Gold Rush

When gold was discovered in California, the news traveled fast. Soon many people came to California to get rich. About 80 percent of these people were American. Others were from Mexico, South America, Europe, Australia, and even China. They were called the **forty-niners** because most got there in 1849.

The people already living there were the Californios. They were Mexican citizens living in California. The Treaty of Guadalupe Hidalgo ended the Mexican War. It said that the Californios would keep their land. The Land Law of 1851 said that if a new settler claimed their land, they had to go to court to prove the land belonged to them. Many Californios lost their land to newcomers.

When miners rushed to new areas to look for gold, **boomtowns** quickly grew up. These towns were built to house and feed the miners. Life in these towns was hard. Almost all who lived there were rough men. They spent their free time drinking and gambling. There were no laws or police. Sometimes people formed groups of vigilantes to protect themselves. **Vigilantes** took the law into their own hands. They acted as police, judge, and jury.

Few miners got rich. However, other people came west to meet the miners' needs. They sold food, clothing, shelter, and other necessities. They often did become rich. Miners might have gold but they had little food and few supplies. Merchants could charge almost any price they wanted. Many of the miners who did not find gold stayed in California. They became farmers or merchants. The population of cities like San Francisco grew large very quickly.

In 1849 California asked to become a state. Its new constitution banned slavery. This caused a crisis in Congress. Congress wanted there to be a balance of slave and free states. In 1850 a compromise was reached. California became a state.

Miners had to buy equipment and supplies. Often the merchants who supplied these needs became rich, while the miners did not.

A Religious Refuge in Utah

Joseph Smith founded the Mormon religion. He said he had visions that he should build a church. He published *The Book of Mormon*. It said that Mormons should build God's kingdom on earth. Smith gathered followers and formed a church. He called it the Church of Jesus Christ of Latter-day Saints, or Mormons. The Mormons believed in hard work. They also believed that a man could have more than one wife. This belief made them unpopular wherever they went. They created a prosperous community named Nauvoo in Illinois. Then Joseph Smith was killed by an angry mob.

Brigham Young took over as leader of the Mormons. He decided that the Mormons should move again to find religious freedom. He led them westward to the Great Salt Lake. The territory was in present-day Utah. It was part of Mexico at the time. However, no Mexicans lived there. The land was dry and harsh. The Mormons built a successful community through hard work. They

Brigham Young led Mormon settlers from the Midwest to what is now Utah.

- planned their towns,
- built irrigation canals,
- taxed property,
- regulated natural resources,
- founded industries, and
- sold supplies to forty-niners who were on their way to California.

In 1850 Congress set up the Utah Territory. Brigham Young was its governor. The Mormons often had conflicts with the U.S. government. One of the issues was the Mormon belief that a man could have more than one wife. Utah did not become a state until 1896.

 NGSSS Check How did the Gold Rush affect California? SS.8.A.4.1

_____

_____

 NGSSS Check What was Brigham Young's role in the settling of Utah?
SS.8.A.4.1

_____

_____

Think Critically

5. Explain Who were Joseph Smith and Brigham Young?

_____

_____

_____

_____

_____

_____

Mark the Text

6. Underline reasons why the Mormons were successful building a community in Utah.

Reflect on What It Means . . .

Since the European settlement of North America began, Florida's geographic location has had a major impact on its history.

To My Community and the World

Think about the different cultural groups that have affected Florida's history. Make your own cultural history map of Florida. Add labels for each of the cultural groups that arrived in Florida. Use arrows to indicate the direction traveled by each group in order to reach Florida.

To Me

On the map above, add a label for your own community. What is one way in which your own life has been affected by Florida's unique geographic location and history?

TAKE THE CHALLENGE

As a class, make a cultural history map of Florida on the computer. If possible, make the map interactive, so that a user could click on a particular town and hear an audio file or play a video file related to the cultural history of that town.

CHAPTER 14

NORTH AND SOUTH

NGSSS

SS.8.A.4.7 Explain the causes, course, and consequences (industrial growth, subsequent effect on children and women) of New England's textile industry.

SS.8.A.4.8 Describe the influence of individuals on social and political developments of this era in American History.

SS.8.A.4.10 Analyze the impact of technological advancements on the agricultural economy and slave labor.

ESSENTIAL QUESTIONS *How does technology change the way people live? How do people adapt to their environment? Why do people make economic choices?*

In 1793 Eli Whitney wrote a letter to his father explaining how he thought of the idea for the cotton gin.

> " I heard much said of the extreme difficulty of ginning Cotton, that is, separating it from its seeds. There were a number of very respectable Gentlemen at Mrs. Greene's who all agreed that if a machine could be invented which would clean the cotton with expedition , it would be a great thing both to the Country and to the inventor. I involuntarily happened to be thinking on the subject and struck out a plan of a Machine in my mind. "
>
> — ELI WHITNEY

PHOTO: Kevin Fleming/CORBIS

Copyright © by The McGraw-Hill Companies, Inc.

ginning

What context clues are given to help understand the meaning of *ginning*?

_____

with expedition

What word might be a good replacement for *with expedition*?

_____

DBQ BREAKING IT DOWN

A few days after thinking of the idea for the cotton gin, Whitney sketched it. Within 10 days he had built a simple model. What do you think are the character traits of an inventor?

_____

The cotton gin solved a problem in Whitney's time. What problem in society today needs a great invention to solve?

_____

McGraw-Hill
networks™
There's More Online!

LESSON 1
THE INDUSTRIAL NORTH

NGSSS

SS.8.A.4.5 Explain the causes, course, and consequences of the 19th century transportation revolution on the growth of the nation's economy.

SS.8.A.4.10 Analyze the impact of technological advancements on the agricultural economy and slave labor.

Essential Question

How does technology change the way people live?

Guiding Questions

1. How did technology and industry change during the 1800s?
2. What changes made agriculture more profitable in the 1830s?

Terms to Know

clipper ship
ship with sleek hulls and tall sails that "clipped" time from long journeys

telegraph
a device that used electric signals to send messages

Morse code
a system of dots and dashes that represent the alphabet

What Do You Know?

Directions: In the first column, answer the questions based on what you know before you study. After this lesson, complete the last column.

Before You Read	Questions	After You Read
	What was one change as a result of the Erie Canal?	
	In which part of the country was there more industry?	
	What was the telegraph?	

When Did It Happen?

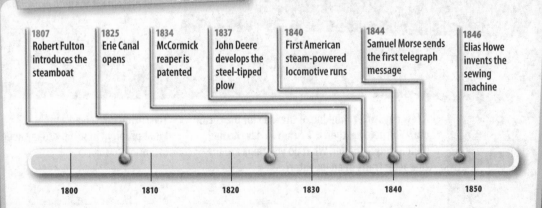

1807	1825	1834	1837	1840	1844	1846
Robert Fulton introduces the steamboat	Erie Canal opens	McCormick reaper is patented	John Deere develops the steel-tipped plow	First American steam-powered locomotive runs	Samuel Morse sends the first telegraph message	Elias Howe invents the sewing machine

1800   1810   1820   1830   1840   1850

netw⊙rks™ Read Chapter 14 Lesson 1 in your textbook or online.

Technology and Industry

In the early 1800s, there were many innovations in industry. There were new machines and new ways of using them. The ways in which Americans worked, traveled, and communicated with each other went through great change. Many of the changes in industry took place in the North.

At the start of the 1800s, most goods, or products, were made one at a time. Each worker would make a product from start to finish. To make clothes, a worker might spin the thread, weave the cloth, then cut and sew the fabric. Innovations in industry changed that way of working.

The North's industrialization took place in three phases, or parts. In the first phase, employers divided jobs into smaller steps. For example, one worker would spin all the thread. Another worker would weave cloth. Each worker specialized in one step and became expert in it. This way of working allowed workers to make more goods faster.

In the second phase, employers built factories to bring specialized workers together. The product could then be moved more quickly from one worker to the next.

In the third phase, workers used machines to do some of their work. For example, looms powered by flowing water did the task of weaving. The machines worked much faster than any human could. The worker's job changed from weaving to running the machine.

Industrialization in the 1800s

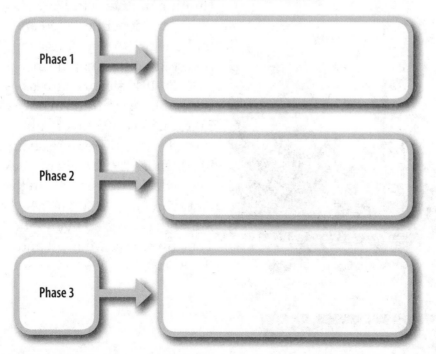

Phase 1 →

Phase 2 →

Phase 3 →

Mark the Text

1. Complete the chart to show the phases of industrialization.

Think Critically

2. **Predict** How do you think industrialization changed the lives of workers?

_____

_____

_____

_____

_____

_____

Show Your Skill

3. Identify Cause and Effect
What caused the growth of cities such as Cincinnati, Buffalo, and Chicago between 1840 and 1860?

_____

_____

_____

_____

Take the Challenge

4. Research some of the most famous clipper ships such as the *Flying Cloud, Glory of the Seas*, or *Challenge*. Create a drawing of one of the ships and write about some of the accomplishments.

Mass production of cotton cloth began in New England in the early 1800s. Mass production means making goods in large numbers using machinery. Elias Howe's invention of the sewing machine in 1846 transformed, or changed, the clothing industry. Workers could now make more clothing faster by using this machine and machine-made cloth.

During this time period, similar changes were transforming other industries. By 1860 the Northeast's factories made at least two-thirds of the country's manufactured goods.

Many changes in transportation also took place during this time period. Between 1800 and 1850, crews built thousands of miles of roads and canals. Many new shipping routes were created by connecting lakes and rivers with canals. In 1807, inventor Robert Fulton introduced his first steamboat, the *Clermont*, on the Hudson River. Steamboats could carry goods and people more cheaply and quickly along inland waterways than other ships of the time.

In the 1840s, builders began to make the canals wider and deeper so that steamboats could travel on them. By 1860 about 3,000 steamboats traveled the country's major rivers and canals, as well as the Great Lakes. This encouraged the growth of cities such as Cincinnati, Buffalo, and Chicago.

Sailing technology also improved in the 1840s. The new clipper ships had tall sails and smooth bodies. They could sail as fast as most steamships at that time. **Clipper ships** got their name because they "clipped" time from long trips.

The first railroads in the United States connected mines with nearby rivers. Horses pulled these early trains. The first steam-powered railroad engine began running in Britain in 1829.

Peter Cooper designed and built the first American steam-powered railroad engine in 1830. By 1840 steam engines were pulling trains on about 3,000 miles (1860 km) of railroad track. By 1860 there were about 31,000 miles (19,220 km) of track. These tracks were mostly in the North and Midwest. The new rail lines connected many cities. They united the Midwest and the East.

The arrival of the train signaled big changes to many small towns.

Improved transportation also affected people in the western areas of the country. Before canals and railroads, farmers sent their crops down the Mississippi River to New Orleans. From there goods sailed to the East Coast or to other countries. Railways and canals transformed trade in these areas.

The Erie Canal opened in 1825. With the railroads and the canal, farm products could be moved directly from the Midwest to the East. Farmers and manufacturers could move goods faster and more cheaply. As a result, people could buy them at lower prices than in the past.

The railroads also played an important role in the settlement of the Midwest and the growth of business there. Fast train travel at good prices brought people into Ohio, Indiana, and Illinois. The populations of these states grew. New towns and industries developed as more people moved into the area.

Effects of Canals and Railroads

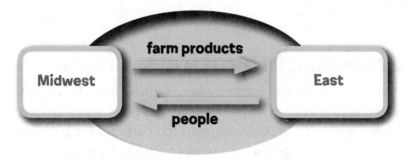

People could move more quickly along railways and waterways. This caused some tragic events to happen. For example, the *SS Central America* was a steamship that carried people and goods between New York and Panama, in Central America. In September 1857, this ship steamed into a hurricane and sank. Hundreds of people went down with the ship off the coast of the Carolinas.

The Great Train Wreck of 1856 happened between Camp Hill and Fort Washington, Pennsylvania, on July 17, 1856. Two trains slammed head-on into each other. About 60 people were killed, and more than 100 were injured. The tragedy shocked the entire nation. Newspapers demanded that railroad companies improve their methods and equipment. They had to make the safety of passengers their first concern

Show Your Skill

5. Identify Cause and Effect What effect did the invention of the steam-powered railroad engine have on the country?

_____

_____

_____

_____

Think Critically

6. Conclude Why does a tragedy sometime lead to changes in an industry?

_____

_____

_____

_____

Think Critically

8. Analyze What were two reasons that farmers were able to make more money growing wheat in the early 1800s?

_____

_____

_____

_____

_____

_____

9. Evaluate Do you think the steel-tipped plow, the mechanical reaper, or the thresher was most useful to farmers? Explain your choice.

_____

_____

_____

_____

The growth of industry and the speed of travel created a need for faster ways to send messages to people at great distances. The **telegraph**—a machine that used electric signals to send messages—filled that need.

Samuel Morse was an American inventor. He had shown that he could send a coded message instantly along electrical wires from one side of a building to another. On May 24, 1844, as a crowd of people in the Capitol watched, Morse tapped in a message to run along a telegraph line to Baltimore. A few moments later, the telegraph operator in Baltimore sent the same message back in reply. The telegraph worked! Soon telegraph messages were flashing back and forth between Washington, D.C., and Baltimore on a system of telegraph lines.

Telegraph operators sent messages by using **Morse code.** This code uses short and long signals—dots and dashes—in place of letters of the alphabet. Telegraph companies formed, and workers put up telegraph lines across the country. By 1852, there were about 23,000 miles (37,015 km) of telegraph lines in the United States.

Farming Innovations

By the early 1800s, few farmers were willing to settle in certain areas west of Missouri, Iowa, and Minnesota. Even some areas west of Ohio and Kentucky seemed too difficult for farming. Settlers worried that their old plows could not break the prairie's hard-packed sod. They also worried that the soil would not be fertile enough to grow fields of crops.

Three inventions of the 1830s helped farmers overcome these difficulties in farming the land. Because of this, more people moved to the Midwest.

One of these inventions was the steel-tipped plow developed by John Deere in 1837. It easily cut through the hard-packed prairie ground. Also important were the mechanical reaper and the thresher. The mechanical reaper sped up the harvesting, or gathering, of wheat. The thresher quickly separated the grain from the stalk, or stem, of the wheat.

Cyrus McCormick invented the mechanical reaper. Before this invention, farmers had harvested grain with cutting tools held in their hands. McCormick's reaper greatly increased the amount of grain a farmer could harvest. Because farmers could harvest more, they could plant more. Growing wheat brought more money than before. Raising wheat became and would stay the main economic activity on the Midwestern prairies.

Cyrus McCormick's reaping machine reduced some of the hours of back-breaking work harvesting required.

Because of the new machines and the railroads, farmers could plant more acres with cash crops. Midwestern farmers grew wheat and shipped it east by train and canal barge. Northeast and Middle Atlantic farmers grew more fruits and vegetables.

Despite improvements in farming, the North turned away from farming and toward industry. The number of people working in factories continued to rise.

Inventions that Helped Farmers	
	cut through hard ground
	sped up harvesting
	separated grain and stalk

Mark the Text

10. Complete the chart by adding the name of each invention that is described.

Show Your Skill

11. **Interpret Art** Based on the image, describe how an early reaper worked.

_____

_____

_____

NGSSS Check What effect did canals and railways have on transportation from the East to the Midwest? SS.8.A.4.5

_____

_____

_____

PEOPLE OF THE NORTH

NGSSS

SS.8.A.4.7 Explain the causes, course, and consequences (industrial growth, subsequent effect on children and women) of New England's textile industry.

Essential Question

How do people adapt to their environment?

Guiding Questions

1. Why did many Americans push for reform in the workplace during this era?
2. What challenges did European immigrants face in Northern cities?

Terms to Know

trade unions
groups of workers with the same trade or skill

strike
a refusal to work in order to force an employer to make changes

prejudice
an unfair opinion not based on facts

discrimination
unfair treatment

famine
an extreme shortage of food

nativist
person opposed to immigration

Where in the World?

Territorial Expansion, 1840

What Do You Know?

Directions: Circle the problems you think that people faced with the growth of industries in the 1800s. When you finish the lesson, come back and circle using a different color.

low wages	new forms of communication	child labor
long working hours	government regulations	faster transportation
unfair treatment	excess vacations	

networks Read Chapter 14 Lesson 2 in your textbook or online.

The Factories of the North

Machines did more and more of the manufacturing of products in the mid-1800s. Workers were brought together in the factories to do specialized tasks. The range of goods produced in this way increased. American factories began to produce goods ranging from clothing to shoes, watches, guns, and farming machines.

Working conditions got worse as the factory system developed. Employees worked long hours. By 1840, a worker's average day was 11.4 hours. Factories had many dangers. Longer workdays made workers extremely tired—and more likely to have accidents on the job. For example, many factory machines had rapidly moving belts and other parts. These belts had no shields to protect workers. Workers, especially children, were often hurt by these belts.

Employees often worked under harsh conditions. In the summer, factories were very hot. In the winter, workers were often cold because most factories had no heating.

There were no laws to control working conditions or protect workers. Factory owners often cared more about profits than about employees' comfort and safety.

Child labor was also a serious problem. Children in factories worked six days a week and 12 hours or more a day. The work was dangerous and hard. Young workers tended machines in mills. They also worked underground in mines. Reformers called for laws to control child labor, shorten working hours, and improve conditions. However, many years went by before child labor laws were passed.

Factory work, like the work in this textile factory, was hard and dangerous.

Show Your Skill

1. Identify Cause and Effect Name two reasons why workers had accidents in factories.

_____

_____

_____

Think Critically

2. Hypothesize Why might a parent let his or her child work in a factory?

_____

_____

_____

3. Summarize What changes did workers hope to make by forming trade unions?

_____

_____

_____

_____

Mark the Text ✏

4. Underline the meaning of *strike*.

5. Graphic Organizer Complete the graphic organizer with two examples of discrimination against African Americans.

Workers tried different ways to gain better conditions in the workplace. By the 1830s, they began forming unions. Skilled workers formed **trade unions.** These were groups of workers with the same trade, or skill. They thought that they would have more power to change working conditions if they worked together.

In New York City, skilled workers wanted to receive higher wages and limit their working day to 10 hours. The workers began to hold strikes in the mid-1830s. A **strike** is a refusal to work. The goal is to force employers to make changes. Groups of skilled workers formed the General Trades Union of New York.

Going on strike was against the law in the early 1800s. Workers who went on strike could lose their jobs and be punished for breaking the law. In 1842 a Massachusetts court ruled that workers did have the right to strike. However, workers would not receive other legal rights for many years.

In the North, slavery was mostly gone by the 1830s. However, racial **prejudice**—an unfair opinion of a group—and **discrimination**—unfair treatment of a group—remained. For example, white men in New York could vote even if they did not own property. However, few African Americans had this right. Rhode Island and Pennsylvania passed laws to keep African Americans from voting.

Most communities in the North did not allow African Americans to go to public schools. Many communities also kept them from using other public services. African Americans often had to go to poor-quality schools and hospitals that were just for them.

In the business world, a few African Americans found success. In 1845 Macon B. Allen became the first African American licensed, or given the official right, to practice law in the United States. Most African Americans, however, lived in poverty in the mid-1800s.

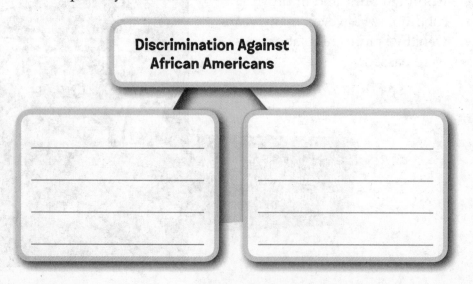

Discrimination Against African Americans

Women also faced discrimination in the workplace. Employers paid women less than male workers. Men kept women from joining unions. They also wanted to keep them out of the workplace.

In the 1830s and 1840s, some female workers tried to organize. Sarah G. Bagley, a weaver from Massachusetts, started the Lowell Female Labor Reform Organization. In 1845 her group petitioned—asked people in authority— for a 10-hour workday. Because most of the workers were women, the legislature did not pay any attention to the petition. However, because Sarah Bagley took this action, she led the way and inspired other women.

Mark the Text

6. Complete the graphic organizer with examples of discrimination against women.

Show Your Skill

7. **Identify Cause and Effect** What was one cause of the growth of cities in the early 1800s?

_____

_____

_____

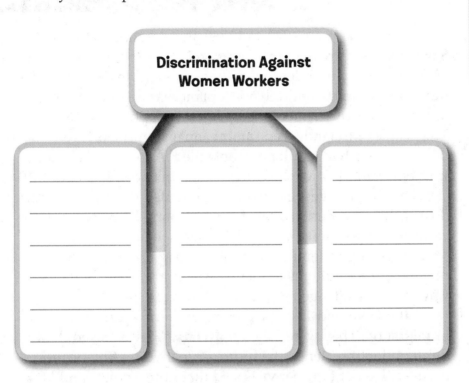

Discrimination Against Women Workers

The Growth of Cities

Industrialization had a big effect on cities. Factories were usually in cities. Because factories drew workers, Northern cities became much bigger in the early 1800s. Industrialization helped small cities in the West to grow.

Between 1820 and 1840, some Midwestern towns that had been small villages located along rivers became cities. St. Louis is located on the Mississippi River just south of where that river meets the Illinois and Missouri Rivers. By the mid-1800s, many steamboats chugged into St. Louis from north and south. Pittsburgh, Cincinnati, and Louisville also profited because they were located on waterways. These cities became centers of trade that linked Midwest farmers with cities of the Northeast.

8. Explain Why did so many people emigrate from Ireland and Germany in the mid-1800s?

_____

_____

_____

Mark the Text

9. Underline what nativists believed.

Show Your Skill

10. Generalize How were immigrants generally treated in the United States?

_____

_____

_____

_____

_____

Take the Challenge

11. You and your family are preparing to leave your homeland in the 1840s and go to the United States. Write a letter to your neighbors explaining your decision.

This engraving depicts Italian immigrants arriving in New York City in the 1860s.

PHOTO: PRISMA ARCHIVO/Alamy

Between the years 1840 and 1860, immigration to the United States greatly increased. Immigration is the process of entering another country in order to live there. The greatest number of immigrants came from Ireland. A plant disease—the potato blight—destroyed most of the Irish food supply in the 1840s. The people of Ireland faced **famine,** an extreme shortage of food. More than a million people died. Another 1.5 million Irish emigrants left for the United States between 1846 and 1860.

The second-largest group of immigrants in the United States during this time period came from Germany. Some wanted work and opportunity. Others left to escape political problems.

European immigrants brought languages, customs, religions, and traditions to their new country. Some of their ways of living changed the way of American life.

In the 1830s and 1840s, some people were against immigration. They were called **nativists.** They believed that immigration threatened the future of "native"— American-born—citizens. Some nativists said that immigrants would take jobs from "real" Americans. They were angry that immigrants would work for lower wages. Others said that immigrants brought crime and disease to American cities.

In the 1850s, nativists formed a new political party, the American Party. Because party members often answered questions about their group with the statement "I know nothing," their American Party came to be known as the Know-Nothing Party. The Know-Nothings called for laws making it harder to become a citizen.

 NGSSS Check What did many Americans want to change in the workplace? SS.8.A.4.7

_____

_____

NGSSS

SS.8.A.4.10 Analyze the impact of technological advancements on the agricultural economy and slave labor.

Essential Question
Why do people make economic choices?

Guiding Questions
1. How were the economies of the South and North different?
2. Why did industry develop slowly in the South?

Terms to Know

productivity
a measure of how much a worker can produce with a given amount of time and effort

domestic slave trade
the trade in enslaved people between states of the United States

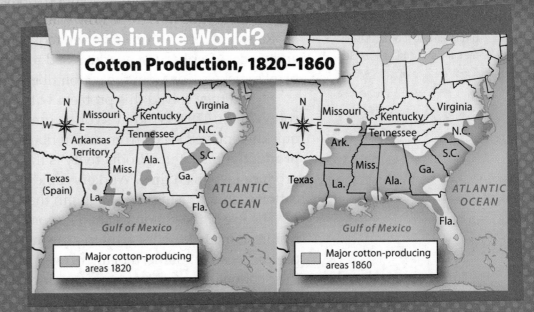

Where in the World?
Cotton Production, 1820–1860

Major cotton-producing areas 1820

Major cotton-producing areas 1860

What Do You Know?

Directions: Choose any four of the words below and write a sentence or two about slavery. When you finish the lesson, write another sentence using four different words from the list.

enslaved	plantation	cotton	South	sugar	master
own	sell	power	agricultural	labor	families

_____

_____

_____

_____

_____

Rise of the Cotton Kingdom

In the early years of the United States, the economy of the South was based mostly on farming. Most Southerners lived in the Upper South. This was an area along the Atlantic coast in Maryland, Virginia, and North Carolina.

By 1850, the South had changed. People had spread inland to the Deep South. The Deep South included Georgia, South Carolina, Alabama, Mississippi, Louisiana, and Texas. The economy of the South was booming. That economy depended, however, on slavery. In fact, slavery was growing stronger than ever in the South, even though it had almost ended in the North.

Southern planters grew mostly rice and tobacco in colonial times. After the American Revolution, demand for these crops got smaller. Mills in Europe now wanted Southern cotton.

Raising a cotton crop, however, took a large amount of time and work. After harvest, workers had to carefully remove the plant's sticky seeds from the cotton fibers.

Eli Whitney solved this problem with his invention of the cotton gin in 1793. Whitney's cotton gin was a machine that quickly removed seeds from cotton fibers. With a cotton gin, **productivity** shot up. Productivity is the amount a worker can produce in a given time. Workers could process 50 times more cotton each day using the cotton gin than they could by hand.

The use of the cotton gin had important consequences, or results. It made farmers want to grow more cotton in more places. Because Southern planters used slaves to plant and pick their cotton, the need for slave labor increased. Slavery spread across a larger area of the South.

Think Critically

1. Explain On what two things did the economy of the South depend?

_____

_____

Mark the Text

2. Underline the definition of productivity.

Show Your Skill

3. Identify Cause and Effect How did the invention of the cotton gin lead to an increase in the number of enslaved people?

_____

_____

_____

_____

_____

_____

_____

Effects of Cotton Gin on Slavery

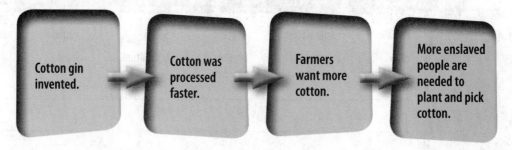

Cotton gin invented. → Cotton was processed faster. → Farmers want more cotton. → More enslaved people are needed to plant and pick cotton.

By 1860, the Deep South and Upper South remained farming areas, but each area grew different crops. The Upper South produced tobacco, hemp, wheat, and vegetables. The Deep South produced rice and sugarcane. Cotton was grown in every slave state.

Because more workers were needed to produce cotton and sugar, the sale of enslaved Africans became a big business. The Upper South became a center for the sale and movement of enslaved people. Because this trade was happening within the country, this trade became known as the **domestic slave trade.**

Southern Industry

Industry grew more slowly in the South than in the North. One reason was the boom in cotton. Farming cotton brought great profits. Secondly, building new industry is costly. Planters would have had to sell enslaved people or land to raise the money to build factories. There was little reason for people to do this. They made plenty of money growing cotton, rice, sugar, and tobacco. They also made money selling enslaved people.

The market, or demand, for factory goods in the South was small. Many people in the South were enslaved people. They had no money to buy goods. This limited local markets and discouraged industries from growing.

For these reasons, it is little surprise that some white Southerners just did not want industry.

Some Southern leaders wanted to develop industry in the region. They thought that the South depended too much on the North for factory goods. These leaders also thought that factories would improve the economy of the Upper South. A few men opened factories, but this was not typical of the South.

Show Your Skill

4. Compare and Contrast
In what ways was agriculture the same in the Upper South and the Lower South? In what ways was it different?

_____

_____

_____

_____

_____

5. Identify Cause and Effect
Why did the sale of enslaved Africans become a big business?

_____

_____

_____

Mark the Text

6. Graphic Organizer Write two reasons for the slow growth of industry in the South. One reason is already filled in for you.

Reasons for Slow Growth of Industry

_____

_____

_____

_____

_____

_____

_____

_____

Building new industry is costly.

Farmers and the few factory owners of the South used natural waterways to transport, or move, their goods. Most towns were located on coasts or along rivers. There were few canals, and roads were poor.

Southern rail lines were short, local, and not linked together. The South had fewer railroads than the North. This caused Southern cities to grow more slowly. In the North, railroads were major routes for transportation. By 1860, only about one-third of the nation's rail lines lay within the South. This rail shortage would hurt the South in the years to come.

Think Critically

8. Contrast How did Southern railroads and cities differ from Northern railroads and cities?

_____

_____

_____

_____

_____

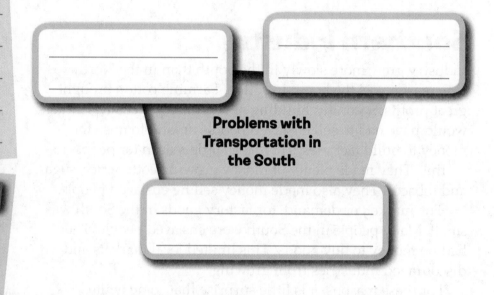

Problems with Transportation in the South

Take the Challenge

9. Take the role of someone from the North who is visiting the South in the mid-1800s. Write a letter back home and describe what you see on your travels.

 NGSSS Check How was the South's economy and development of industry different from the North's? SS.8.A.4.10

North	South
• The economy included agriculture and industry. • Slavery was not allowed. • People favored industry. • The transportation system was fairly well-established.	

PEOPLE OF THE SOUTH

NGSSS

SS.8.A.4.8 Describe the influence of individuals on social and political developments of this era in American History.

SS.8.A.4.11 Examine the aspects of slave culture including plantation life, resistance efforts, and the role of the slaves' spiritual system.

Essential Question

How do people adapt to their environment?

Guiding Questions

1. How were Southern farms different from Southern plantations?
2. How did enslaved African Americans try to cope with their lack of freedom?
3. What changes did urbanization introduce in the South by the mid-1800s?

Terms to Know

yeomen
farmers who owned small farms

overseer
plantation manager

spiritual
an African American religious folk song

slave codes
laws in Southern states that controlled enslaved people

Underground Railroad
a system of aid to enslaved people who had escaped

literacy
the ability to read and write

When Did It Happen?

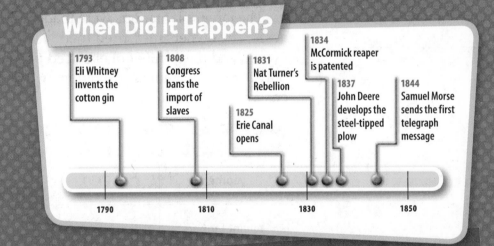

1793 Eli Whitney invents the cotton gin

1808 Congress bans the import of slaves

1825 Erie Canal opens

1831 Nat Turner's Rebellion

1834 McCormick reaper is patented

1837 John Deere develops the steel-tipped plow

1844 Samuel Morse sends the first telegraph message

1790   1810   1830   1850

What Do You Know?

Directions: In the first column, answer the questions based on what you know before you study. After this lesson, complete the last column.

Before the Lesson		After the Lesson
	What were Southern farmers like in the 1800s?	
	What kind of family life did enslaved African Americans have?	

Mark the Text

1. Chart Complete the chart by writing a fact about each type of white Southerner.

Think Critically

2. Analyze Which group made up the largest number of whites in the South?

_____

_____

3. Hypothesize If most white people in the South did not own enslaved Africans, why do you think most supported the practice of slavery?

_____

_____

_____

_____

netw⊙rks Read Chapter 14 Lesson 4 in your textbook or online.

Southern Agriculture

Slavery was at the heart of the Southern economy. That does not mean that every white person owned large numbers of enslaved people. Most white Southerners were one of four kinds: yeomen, tenant farmers, the rural poor, or plantation owners. Plantations were large farms.

Most white people in the South were **yeomen.** They generally owned small farms of 50 to 200 acres. They lived mostly in the Upper South and hilly parts of the Deep South. They grew crops to use for their own families and to trade with local business people.

Another group of Southern whites worked as tenant farmers. They rented land from land owners. Most white people of the South were yeomen and tenant farmers. They lived in simple homes. Poorer members of these groups lived in cabins. These rural poor would not do work done by enslaved people.

The larger plantations were made up of several thousand acres. The owners measured their wealth by the land they owned and the number of enslaved people they had. In 1860 only about 4 percent of plantation owners held 20 or more enslaved workers.

White Southerners in the Mid-1800s	
yeomen	
tenant farmers	
rural poor	
plantation owners	

A few free African Americans also held enslaved workers. Some free African Americans bought members of their own families to free them.

Earning profits was the goal for owners of large plantations. To make a profit, they needed to bring in more money than they spent to run their plantations. Large plantations had fixed costs. These are costs of running a business that remain much the same year after year. For example, the cost of housing and feeding workers is a fixed cost.

The price of cotton, however, changed from season to season. A change in price often meant the difference between a good year for a plantation and a bad one.

Plantation owners were almost always men. They traveled often to make sure their deals with traders were fair. Their wives often led difficult and lonely lives. They took charge of their households and watched over the buildings. They managed the enslaved domestic workers. Women also often kept the plantation's financial records.

Many different tasks needed to be done to keep a plantation running. Some enslaved people cleaned the house, cooked, did laundry and sewing, and served meals. Others were trained as blacksmiths, carpenters, shoemakers, or weavers. Others took care of the livestock. Animals kept on a farm, such as sheep and cows, are called livestock. Most enslaved African Americans were field hands. They worked from sunrise to sunset to plant, tend, and harvest crops. An **overseer,** or plantation manager, supervised them.

The Lives of Enslaved People

Hardship and misery filled the lives of most enslaved African Americans. They worked hard, earned no money, and had little hope of freedom. They lived with the fear that an owner could sell them or members of their family without warning. In the face of all this, enslaved African Americans kept up their family lives as best they could. They developed a culture, or way of life, all their own. It blended African and American elements. They came up with clever ways to resist slavery.

Even though it was not accepted by law, enslaved people married and raised families. This offered some comfort and support. Uncertainty and danger, however, were always present. There were no laws that would stop a slave owner from breaking apart a family. If a slaveholder chose to—or if the slaveholder died— families could be separated.

Show Your Skill

4. Identify Cause and Effect
Why did many plantation wives manage the plantation alone?

_____

_____

_____

Think Critically

5. Describe What kind of work was done by most enslaved African Americans?

_____

_____

6. Explain What was one reason enslaved people needed extended families?

_____

_____

_____

Artists chose to depict life for enslaved people in different ways. Here, one image shows life on a cotton plantation in Mississippi while the other shows the home of an enslaved family.

Mark the Text ✏️

7. Underline two ways that enslaved people tried to keep African customs.

8. **Chart** Complete the chart. Write a fact about each type of African American song.

Show Your Skill

9. **Contrast** Write a sentence that explains how a spiritual is different from a field holler.

_____

_____

_____

_____

_____

In the face of this, enslaved people set up a group of relatives and friends to act as family. If an owner sold a father or mother, then an aunt, an uncle, or a close friend stepped in to raise the children left behind. Large, close-knit, extended families became an important part of African American culture.

In 1808 Congress banned the import of slaves. Slavery remained legal, but traders could no longer bring enslaved people to the United States from other countries. By 1860, almost all the enslaved people in the South had been born there.

Though most enslaved people were born in the United States, they tried to keep African customs. They told traditional African folk stories to their children. They performed African music and dance.

Enslaved people also created musical forms that were new to the United States. They used their African music styles. One form was the work song or field holler. A worker led a call-and-response song with a regular beat, which sometimes included shouts and moans. The beat set the pace, or speed, for their work in the fields.

Many enslaved African Americans followed traditional African religious beliefs and practices. Others, however, accepted the Christian religion that was practiced widely in the United States. Christianity became a religion of hope. Enslaved people prayed for their freedom. They expressed their beliefs in the **spiritual,** an African American religious folk song.

Spirituals helped enslaved people express joy—but also sadness about their suffering here on Earth. Enslaved people also used spirituals as a way to communicate secretly among themselves.

African American Songs	
field holler	
spiritual	

The **slave codes** were laws in the Southern states that controlled enslaved people. They were sometimes called "black laws." These laws had existed since colonial times.

One purpose of the codes was to prevent slave rebellions. This was what white people feared the most. A rebellion is a violent attack against people in charge. For this reason, slave codes did not allow enslaved people to meet in large groups. The codes also required enslaved people to have written passes to leave the slaveholder's property.

Teaching enslaved people to read or write was a crime. White Southerners feared that an educated enslaved person might start a rebellion. They thought an enslaved person who could not read and write was less likely to rebel.

White people did have some reason to fear slave rebellion. Enslaved African Americans did sometimes rebel openly against their owners.

Nat Turner was a popular religious leader among enslaved people. Turner had taught himself to read and write. In 1831 he led a group of followers on a brief, violent rebellion in Virginia. Turner and his followers killed at least 55 whites. Authorities captured and hanged Nat Turner, but his rebellion terrified white Southerners. White mobs killed more than 100 African Americans. Many of the victims had nothing to do with the rebellion. Whites also passed stricter slave codes. Life under slavery became even more difficult.

Effects of Nat Turner's Rebellion

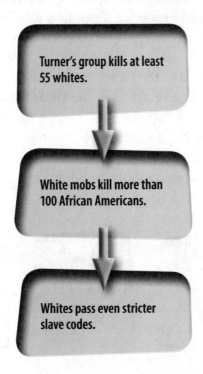

Turner's group kills at least 55 whites.

White mobs kill more than 100 African Americans.

Whites pass even stricter slave codes.

10. Draw Conclusions What were slave codes, and why were they created?

_____

_____

_____

_____

_____

11. Draw Conclusions Why was it seen as important to not encourage enslaved people to learn to read?

_____

_____

_____

_____

Nat Turner was captured after leading a slave uprising in 1831.

PHOTO: MPI/Archive Photos/Getty Images

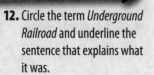

Mark the Text

12. Circle the term *Underground Railroad* and underline the sentence that explains what it was.

Take the Challenge

13. Make a list of factors that an enslaved African American would have to consider when deciding if trying to escape was worth the risk. Label the two columns on your list "Reasons to Stay" and "Reasons to Try to Escape."

Armed revolts such as Turner's were rare because enslaved African Americans knew they had little chance of winning. For the most part, enslaved people resisted slavery by working slowly or by pretending to be sick. Sometimes, they might set fire to a plantation building or break tools. Such acts helped enslaved African Americans deal with their lack of freedom.

Enslaved people also resisted by running away from their owners. Sometimes, their goal was to find family members on other plantations. Sometimes, they left to escape being punished.

Less often, enslaved African Americans tried to run away to freedom in the North. Getting to the North was very hard. Harriet Tubman and Frederick Douglass were among those who made it. They became important African American leaders.

Most who made it to the North escaped from the Upper South. A runaway might receive aid from the **Underground Railroad.** This was a network of "safe houses" owned by people who were against slavery. The big danger, of course, was capture. Most runaways were caught and returned to their owners. The owners punished them severely, usually by whipping.

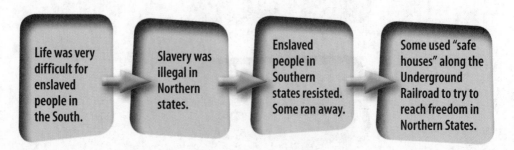

Life was very difficult for enslaved people in the South. → Slavery was illegal in Northern states. → Enslaved people in Southern states resisted. Some ran away. → Some used "safe houses" along the Underground Railroad to try to reach freedom in Northern States.

Southern Cities

The South had several large cities by the mid-1800s, including Baltimore and New Orleans. The ten largest cities in the South were either seaports or river ports. Cities located where railways crossed also started to grow.

In the cities, the South's free African Americans were able to form their own communities. They practiced trades and founded churches and institutions. Yet their rights were limited. Most states did not allow them to move from state to state. Free African Americans did not share equally in economic and political life.

In the early 1800s, there were no statewide public school systems in the South. People with enough money sent their children to private schools. Some larger cities set up public schools. By the mid-1800s, however, education was growing. North Carolina and Kentucky set up and ran public schools.

The South was behind other parts of the country in **literacy,** the ability to read and write. One reason was that people in the South were spread out over wide areas. A school would have to serve a wide area. Many families were not willing or not able to send their children so far to school. Many Southerners also believed that education should be private and not public.

Mark the Text

14. Graphic Organizer Complete the graphic organizer. Write two reasons for low literacy in the South in the circles. One reason has already been provided.

Think Critically

15. Infer Why did major cities in the South develop where they did?

_____

_____

_____

_____

_____

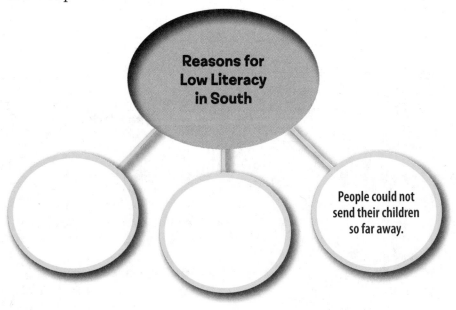

Reasons for Low Literacy in South

People could not send their children so far away.

NGSSS Check Describe life on the plantation for most enslaved Africans. SS.8.A.4.11

_____

_____

_____

MY REFLECTIONS

ESSENTIAL QUESTION *How does technology change the way people live?*

Reflect on What It Means . . .

The Industrial Revolution not only revolutionized manufacturing but also revolutionized people's lives. Inventors have not stopped developing new technology since then. In the last century, several inventions have revolutionized life for the average person.

To Me, My Community, and the World

Pick an invention that you feel has revolutionized life in the last 100 years. Then fill out the spider map below to show how the invention that you chose has revolutionized life in your community, the world, and how it has affected your own life.

Me

Invention:

_____

_____

My Community

The World

TAKE THE CHALLENGE

As a class, have an invention workshop. Bring in any materials that you think might be useful in making an invention (empty spools of thread, clothespins, pulleys, etc.). Try to come up with your own simple invention. When the inventions are complete, hold an invention fair. Explain what problem each invention is designed to solve.

THE SPIRIT OF REFORM

NGSSS

SS.8.A.4.8 Describe the influence of individuals on social and political developments of this era in American History.

SS.8.A.4.11 Examine the aspects of slave culture including plantation life, resistance efforts, and the role of the slaves' spiritual system.

ESSENTIAL QUESTIONS *Why do societies change? What motivates people to act? How do new ideas change the way people live?*

Writing to one of her children, Harriet Beecher Stowe explained why she was inspired to write *Uncle Tom's Cabin:*

PHOTO: Library of Congress

Copyright © by The McGraw-Hill Companies, Inc.

" My heart was bursting with the anguish excited by the cruelty and injustice our nation was showing to the slave, and praying God to let me do a little and to cause my cry for them to be heard. "

HARRIET BEECHER STOWE

anguish

Write another word (synonym) for *anguish* below.

_____

_____

To whom is Stowe referring as *them?*

_____

_____

DBQ BREAKING IT DOWN

When *Uncle Tom's Cabin* was published, many of its critics argued that Stowe was exaggerating the conditions in which American slaves were living. Suppose that you are an abolitionist living in the 1800s. Write a response to Stowe's critics.

_____

_____

McGraw-Hill
networks™
There's More Online!

LESSON 1

SOCIAL REFORM

NGSSS

SS.8.A.4.8 Describe the influence of individuals on social and political developments of this era in American History.

SS.8.A.4.9 Analyze the causes, course, and consequences of the Second Great Awakening on social reform movements.

SS.8.A.4.15 Examine the causes, course, and consequences of literature movements significant to this era of American history.

Essential Question

Why do societies change?

Guiding Questions

1. What was the effect of the Second Great Awakening?
2. What type of American literature emerged in the 1820s?

Terms to Know

revival
religious meeting

utopia
community based on a vision of the perfect society

temperance
drinking little or no alcohol

normal school
state-supported school for training high school graduates to become teachers

civil disobedience
refusing to obey laws considered unjust

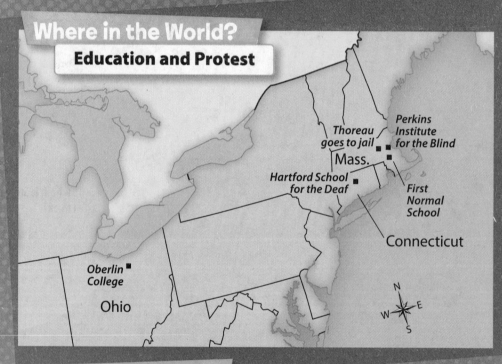

Where in the World?
Education and Protest

Thoreau goes to jail

Perkins Institute for the Blind

Mass.

Hartford School for the Deaf

First Normal School

Connecticut

Oberlin College

Ohio

When Did It Happen?

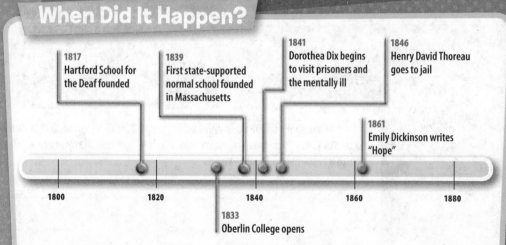

1817 Hartford School for the Deaf founded

1839 First state-supported normal school founded in Massachusetts

1841 Dorothea Dix begins to visit prisoners and the mentally ill

1846 Henry David Thoreau goes to jail

1861 Emily Dickinson writes "Hope"

1833 Oberlin College opens

1800   1820   1840   1860   1880

Religion and Reform

Religious camp meetings, called **revivals,** were popular in the early 1800s. This era was a time of great religious interest known as the Second Great Awakening. People believed that they should work to improve or reform society.

Some reformers wanted to improve society by setting up **utopias.** These were communities based on the idea of a perfect society. Most of these communities did not last.

Several social reform movements came about in the 1800s. Some reformers, like Lyman Beecher, called for **temperance.** This meant drinking little or no alcohol. These reformers used lectures and booklets to warn people about the dangers of liquor. The temperance movement led to the passage of some laws, but most of them were later repealed.

In the mid-1800s, most people did not believe in required education. Education also was usually not available to girls and many African Americans. Some reformers wanted to improve education. In Massachusetts, Horace Mann founded the nation's first state-supported **normal school.** This was a school in which people were trained to be teachers. Many colleges and universities were also set up during this time.

Some reforms helped people with disabilities. Thomas Gallaudet (GA•luh•DEHT) developed a way to teach people who could not hear. Samuel Gridley Howe helped teach people who could not see. He created books with large raised letters that people could "read" with their fingers. Dorothea Dix educated people about the poor conditions in which prisoners and mentally ill people lived.

Reformer	Contributions
Lyman Beecher	
Horace Mann	
Thomas Gallaudet	
Dorothea Dix	

Mark the Text

1. **Graphic Organizer** Complete the graphic organizer to describe the contributions of four reformers during the 1800s.

Show Your Skill

2. **Identify the Main Idea** Place a check mark next to the better statement of the main idea of this page.

_____ Several social reform movements started in the 1800s.

_____ Some reformers worked for temperance.

Think Critically

3. **Evaluate** Which reformer do you think made the most important contribution to American society? Why?

_____

_____

_____

_____

Mark the Text

4. Circle the names of three people who worked for reforms for people with disabilities.

5. Classify Information Identify the person described in each of the following:

A transcendentalist who supported women's rights in her writings

_____

An American poet who wrote story poems

_____

Author of *Uncle Tom's Cabin*

_____

Think Critically

6. Conclude How did art in the United States change in the 1800s?

_____
_____
_____
_____

Take the Challenge

7. Read a poem by Longfellow and one by Whitman. Compare and contrast the content of the two poems.

Culture Changes

The changes in American society made an impact on art and literature. American artists started to develop their own style of art. Their art had to do with American themes.

The reform spirit had an effect on the transcendentalists. These thinkers and writers stressed the relationship between humans and nature. They also wrote about the importance of the individual conscience. The conscience deals mainly with a person's values or sense of right and wrong. In her writings, Margaret Fuller supported women's rights. Ralph Waldo Emerson pushed for people to listen to their conscience and to rise above their prejudice. Henry David Thoreau practiced **civil disobedience.** He refused to obey laws he thought were unjust.

American poets also created great works. Henry Wadsworth Longfellow wrote story poems, such as the *Song of Hiawatha.* In *Leaves of Grass,* Walt Whitman captured the new American spirit. Emily Dickinson wrote personal poems. Harriet Beecher Stowe wrote the best-selling novel in the mid-1800s. In her novel, *Uncle Tom's Cabin,* she wrote about the injustice of slavery.

Walt Whitman wrote poems that celebrated the senses.

NGSSS Check List four areas of reform in the 1800s. SS.8.A.4.9

_____
_____

NGSSS

SS.8.A.4.8 Describe the influence of individuals on social and political developments of this era in American History.

SS.8.A.4.11 Examine the aspects of slave culture including plantation life, resistance efforts, and the role of the slaves' spiritual system.

SS.8.A.5.2 Analyze the role of slavery in the development of sectional conflict.

Essential Question
What motivates people to act?

Guiding Questions
1. How did Americans' attitudes toward slavery change?
2. Why did the reform movement gain momentum?
3. Who opposed the abolition of slavery?

Terms to Know

abolitionists
reformers who worked to abolish, or end, slavery in the early 1800s in the United States

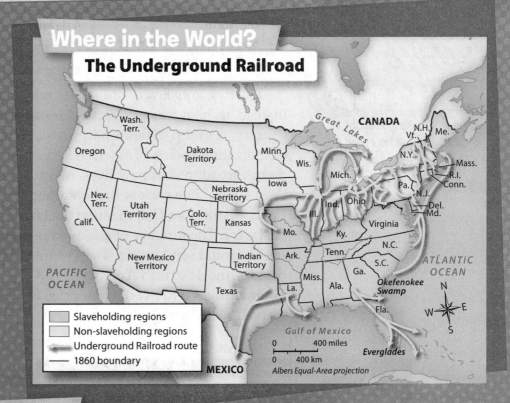

Where in the World?

The Underground Railroad

Slaveholding regions
Non-slaveholding regions
Underground Railroad route
1860 boundary

0   400 miles
0   400 km
Albers Equal-Area projection

When Did It Happen?

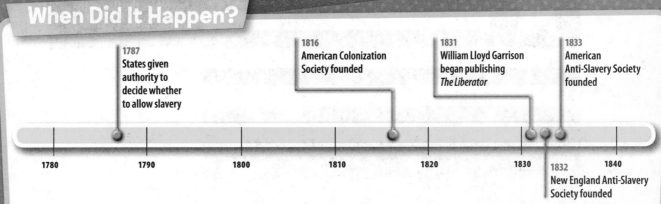

1787
States given authority to decide whether to allow slavery

1816
American Colonization Society founded

1831
William Lloyd Garrison began publishing *The Liberator*

1833
American Anti-Slavery Society founded

1832
New England Anti-Slavery Society founded

1780   1790   1800   1810   1820   1830   1840

PHOTO: Image Source/Alamy

Show Your Skill

2. **Identify Cause and Effect**
Explain why the efforts of the American Colonization Society were not more successful.

_____

_____

_____

_____

_____

Take the Challenge

3. Research the country of Liberia today. Learn five fascinating facts to share with the class.

networks Read Chapter 15 Lesson 2 in your textbook or online.

The Start of the Abolition Movement

The spirit of reform in the early 1800s included the work of **abolitionists.** Abolitionists were reformers who worked to abolish, or end, slavery. Even before the American Revolution, some Americans worked to end slavery. By the early 1800s, Northern states had ended slavery. However, it was an important part of the South's economy. By the mid-1800s, more and more Americans came to believe that slavery was wrong. The conflict over slavery grew.

North	South
Slavery is over throughout the North. Slavery is morally wrong.	Our economy depends on slavery.

The first antislavery effort was not about ending slavery. Instead, its goal was to resettle African Americans out of the country. A group of white Virginians founded the American Colonization Society. They freed enslaved people and sent them abroad to start new lives. Many were sent to Liberia in West Africa. The society had obtained land for a colony there.

The American Colonization Society did not stop the growth of slavery. The number of enslaved people kept growing. The society could send only a small number of them to Africa. Besides, most African Americans did not want to go to Africa. Their families had lived in America for many years. They just wanted to be free.

The Liberian flag strongly resembles the flag of the United States.

Republic of Liberia

The Movement Builds Strength

Around 1830, slavery became the most important issue for reformers. William Lloyd Garrison had a big impact on the antislavery movement. He started *The Liberator* and the American Anti-Slavery Society. He was one of the first white abolitionists to call for an immediate end to slavery.

Sarah Grimké and her sister worked to free enslaved workers.

Sisters Sarah and Angelina Grimké lectured and wrote against slavery. They used their inheritance money to free several of the family's enslaved workers. Their book, *American Slavery As It Is*, was one of the most powerful abolitionist works of the time.

Free African Americans also played an important role in the abolitionist movement. They helped set up and direct the American Anti-Slavery Society. Samuel Cornish and John Russwurm began the first African American newspaper, *Freedom's Journal*. Writer David Walker urged African Americans to rebel against slavery. In 1830, free African American leaders held their first convention in Philadelphia.

Frederick Douglass was the best-known African American abolitionist. Douglass escaped from slavery in Maryland in 1838. He settled in Massachusetts. Later he moved to New York. He was a powerful speaker. He spoke at many meetings in the United States and abroad. Douglass was also the editor of the antislavery newspaper *North Star.*

Show Your Skill

4. Draw Conclusions How did William Lloyd Garrison influence the abolition movement?

_____

_____

_____

_____

_____

5. Classify Information How did Samuel Cornish, John Russwurm, and David Walker work for abolition?

_____

_____

_____

_____

_____

Frederick Douglass lectured and wrote extensively on the evils of slavery.

6. Infer Why do you think both Frederick Douglass and Sojourner Truth were so effective in inspiring support for abolition?

_____

_____

_____

7. Summarize How did the Underground Railroad help enslaved African Americans?

_____

_____

_____

_____

8. Categorize List two reasons Northerners gave for opposing abolition.

_____

_____

_____

_____

_____

Sojourner Truth escaped slavery in 1826. She worked with Frederick Douglass and William Lloyd Garrison to end slavery. She traveled throughout the North. She spoke about her experiences as an enslaved person. She also worked in the women's rights movement.

Some abolitionists helped African Americans escape slavery. The network of escape routes from the South to the North was called the Underground Railroad. Along the routes, whites and African Americans guided the runaways to freedom in Northern states or Canada. Harriet Tubman became the most famous conductor on the Underground Railroad.

Reaction to the Abolitionists

Only a small number of Northerners were abolitionists. Many Northerners believed that freed African Americans could never blend into American society. Some Northerners were afraid that the abolitionists could begin a war between the North and South. Other Northerners feared that freed African Americans would take their jobs.

Opposition toward abolitionists turned cruel at times. Angry whites tore up Elijah Lovejoy's antislavery newspaper offices three times. The fourth time, the mob set fire to the building and killed Lovejoy.

Many Southerners said that abolition threatened their way of life. Southerners defended slavery. They thought it was necessary for the Southern economy. Southerners also said that they treated enslaved people well, providing food and medical care. Some defenses of slavery were based on racism. Many whites believed that African Americans could not take care of themselves and were better off under the care of white people.

NGSSS Check Complete the graphic organizer by identifying the contributions of each person. SS.8.A.4.8

Abolitionists

1. Harriet Tubman
5. William Lloyd Garrison
2. Sojourner Truth
4. Angelina Grimké
3. Frederick Douglass

NGSSS

SS.8.A.4.8 Describe the influence of individuals on social and political developments of this era in American History.

SS.8.A.4.14 Examine the causes, course, and consequences of the women's suffrage movement.

Essential Question
How do new ideas change the way people live?

Guiding Questions
1. What did women do to win equal rights?
2. In what areas did women make progress in achieving equality?

Terms to Know

suffrage
the right to vote

coeducation
the teaching of males and females together

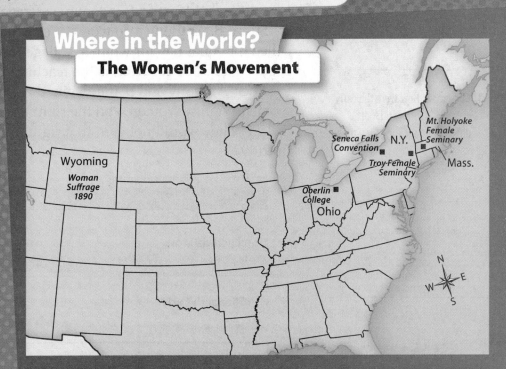

Where in the World?
The Women's Movement

Wyoming
Woman Suffrage 1890

Seneca Falls Convention N.Y.

Mt. Holyoke Female Seminary

Troy Female Seminary   Mass.

Oberlin College
Ohio

When Did It Happen?

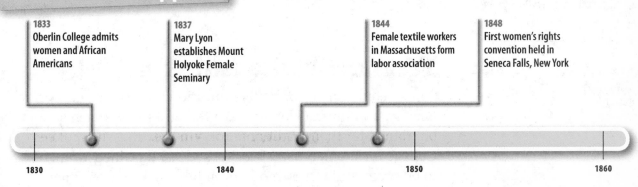

1833
Oberlin College admits women and African Americans

1837
Mary Lyon establishes Mount Holyoke Female Seminary

1844
Female textile workers in Massachusetts form labor association

1848
First women's rights convention held in Seneca Falls, New York

1830   1840   1850   1860

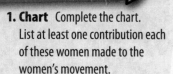

Mark the Text

1. **Chart** Complete the chart. List at least one contribution each of these women made to the women's movement.

Think Critically

2. **Summarize** What were the goals of the early women's movement?

_____

_____

_____

_____

_____

3. **Contrast** How were the early views of Stanton and Mott different on suffrage for women?

_____

_____

_____

_____

_____

_____

Show Your Skill

4. **Make Connections** Do most schools in Florida offer coeducation today? Does yours?

_____

_____

_____

netw**rks** Read Chapter 15 Lesson 3 in your textbook or online.

Reform for Women

Many women abolitionists also worked for women's rights. In July of 1848, Lucretia Mott and Elizabeth Cady Stanton set up the first women's rights convention. It was in Seneca Falls, New York. The Seneca Falls Convention paved the way for the women's rights movement. The convention issued a declaration that called for an end to laws that discriminated against women. It called for women to be allowed to enter jobs and businesses that mostly men held.

Suffrage, or the right to vote, became an issue at the convention. Elizabeth Stanton wanted the declaration to demand the right to vote for women. Lucretia Mott believed that letting women vote was too radical an idea. The convention decided to include the demand for woman suffrage in its declaration.

Susan B. Anthony also worked for women's rights. She called for equal pay for women, college training for girls, and coeducation. **Coeducation** is the teaching of males and females together. Anthony and Stanton joined together to work for women's rights. Women won the right to vote in Wyoming in 1890. They would not gain that right in the whole country until 1920.

Individual	Contribution
Lucretia Mott	
Elizabeth Cady Stanton	
Susan B. Anthony	

Women Make Gains

Some people called for better education for women. Catherine Beecher and Emma Hart Willard thought that women should be trained for their traditional roles in life. The Milwaukee College for Women used Beecher's ideas. It trained women to be successful wives, mothers, and housekeepers. Other people thought that women would make capable teachers.

Some young women began to make their own opportunities. Emma Willard taught herself science and mathematics. She set up the Troy Female Seminary in New York. There, girls learned math, history, geography, and physics, as well as homemaking subjects. Mary Lyon set up Mount Holyoke Female Seminary in Massachusetts.

In the 1800s, women made some gains in marriage and property laws. Some states began to recognize women's rights to own property after they married. Some states passed laws that allowed divorced women to share the custody of their children with their husbands. Some states also allowed women to get a divorce if their husbands abused alcohol.

At the time, women had few career choices. They struggled to enter some professions, such as medicine and the ministry. Some women began to break through those barriers. Elizabeth Blackwell was finally accepted to a medical school in New York. She had been turned down several times. She graduated first in her class and became a famous doctor.

Elizabeth Blackwell was the first female doctor in the United States.

Gains in Three Areas		
Education	**Marriage and Family**	**Career**
• better training for traditional roles • can be good teachers • Troy Female Seminary offers traditional "male" subjects: math, history, and so on	• married women gain right to own property • divorced women gain right to share custody of their children • women gain right to divorce husbands who abuse alcohol	• Elizabeth Blackwell breaks the barrier to women training in medicine

NGSSS Check What were some of the major events related to the women's suffrage movement? SS.8.A.4.14

_____

_____

_____

_____

Think Critically

5. Categorize Match the education reformer with the school she is associated with.

_____ Catherine Beecher

_____ Emma Willard

_____ Mary Lyon

a. Troy Female Seminary

b. Milwaukee College for Women

c. Mount Holyoke Female Seminary

Mark the Text

6. Underline the text to show the progress women in the middle to late 1800s made regarding marriage and property laws.

Take the Challenge

7. Research five famous firsts for women. Prioritize them according to which you feel had the most lasting effect.

ESSENTIAL QUESTION *Why do societies change?*

Reflect on What It Means . . .

The abolitionist movement, the temperance movement, and the women's movement were all started by people who wanted to make the world a better place. But they could not impose their ideas on others—they had to find ways to persuade others that change was moral and right.

To Me, My Community, and the World

Think of an issue that touches you, your community, and the world. It needs to be an issue you really care about. Design a mascot or create a superhero that could be used to convince younger kids that your issue is important. Think of symbols that can help you make your points visually. Add at least two speech bubbles showing what the character says to provide evidence related to your cause or to ask people to take action.

TAKE THE CHALLENGE

As a class, choose an issue that has good points which could be made on both sides. Organize a debate about your issue, with half the class taking one side and half the class taking the other side.

CHAPTER 16

TOWARD CIVIL WAR

NGSSS

SS.8.A.5.1 Explain the causes, course, and consequence of the Civil War (sectionalism, slavery, states' rights, balance of power in the Senate).

SS.8.A.5.7 Examine key events and peoples in Florida history as each impacts this era of American history.

ESSENTIAL QUESTION ***Why does conflict develop?***

On January 10, 1861, Florida became the third state to secede from the Union. Read an excerpt from Florida's Ordinance of Secession:

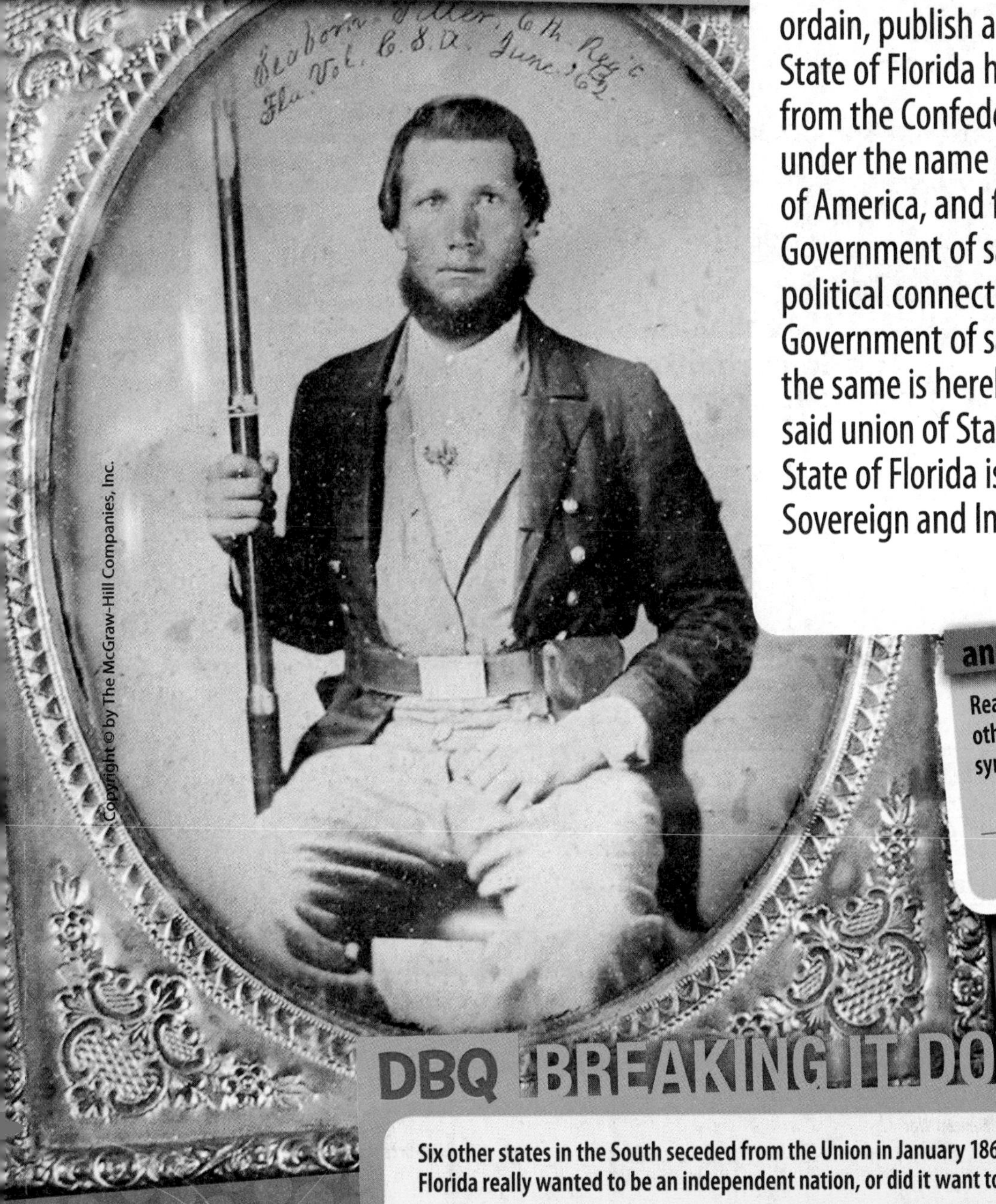

"We, the people of the State of Florida in Convention assembled, do solemnly ordain, publish and declare: That the State of Florida hereby withdraws herself from the Confederacy of States existing under the name of the United States of America, and from the existing Government of said States: and that all political connection between her and the Government of said States ought to be and the same is hereby totally annulled, and said union of States dissolved: and the State of Florida is hereby declared a Sovereign and Independent Nation. . . ."

—ORDINANCE OF SECESSION

annulled

Read the rest of the Ordinance. Which other word in the Ordinance is a synonym for *annulled*?

____

DBQ BREAKING IT DOWN

Six other states in the South seceded from the Union in January 1861. Do you think that the state of Florida really wanted to be an independent nation, or did it want to break free from the Union, or both?

____

____

McGraw-Hill **networks**™ *There's More Online!*

PHOTO: Florida Photographic Collection

THE SEARCH FOR COMPROMISE

NGSSS

SS.8.A.4.1 Examine the causes, course, and consequences of United States westward expansion and its growing diplomatic assertiveness (War of 1812, Convention of 1818, Adams-Onís Treaty, Missouri Compromise, Monroe Doctrine, Trail of Tears, Texas annexation, Manifest Destiny, Oregon Territory, Mexican American War/ Mexican Cession, California Gold Rush, Compromise of 1850, Kansas Nebraska Act, Gadsden Purchase).

SS.8.A.4.2 Describe the debate surrounding the spread of slavery into western territories and Florida.

SS.8.A.4.8 Describe the influence of individuals on social and political developments of this era in American History.

SS.8.A.5.1 Explain the causes, course, and consequence of the Civil War (sectionalism, slavery, states' rights, balance of power in the Senate).

SS.8.A.5.2 Analyze the role of slavery in the development of sectional conflict.

Essential Question

Why does conflict develop?

Guiding Questions

1. What political compromises were made because of slavery?
2. What is the Kansas-Nebraska Act?

Terms to Know

fugitive
person who runs away from the law

secede
leave

border ruffians
armed pro-slavery supporters who crossed the border from Missouri to vote in Kansas

civil war
fighting between citizens of the same country

Where in the World?

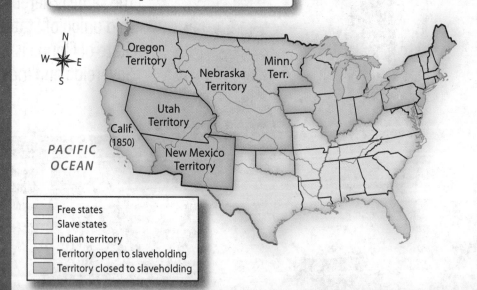

The Compromise of 1850

Oregon Territory, Nebraska Territory, Minn. Terr., Utah Territory, Calif. (1850), New Mexico Territory, PACIFIC OCEAN

Free states
Slave states
Indian territory
Territory open to slaveholding
Territory closed to slaveholding

When Did It Happen?

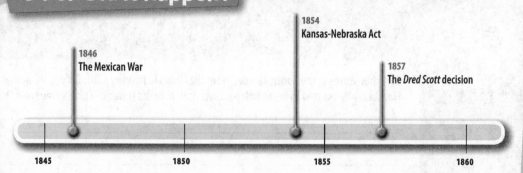

1846 The Mexican War
1854 Kansas-Nebraska Act
1857 The *Dred Scott* decision

1845   1850   1855   1860

networks Read Chapter 16 Lesson 1 in your textbook or online.

Political Conflict Over Slavery

The question of slavery divided Americans. Many Northerners wanted to ban it. Most Southerners wanted Northerners to stay out of the issue of slavery. Each time there was a debate over slavery, the nation's leaders came up with a compromise. For example, Congress passed the Missouri Compromise in 1820. It kept a balance of power in the Senate. It also stopped the debate over slavery—for a little while.

In 1845 there was a debate over slavery in new territories. Texas, where slavery was legal, became a state. This angered Mexico. The United States and Mexico fought over the boundary between Texas and Mexico in the Mexican War. The United States won and gained New Mexico and California as a result.

Representative David Wilmot wanted slavery banned in any lands taken from Mexico. His plan was called the Wilmot Proviso. Southerners protested. They wanted California and New Mexico open to slavery. Senator John C. Calhoun stated that Congress could not ban slavery in any territory.

In 1848 both presidential candidates ignored the slavery issue, which made voters angry. Many antislavery Whigs and Democrats formed the Free-Soil Party. The new party's slogan was "Free Soil, Free Speech, Free Labor, and Free Men." Former president Martin Van Buren was the party's candidate. He lost to Zachary Taylor, but the party gained some seats in Congress.

The debate over slavery came up again in 1849 because

- California applied to become a free state;
- antislavery groups wanted to ban slavery in Washington, D.C.;
- Southerners wanted a stronger **fugitive,** or runaway slave, law. It would require all states to return runaway slaves.

Mark the Text

1. Underline the name of the plan that would ban slavery from any lands taken from Mexico.

Think Critically

2. **Draw Conclusions** Why did the United States and Mexico have a dispute over the boundary between Mexico and Texas?

_____

_____

_____

_____

_____

Take the Challenge

3. Make a campaign poster for the Free-Soil Party. Include slogans and illustrations to show the position of the party on the issue of slavery.

Both Florida and Texas were admitted to the Union in 1845. The Florida quarter includes that date in its design.

Show Your Skill

4. Compare and Contrast
How did Clay's proposal for Washington, D.C., appeal to both the North and the South?

_____

_____

_____

_____

_____

Think Critically

5. Summarize In your own words, summarize the meaning of the term *popular sovereignty*.

_____

_____

_____

_____

_____

_____

_____

If California entered as a free state, the slave states would be outvoted in the Senate. Angry Southerners talked about **seceding** from, or leaving, the Union.

Senator Henry Clay tried to find a compromise. He suggested that:

- California be a free state.
- slavery would not be limited in any new territories.
- slave trade would be banned in Washington, D.C., but not slavery.
- there be a stronger fugitive slave law.

Congress debated the ideas. To end the debate, Senator Stephen A. Douglas divided Clay's plan into parts. Congress passed five separate bills. Together, they are called the Compromise of 1850.

The Kansas-Nebraska Act

In 1854 Senator Douglas suggested making the lands west of Missouri into two territories. They would be called Kansas and Nebraska. They were north of the line that limited slavery, so the two states would be free states. Douglas suggested that Congress repeal the Missouri Compromise. Instead, settlers in those areas would vote on whether to allow slavery. Douglas called this popular sovereignty. That means the decision is for the people of the territory to make, not the government.

Many Northerners did not like Douglas's plan. It would allow slavery in places that had been free for years. Southerners liked the plan. They thought Kansas would be settled mostly by slaveholders from Missouri. Since slavery was legal in Missouri, those settlers would vote to make slavery legal in Kansas, too. The Kansas-Nebraska Act passed in 1854.

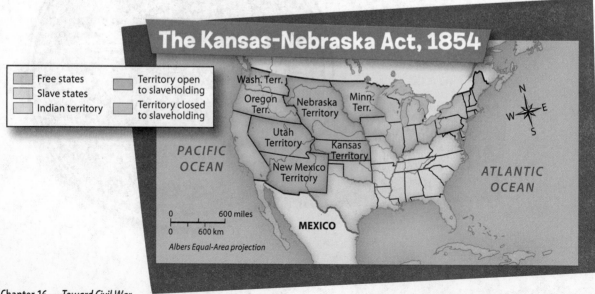

The Kansas-Nebraska Act, 1854

Free states
Slave states
Indian territory
Territory open to slaveholding
Territory closed to slaveholding

Wash. Terr.
Oregon Terr.
Nebraska Territory
Minn. Terr.
Utah Territory
Kansas Territory
New Mexico Territory

PACIFIC OCEAN
ATLANTIC OCEAN
MEXICO

0   600 miles
0   600 km
Albers Equal-Area projection

Pro-slavery and antislavery groups rushed to Kansas. Thousands of pro-slavery supporters crossed the border from Missouri just to vote in Kansas. They traveled in armed groups. They were known as **border ruffians.**

The pro-slavery group won the election and Kansas passed laws in favor of slavery. People opposed to slavery refused to accept the laws. Instead, they held their own election. They adopted a constitution that banned slavery. By 1856, Kansas had two rival governments.

Both antislavery and pro-slavery groups were armed. Soon fighting broke out. Pro-slavery supporters attacked a town where many antislavery supporters lived. Then John Brown, an abolitionist, led an attack on a pro-slavery group. Brown's group killed five slavery supporters. Newspapers called the conflict "Bleeding Kansas" and the "Civil War in Kansas." A **civil war** is a conflict between people of the same country.

Think Critically

6. Sequence What events led to "Bleeding Kansas"?

_____

_____

_____

_____

_____

_____

Mark the Text

7. Underline the two groups that were involved in a "civil war" in Kansas.

Fort Scott, Kansas was just one of many scenes of violent disagreement over the issue of slavery during the 1850s.

NGSSS Check Why did Senator Douglas suggest that Congress repeal the Missouri Compromise? What political concept did his actions support? SS.8.A.4.1

_____

_____

CHALLENGES TO SLAVERY

NGSSS

SS.8.A.5.2 Analyze the role of slavery in the development of sectional conflict.

Essential Question
Why does conflict develop?

Guiding Questions
1. How did a new political party affect the challenges to slavery?
2. Why was the *Dred Scott* case important?
3. How did Abraham Lincoln and Stephen A. Douglas play a role in the challenges to slavery?

Terms to Know

arsenal
a place to store weapons

martyr
a person who dies for a great cause

Where in the World?

The Election of 1856

Washington Territory
Oregon Territory
Minnesota Territory
Nebraska Territory
NH 5
VT 5
ME 8
WI 5
MI 6
NY 35
MA 13
RI 4
CT 6
IA 4
PA 27
NJ 7
DE 3
MD 8
Utah Territory
IL 11
IN 13
OH 23
CA 4
Kansas Territory
MO 9
KY 12
VA 15
NC 10
New Mexico Territory
Indian Terr.
AR 4
TN 12
SC 8
MS 7
AL 9
GA 10
TX 4
LA 6
FL 3

ELECTORAL VOTE
TOTAL: 296
2.7% 8
38.5% 114
58.8% 174

POPULAR VOTE
TOTAL: 4,051,605**
21.6% 872,703
33.1% 1,340,668
45.3% 1,835,140

Buchanan (Democrat)
Frémont (Republican)
Fillmore (Whig-American)

* Numbers on map show electoral votes per state.
** Popular vote includes 3,094 votes for candidates other than Buchanan, Frémont, or Fillmore.

When Did It Happen?

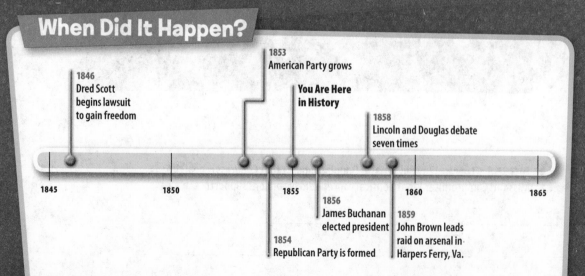

1846
Dred Scott begins lawsuit to gain freedom

1853
American Party grows

You Are Here in History

1858
Lincoln and Douglas debate seven times

1845
1850
1855
1860
1865

1854
Republican Party is formed

1856
James Buchanan elected president

1859
John Brown leads raid on arsenal in Harpers Ferry, Va.

Birth of the Republican Party

The Kansas-Nebraska Act drove the North and South further apart. Many Northern Democrats left the party. In 1854 antislavery Whigs and Democrats joined with Free-Soilers. They started the Republican Party. They wanted to ban slavery in new territories. Northerners liked the party's message. The Republicans won seats in Congress. The Democratic Party became mostly a Southern party.

In the presidential election of 1856:

- the Republicans chose John C. Frémont as their candidate. Frémont was a military officer and a U.S. senator from California. The party called for free territories.

- the Democrats nominated James Buchanan. Buchanan served as a U.S. senator from Pennsylvania and had also been Secretary of State. The party wanted popular sovereignty.

- the American Party, or Know Nothings, nominated former president Millard Fillmore. Fillmore had served as president for three years after the death of President Zachary Taylor.

- the Whigs were very divided over slavery. They did not have a candidate.

Buchanan won the most electoral votes. He won all Southern states except Maryland. None of Frémont's electoral votes came from south of the Mason-Dixon line.

Candidate	Popular Vote (%)	Electoral Vote (%)
Buchanan	1,838,169 (45%)	174 (59%)
Frémont	1,341,264 (33%)	114 (38%)
Fillmore	874,534 (22%)	8 (3%)

1. Identify the Main Idea
Who joined together to form the Republican Party? What was their main goal?

_____

_____

_____

2. Interpret Charts Who was the American Party's candidate? According to the chart, how much of the popular vote did he receive? How many electoral votes did he get?

_____

_____

Challenges to Slavery Lesson 2 **273**

Following the loss of his case in the Supreme Court, Dred Scott and his wife were freed. The sons of the doctor, who had also funded much of the legal fees, "purchased" the Scotts and gave them their freedom.

Think Critically

3. **Sequence** Number these events in the order in which they happened.

_____ The doctor and Scott move to Illinois.

_____ The doctor and Scott return to Missouri.

_____ A doctor buys Scott in Missouri.

_____ The doctor and Scott live in the Wisconsin Territory.

Show Your Skill

4. **Make Inferences** Why did the *Dred Scott* decision say voters could not ban slavery?

_____

_____

_____

Mark the Text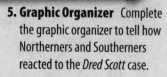

5. **Graphic Organizer** Complete the graphic organizer to tell how Northerners and Southerners reacted to the *Dred Scott* case.

Dred Scott v. Sandford

Dred Scott was an enslaved African American. A doctor in Missouri, a slave state, bought him. In the 1830s, the doctor and Scott moved to Illinois, a free state. Then they moved to the Wisconsin Territory. Slavery was banned there. Later the doctor and Scott returned to Missouri, where the doctor died.

In 1846 Dred Scott sued for his freedom. He said he should be free because he had lived where slavery was illegal. The case finally reached the Supreme Court in 1857. The case gained a lot of attention. It gave the Court a chance to rule on the question of slavery itself.

The Court ruled that:

- Scott was not free just because he had lived in free areas.
- he was not a citizen, so he had no right to bring a lawsuit.
- slaves were property.
- the Missouri Compromise and popular sovereignty were unconstitutional. Neither Congress nor voters could ban slavery. That would be like taking away a person's property.

The Court's decision outraged Northerners. Southerners were pleased. They believed that now nothing could stop the spread of slavery.

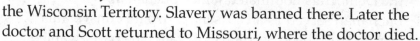

Dred Scott Decision

Northerners	Southerners
_____	_____
_____	_____
_____	_____
_____	_____

Lincoln and Douglas held a series of debates throughout Illinois. The debates were so popular that people even came from outside the state to hear them.

Lincoln and Douglas

In 1858 the Illinois Senate race had national attention. Senator Stephen A. Douglas, a Democrat, was running against Abraham Lincoln, a Republican. Douglas was popular. People thought he might run for president in 1860. Lincoln was not as well known. He challenged Douglas to a series of debates.

Slavery was the main topic of each debate. Douglas was for popular sovereignty. He believed people could vote to limit slavery. Lincoln said that African Americans had rights and that slavery was wrong.

Douglas won the election. Even though he lost, Lincoln became popular with people around the nation. His arguments against Douglas had been forceful and persuasive. Lincoln gained a national reputation as a man of clear thinking.

Southerners felt threatened by Republicans. In 1859 an act of violence added to their fears. Abolitionist John Brown led a raid on Harpers Ferry, Virginia. The target was an **arsenal,** or place where weapons are stored. Brown hoped to arm enslaved African Americans. He hoped they would revolt against slaveholders.

Local citizens and troops stopped the raid. Brown was tried and convicted of treason and murder. He was given the death penalty. His death divided the North. Some antislavery groups had never approved of Brown's violence. Others saw him as a **martyr**—a person who dies for a great cause.

NGSSS Check List a reason given by the Supreme Court for the decision in the *Dred Scott* case. SS.8.A.5.2

_____

_____

_____

Think Critically

6. Contrast How did Douglas and Lincoln differ in their opinions on slavery?

_____

_____

_____

_____

_____

7. Summarize Why did John Brown raid the arsenal at Harpers Ferry?

_____

_____

_____

_____

Take the Challenge

8. With a partner, take the role of either Lincoln or Douglas and debate the issues in 1858.

SECESSION AND WAR

NGSSS

SS.8.A.5.1 Explain the causes, course, and consequence of the Civil War (sectionalism, slavery, states' rights, balance of power in the Senate).

SS.8.A.5.2 Analyze the role of slavery in the development of sectional conflict.

SS.8.A.5.3 Explain major domestic and international economic, military, political, and socio-cultural events of Abraham Lincoln's presidency.

SS.8.A.5.4 Identify the division (Confederate and Union States, Border states, western territories) of the United States at the outbreak of the Civil War.

SS.8.A.5.7 Examine key events and peoples in Florida history as each impacts this era of American history.

Essential Question
Why does conflict develop?

Guiding Questions
1. What was the importance of the election of 1860?
2. What did the attack on Fort Sumter signify?

Terms to Know

secession
withdrawal

states' rights
idea that states are independent and have the right to control their own affairs

Where in the World?

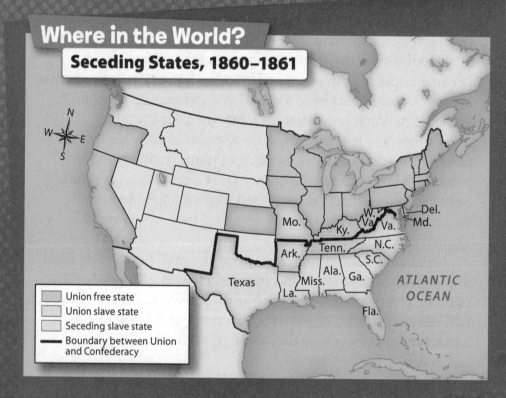

Seceding States, 1860–1861

Mo. • Ky. • W. Va. • Va. • Del. • Md. • Ark. • Tenn. • N.C. • S.C. • Texas • Miss. • Ala. • Ga. • La. • Fla.

ATLANTIC OCEAN

Legend:
- Union free state
- Union slave state
- Seceding slave state
- Boundary between Union and Confederacy

When Did It Happen?

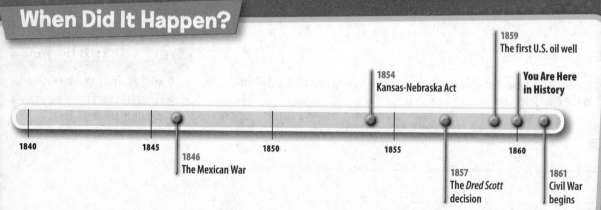

- 1840
- 1845
- **1846** The Mexican War
- 1850
- **1854** Kansas-Nebraska Act
- 1855
- **1857** The *Dred Scott* decision
- **1859** The first U.S. oil well
- 1860
- **You Are Here in History**
- **1861** Civil War begins

The 1860 Election

The issue of slavery split the Democratic Party in the presidential election of 1860.

- Democrats in the North supported popular sovereignty. They chose Stephen A. Douglas as their candidate.
- Democrats in the South favored slavery. They chose John Breckinridge.
- Moderates in the North and South started the Constitutional Union Party. They chose John Bell. The party took no position on slavery.
- Republicans chose Abraham Lincoln. They wanted to leave slavery where it existed. However, they wanted to ban it in the territories. Lincoln's name was not even on the ballot in most Southern states.

Lincoln won, and he took every Northern state. Many Southerners believed the Republicans would try to stop slavery where it existed. On December 20, 1860, South Carolina left the Union. Other Southern states debated **secession,** or withdrawing from the Union, too.

Congress worked to hold the Union together. Senator John Crittenden suggested amendments to the Constitution. They protected slavery south of the line set by the Missouri Compromise. Neither Republicans nor Southern leaders accepted Crittenden's plan.

By February 1861, Texas, Louisiana, Mississippi, Alabama, Florida, and Georgia had seceded. Delegates from these states met with South Carolina leaders. Together they formed the Confederate States of America. They chose Jefferson Davis as their president.

Mark the Text

1. Underline each of the 1860 presidential candidates and his party.

Think Critically

2. **Summarize** What was John Crittenden's plan to stop secession?

_____

_____

_____

_____

_____

Show Your Skill

3. **Draw Conclusions** Why did the Confederacy choose its own president?

_____

_____

_____

_____

The four candidates for president in 1860 *left to right:* Douglas, Breckinridge, Lincoln, and Bell

Think Critically

4. Sequence Number the events in the order they happened.

_____ Lincoln issues a call for troops.

_____ Lincoln sends supplies to the fort.

_____ Fort Sumter surrenders.

_____ Lincoln becomes president.

_____ Jefferson Davis orders Confederate troops to attack.

_____ Lincoln gets a message from the commander at Fort Sumter.

5. Explain What are two reasons that the Confederate forces were able to beat the Union forces at Fort Sumter in just a few days?

_____

_____

_____

Take the Challenge

6. Write a journal entry from the point of view of a Confederate or Union soldier at Fort Sumter.

Southerners used the idea of **states' rights** to explain their decision to secede. They argued that

PHOTO: Bettmann/Corbis

- each state had joined the Union voluntarily.
- the Constitution was a contract between the federal government and the states.
- the government broke the contract because it did not give Southern states equal rights in the territories.

Confederate soldiers use cannons to attack Fort Sumter in 1861.

- therefore, a state had the right to leave the Union.

Not all Southerners believed in secession. Northerners also disagreed. Some were glad to see Southern states leave the Union. Most Northerners, however, thought secession would be bad for the country.

In March 1861, Abraham Lincoln took office. He asked the seceding states to rejoin the Union. He pleaded for peace. He also warned that he would enforce federal law in the South.

Fighting at Fort Sumter

The day after Lincoln took office, he received a message. It came from Fort Sumter, a U.S. fort on an island in Charleston Harbor, South Carolina. The commander of the fort warned that supplies were low. He said the Confederates were demanding that he surrender. Lincoln sent an unarmed group with supplies. He ordered Union troops at the fort not to fire unless they were fired upon.

Jefferson Davis made a historic choice. He ordered Confederate troops to attack Fort Sumter before the supplies arrived. On April 12, 1861, the Confederates fired on Fort Sumter. Rough, high seas kept Union ships from coming to help. Two days later, Fort Sumter surrendered. The Civil War had begun.

Lincoln issued a call for troops. Volunteers quickly signed up. Meanwhile, Virginia, North Carolina, Tennessee, and Arkansas joined the Confederacy.

 NGSSS Check What two nations were at war in the Civil War? SS.8.A.5.4

MY REFLECTIONS

ESSENTIAL QUESTION *Why does conflict develop?*

Reflect on What It Means . . .

Different viewpoints and strongly held beliefs on slavery and states' rights broke apart the Union. It brought the Union and the Confederacy to civil war. Reflect on what you and others believe and how that can lead to conflict.

To My Community and the World

Think about a belief or viewpoint of a group in your community or somewhere else in the world. Summarize that viewpoint or belief in the center of the circle. In the four spaces around the center, write actions that the group might take based on those beliefs. In the three spaces next to each action, write possible positive and negative outcomes of the action as well as possible opposition or obstacles to the action.

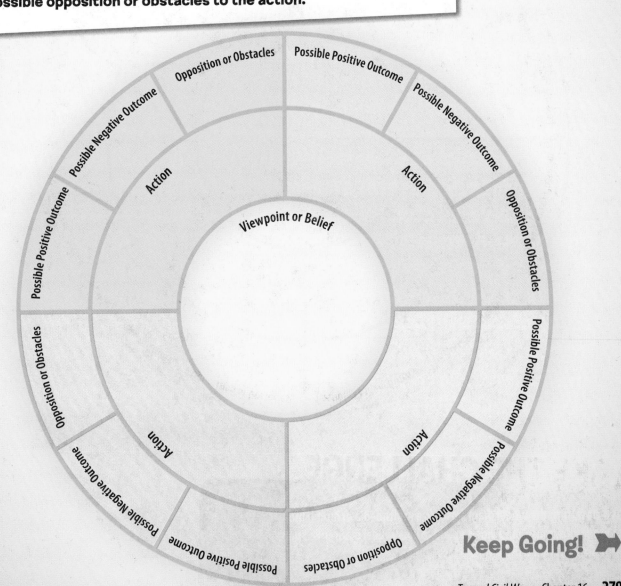

Keep Going!

To Me

Complete this wheel diagram based on one
of your own viewpoints and beliefs.

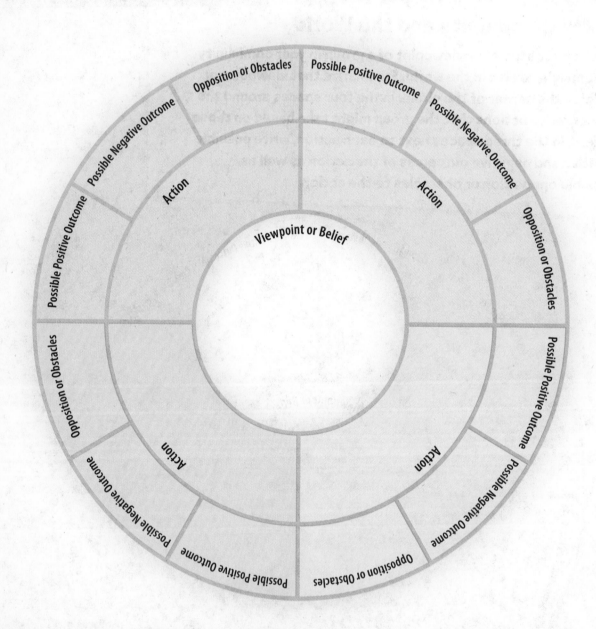

TAKE THE CHALLENGE

As a class, turn the wheel diagrams into a multimedia exhibit. Find
photographs, music, and video to add to your wheel diagrams. Share
your presentation with another class.

CHAPTER 17

THE CIVIL WAR

NGSSS

SS.8.A.5.6 Compare significant Civil War battles and events and their effects on civilian populations.

SS.8.A.5.7 Examine key events and peoples in Florida history as each impacts this era of American history.

ESSENTIAL QUESTION *Why does conflict develop?*

The Civil War was on the verge of beginning when author and historian Caroline Mays Brevard was born in Tallahassee in 1860. Later, Brevard wrote a history of Florida that included the following description of the state's preparations to defend itself:

" Governor Perry began preparations for the war by ordering volunteer companies to organize into battalions and regiments, and all citizens subject to military duty to be ready for the defense of the State. From all over the State men answered the call eagerly, and on April 5 the first regiment, under Colonel Patton Anderson, was sent to Pensacola."

CAROLINE MAYS BREVARD

subject to

What words could be substituted for "subject to" here?

_____

_____

companies, battalions, and regiments

Companies, *battalions*, and *regiments* are all groups of soldiers. A battalion contains several companies, while a regiment can contain several battalions. In the space below, list the three types of soldier groupings in order from smallest to largest.

_____

DBQ BREAKING IT DOWN

Soldiers in the Civil War had to carry their own equipment, some of it issued by the government, and some of it provided by each soldier personally. In the space below, make your own list of the items a Civil War soldier might need to carry.

_____

_____

_____

McGraw-Hill
netw⚬rks™
There's More Online!

PHOTO: Florida Photographic Collection

THE TWO SIDES

LESSON 1

NGSSS

SS.8.A.5.3 Explain major domestic and international economic, military, political, and socio-cultural events of Abraham Lincoln's presidency.

SS.8.A.5.4 Identify the division (Confederate and Union States, Border states, western territories) of the United States at the outbreak of the Civil War.

SS.8.A.5.5 Compare Union and Confederate strengths and weaknesses.

SS.8.A.5.7 Examine key events and peoples in Florida history as each impacts this era of American history

Essential Question

Why does conflict develop?

Guiding Questions

1. What were the goals and strategies of the North and South?
2. What was war like for the soldiers of the North and the South?

Terms to Know

border state
the states on the border between the North and South: Delaware, Maryland, Kentucky, and Missouri

enlist
to formally join a military force

Where in the World?

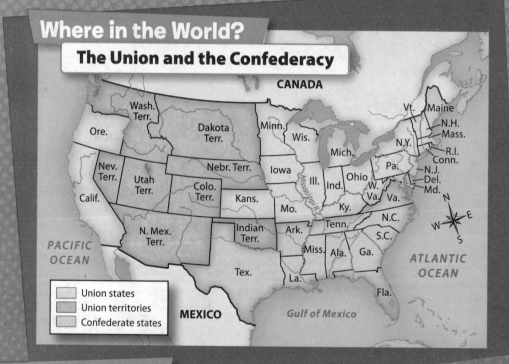

The Union and the Confederacy

Legend:
- Union states
- Union territories
- Confederate states

When Did It Happen?

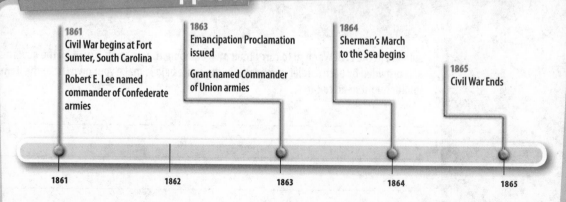

1861
Civil War begins at Fort Sumter, South Carolina

Robert E. Lee named commander of Confederate armies

1863
Emancipation Proclamation issued

Grant named Commander of Union armies

1864
Sherman's March to the Sea begins

1865
Civil War Ends

Timeline: 1861 — 1862 — 1863 — 1864 — 1865

Two Very Different Sides

For most states, choosing sides in the Civil War was easy. This was not true for Delaware, Maryland, Kentucky, and Missouri. They were the **border states.** They had ties to both the North and the South.

These states were important to the Union's plans. Missouri could control parts of the Mississippi River and major routes to the West. Kentucky controlled the Ohio River. Delaware was close to Philadelphia. Maryland was close to Richmond, the Confederate capital. Also, Washington, D.C., lay inside the state. If Maryland seceded, the North's government would be surrounded by Confederate states.

President Lincoln worked hard to keep the border states in the Union. In the end, he succeeded. Still, many people who lived in the border states supported the Confederacy.

Each side had different goals and strategies, or plans for winning the war. The South wanted to be an independent nation. The North wanted to restore the Union. They had to try to force the states to give up independence.

The South had to conduct a defensive war. This meant that the South would hold on to as much territory as possible. Southerners felt that if they fought long and hard enough, Northerners would give up.

The South also expected support from Britain and France. These countries bought cotton from the South. The war cut off the cotton supply, so Southerners hoped these nations might pressure the North to end the war.

Copyright © by The McGraw-Hill Companies, Inc.

Think Critically

1. Explain Why did Lincoln need the support of the border states?

_____

_____

_____

_____

Show Your Skill

2. Compare and Contrast What were the strengths of the North and the South?

North

_____

_____

_____

South

_____

_____

_____

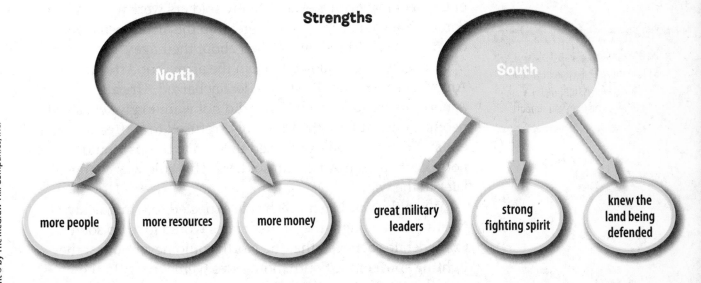

Strengths

North: more people | more resources | more money

South: great military leaders | strong fighting spirit | knew the land being defended

Mark the Text

3. Chart Complete the chart. List the strategies of the two sides.

Think Critically

4. Draw Conclusions In what ways might it have been an advantage for the South to fight on their own territory?

_____

_____

_____

_____

_____

Show Your Skill

5. Identify the Main Idea
What was the main goal of the Anaconda Plan?

_____

_____

_____

_____

Take the Challenge

6. Take the role of a parent writing to a son who is fighting for a different side than you support.

The North's war plan came from General Winfield Scott. Scott's plan had three main parts:

1. to blockade, or close, Southern ports. This would stop supplies from getting to the Confederacy. It also would keep the South from exporting its cotton crop.

2. to gain control of the Mississippi River. This would split the Confederacy in two and cut Southern supply lines.

3. to capture Richmond, Virginia, the Confederate capital. Scott's plan was called the Anaconda Plan. An *anaconda* is a snake that squeezes its prey to death.

Union Strategy	Confederate Strategy

Americans Against Americans

The Civil War was more than a war between the states. Brother fought brother, and neighbor fought neighbor. Kentucky senator John Crittenden had two sons who became generals. One fought for the Confederacy. The other fought for the Union. Even President Lincoln's wife had relatives in the Confederate army.

Many men left their homes to **enlist** in, or join the Union or Confederate armies. Many, many soldiers were under 18. Some were younger than 14. To get into the army, teenagers often ran away from home or lied about their ages.

Teenagers were allowed to join the army, but African Americans were not. The Confederacy barred African Americans from the army. They did not want to give enslaved people guns. At first, the Union also refused to let freed people enlist. Northern leaders worried that white troops would not accept African American soldiers. This rule was changed later in the war.

When the war began, each side expected to win quickly. Northerners thought the Confederates would give up soon. Confederates believed that the North could never outlast the fighting spirit of the South. Both sides were wrong. In the end, the war lasted longer than most Americans guessed.

Union and Confederate soldiers in some cases had friends and even family members fighting on the opposite side.

Soldiers came from every region. Most came from farms. Almost half of the North's troops and almost two-thirds of the South's troops had owned or worked on farms.

Total Troop Strength, 1861—1865	
Union Troops	Confederate Troops
2,100,000	900,000

The Confederate troops were sometimes called Rebels. Union troops were known as Yankees.

Life for soldiers on both sides was very hard. Soldiers wrote letters to family and friends about what they saw. Many wrote about their boredom, discomfort, sickness, fear, and horror.

Most of the time the soldiers lived in camps. There soldiers had some fun times with songs, stories, letters from home, and baseball games. Often, however, a soldier's life was a dull routine of drills, bad food, marches, and rain.

Both sides lost many soldiers during the war. Thousands of casualties crowded hospitals. After the Battle of Shiloh, the wounded lay in the rain for more than 24 hours waiting for treatment. Around them, lay dead and dying soldiers.

Many men deserted, or ran away. About one out of every eleven Union soldiers and one out of every eight Confederate soldiers deserted.

NGSSS Check How was the North's strategy different from the South's?
SS.8.A.5.4

_____

_____

_____

Think Critically

7. Infer Why were Confederate soldiers called "Rebels"?

_____

_____

Show Your Skill

8. Make a Connection How do you think life for a soldier during the Civil War is similar to and different from the life of an American soldier at war today?

_____

_____

_____

_____

_____

_____

_____

_____

2 EARLY YEARS OF THE WAR

NGSSS

SS.8.A.5.3 Explain major domestic and international economic, military, political, and socio-cultural events of Abraham Lincoln's presidency.

SS.8.A.5.5 Compare Union and Confederate strengths and weaknesses.

SS.8.A.5.6 Compare significant Civil War battles and events and their effects on civilian populations

Essential Question
Why does conflict develop?

Guiding Questions
1. What was the outcome of the first major battle of the war?
2. How did the Union respond to important defeats in the East in 1862?
3. What was the effect of the Emancipation Proclamation?

Terms to Know

tributary
stream or smaller river that feeds into a larger river

ironclad
covered in iron armor

casualty
a soldier who is killed or wounded in battle

Emancipation Proclamation
decree issued by President Lincoln freeing slaves in those parts of the Confederacy still in rebellion on January 1, 1863

Where in the World?

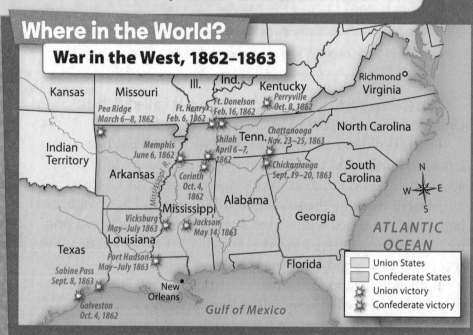

War in the West, 1862–1863

Kansas, Missouri, Ill., Ind., Kentucky, Virginia, Richmond, North Carolina, Indian Territory, Arkansas, Tenn., South Carolina, Mississippi, Alabama, Georgia, Louisiana, Texas, Florida, New Orleans, Gulf of Mexico, ATLANTIC OCEAN

Pea Ridge March 6–8, 1862
Ft. Henry Feb. 6, 1862
Ft. Donelson Feb. 16, 1862
Perryville Oct. 8, 1862
Chattanooga Nov. 23–25, 1863
Memphis June 6, 1862
Shiloh April 6–7, 1862
Corinth Oct. 4, 1862
Chickamauga Sept. 19–20, 1863
Vicksburg May–July 1863
Jackson May 14, 1863
Port Hudson May–July 1863
Sabine Pass Sept. 8, 1863
Galveston Oct. 4, 1862

Union States
Confederate States
Union victory
Confederate victory

What Do You Know?

Directions: Use no more than three words to tell what you know about each of these names or terms. After you finish the lesson, adjust any of your descriptions if needed.

Abraham Lincoln _____

Battle of Bull Run _____

Robert E. Lee _____

Ulysses S. Grant _____

Emancipation Proclamation _____

ironclad ships _____

War on Land and at Sea

The first big battle of the Civil War took place in the summer of 1861. It happened in northern Virginia near a small river called Bull Run. On July 21, about 30,000 Union troops attacked a smaller Confederate force.

At first, the Yankees pushed the Confederates back. But General Thomas Jackson inspired the rebels to keep fighting. Jackson held his position "like a stone wall," so he later became known as "Stonewall" Jackson. The Confederates began fighting back hard. They broke the Union lines.

The loss shocked Northerners. They realized they would not win as easily as they had hoped. President Lincoln named a new general, George B. McClellan, to head the Union army of the East—called the Army of the Potomac—and to train the troops.

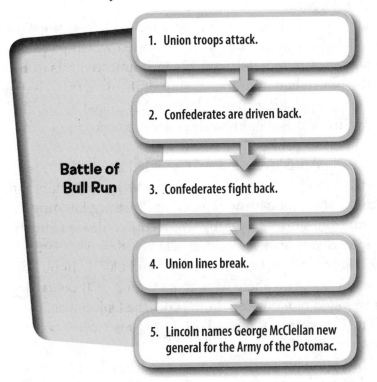

Battle of Bull Run

1. Union troops attack.
2. Confederates are driven back.
3. Confederates fight back.
4. Union lines break.
5. Lincoln names George McClellan new general for the Army of the Potomac.

In the West, the Union wanted control of the Mississippi River and its **tributaries,** the smaller rivers that fed it. That way, Union ships could stop Louisiana, Arkansas, and Texas from supplying the rest of the Confederacy. Union gunboats and troops would also be able to move into the South.

The battle for the rivers began in February 1862. Union forces captured Fort Henry on the Tennessee River. Then, Union Generals Grant and Foote moved against Fort Donelson on the Cumberland River. The Confederates knew they could not save the fort. They surrendered to Grant. This made Grant a hero in the North.

Think Critically

1. Explain What was surprising about the Battle of Bull Run?

_____

_____

_____

Show Your Skill

2. Identify Cause and Effect Why did Lincoln put a new general in charge after Bull Run?

_____

_____

_____

_____

_____

Think Critically

3. Infer Why was controlling the Mississippi River important to both sides?

_____

_____

_____

_____

_____

The battle, shown here, between the *Virginia* and the *Monitor* was the first battle in maritime history fought between two ironclad ships.

Show Your Skill

4. Draw Conclusions Why do you think the *Virginia* was a "secret weapon" for the South?

_____

_____

_____

_____

_____

Think Critically

5. Evaluate Which do you think had more of an impact on the results of the Civil War—the capture of New Orleans or the battle between the ironclad ships? Explain.

_____

_____

_____

_____

_____

_____

Meanwhile, Union and Confederate navies were fighting in the Atlantic Ocean. In April 1861, President Lincoln ordered a blockade of all Confederate ports.

Southerners had a secret weapon, though. It was an old Union warship called the *Merrimack*. The Confederates rebuilt the wooden ship and covered it with iron. Its iron armor would protect it from Union cannon fire. They renamed the **ironclad** ship the *Virginia*.

On March 8, 1862, the *Virginia* attacked Union ships off the coast of Virginia. The North's wooden warships could not damage the Confederate ship. Shells bounced off its iron sides.

The North had an ironclad ship of its own, though: the *Monitor*. The *Monitor* rushed toward Virginia. On March 9, the two ironclads met in battle. The ships could not sink each other, so neither side won.

In early April 1862, General Grant led about 40,000 troops toward Corinth, Mississippi. Corinth was an important railroad junction. The Union army camped at Pittsburg Landing, 20 miles (32 km) from Corinth. Nearby was a church named Shiloh.

Confederate leaders decided to attack first. The Battle of Shiloh lasted two days. It was a hard and bloody fight. Both sides lost many soldiers. There were more than 23,000 **casualties**— people killed or wounded. In the end, the Union won.

The Union troops moved on. They took Corinth on May 30 and Memphis, Tennessee, on June 6.

The Union Navy also won an important battle. On April 25, 1862, Union naval forces under David Farragut captured New Orleans, Louisiana. New Orleans was the largest city in the South. The Confederacy could no longer use the Mississippi River to carry its goods to sea. The Union just had to capture Vicksburg, Mississippi, to get full control of the Mississippi River.

Union Victories in the West: Spring 1862

- Fort Henry
- Shiloh
- Memphis
- Fort Donelson
- Corinth
- New Orleans

War in the Eastern States

As you read about the War in the East, make a list of each battle, the location, and which side won.

Battle	Location	Winner

The South had very good military leaders, especially Generals Robert E. Lee and Stonewall Jackson. These men knew the terrain, could move forces quickly, and inspired their troops. They won several victories in the East.

In 1862 Confederate forces in Virginia won the Seven Days' Battle, the Second Battle of Bull Run, and Fredericksburg. In May 1863, at Chancellorsville, Virginia, Lee's army beat a Union army twice its size.

The Confederates wanted to attack Washington, D.C. The city was too well guarded for Lee to attack, though. Confederate president Jefferson Davis told Lee to move his troops into western Maryland instead. This was Union territory. He planned to move into Pennsylvania and invade the North. Lee knew that McClellan was following him with a large force. He concentrated on moving forward. Soon, Lee's forces crossed into Maryland.

In Maryland, Lee split his army into four parts. He told each part to move in a different direction. He wanted to confuse Union General McClellan. Lee's plan did not work. A Confederate officer lost his copy of the plan. Two Union soldiers found the orders and brought them to McClellan.

McClellan did not attack right away, so Lee gathered his troops again. On September 17, 1862, the two sides met at Antietam near Sharpsburg, Maryland. The Union won this battle.

Antietam was the deadliest single day of fighting in the war. About 6,000 soldiers died. About 17,000 more were wounded. Lee went back to Virginia after the battle. His plan to invade the North had failed.

6. Identify Cause and Effect Why did the Confederate soldiers not attack Washington, D.C.?

_____

_____

_____

Think Critically

7. Explain What was the outcome of the Battle of Antietam?

_____

_____

_____

Take the Challenge

8. Write a newspaper article about what might have happened if General Lee's plans had not fallen into the hands of General McClellan.

Among the thousands killed during the Battle of Antietam, shown below, were six generals: three were Union and three were Confederate.

Lincoln is surrounded by his advisers as he signs the Emancipation Proclamation.

The Emancipation Proclamation

Lincoln hated slavery. He did not want to make the Civil War a battle to end it, though. He needed the support of the border states. If the war had been about slavery, these states may not have sided with the Union. Even many Northerners who did not like slavery would not have risked their lives to end it.

Abolitionists, including Frederick Douglass and Horace Greeley, tried to convince Lincoln to make the war a fight to end slavery. They said that slavery was a moral wrong that should be stopped. They also said that slavery was the cause of the split between North and South. Finally, they said that if Britain and France saw that the Union was focused on ending slavery, they would not support the South. That would help the Union.

Mark the Text

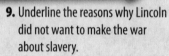

9. Underline the reasons why Lincoln did not want to make the war about slavery.

Think Critically

10. Explain Did the Emancipation Proclamation end slavery in the United States? Explain your answer.

_____

_____

_____

_____

_____

_____

_____

Reasons to Make the War About Slavery

• Slavery is morally wrong.
• Slavery is the main issue that the North and South disagree on.
• Opposing slavery is good foreign policy.

The Constitution did not give Lincoln the power to end slavery, but he had the power to take property from an enemy in wartime. By law, enslaved people were property. On September 22, 1862, Lincoln signed the **Emancipation Proclamation.** This freed all enslaved people in the Confederacy on January 1, 1863.

The Emancipation Proclamation did not really free any enslaved people. It applied only in areas held by the Confederacy. In those areas, Lincoln had no power to enforce his new policy. Still, the proclamation was important. The government had declared slavery to be wrong. If the Union won the war, slavery would be banned forever.

 NGSSS Check Choose two people from this lesson and write how each person influenced the Civil War. SS.8.A.4.8

_____

_____

PHOTO: MPI/Archive Photos/Getty Images

Copyright © by The McGraw-Hill Companies, Inc.

LIFE DURING THE CIVIL WAR

NGSSS

SS.8.A.5.6 Compare significant Civil War battles and events and their effects on civilian populations

SS.8.A.5.7 Examine key events and peoples in Florida history as each impacts this era of American history

Essential Question
Why does conflict develop?

Guiding Questions
1. How did life change during the Civil War?
2. How did Florida participate in the Civil War?
3. What were the conditions of hospitals and prison camps during the Civil War?
4. What political and economic changes occurred during the Civil War?

Terms to Know

habeas corpus
a legal writ, or action, that guarantees a prisoner the right to be heard in court

draft
a system of selecting people for required military service

bounty
reward or payment

greenbacks
paper money issued by the United States government

When Did It Happen?

1862
Union forces get control of Pensacola harbor

1863
Harriet Tubman leads mission to disrupt the Southern supply lines

1864
Battle of Olustee

1865
Andersonville Prison closes

1860   1870

What Do You Know?

Directions: In the first column, circle "True" if you think the statement is true, and circle "False" if you think it is false based on what you know before you read the lesson. After this lesson, complete the last column.

Before the Lesson		After the Lesson
True False	The greatest danger for soldiers was cannon fire.	True False
True False	During the Civil War, many children were not able to attend school.	True False
True False	Being a nurse was a common job for women during the mid-1800s.	True False
True False	Prisoners captured in battle were often held in horrible facilities.	True False

Think Critically

1. Explain Why did many children not go to school during the war?

_____

_____

_____

_____

_____

Mark the Text

2. Graphic Organizer Complete the graphic organizer to show new roles for women during the Civil War.

Think Critically

3. Summarize What challenges did nurses face during the war?

_____

_____

_____

_____

_____

_____

A Different Way of Life

During the Civil War, life in both the North and the South changed dramatically. About half of the school-age children did not go to school. Some schools were closed because they were too close to battle sites or because they were used as hospitals. Many children had to help their families.

Most battles took place in the South, so both armies moved through the South. Wherever they passed through, people lost their homes and crops. Many people had to flee. The South also faced severe shortages of food and supplies.

Women in both the North and the South took on new roles during the war. They kept farms and factories running. They served as teachers and clerks. They often had to make do with little money.

Women also served in other ways in the war:

- **Nurses** Thousands of women served as nurses. They were not welcomed at first. Doctors thought they were too delicate to do the work. Some people thought it was wrong for women to take care of men they did not know.

- **Spies** Some women served as spies. Rose O'Neal Greenhow was a Southern woman who gathered information about Union plans and passed it to the South. Harriet Tubman helped serve as a spy and scout for the Union. She also helped enslaved people escape along the Underground Railroad.

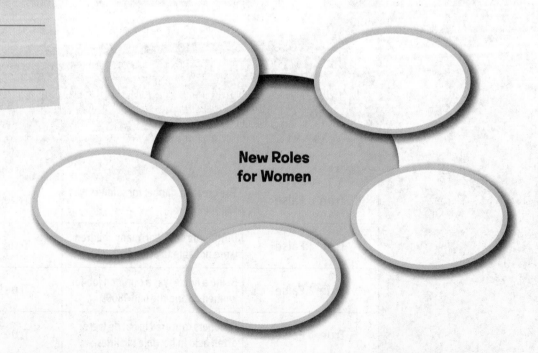

New Roles for Women

Each year at the Olustee Festival, people reenact Florida's largest Civil War battle.

Floridians and the War

When the Civil War began, Florida was not seen as important to either side. Later, though, Florida became an important supplier for the Confederacy. Florida supplied cotton, pork, beef, and vegetables to the Confederacy. Salt work plants provided much-needed salt. Salt was important because it kept meat from spoiling in the days before refrigeration.

The Union controlled Jacksonville for most of the war. Union troops also held some other coastal towns and several forts. Confederates, however, controlled the interior part of Florida. This included Tallahassee, Florida's capital. Tallahassee was the only Confederate capital east of the Mississippi River that did not fall to Union hands.

Soldiers After Battle

Early in the war, the North and the South simply exchanged prisoners. When officials realized that the exchanged prisoners were returning to fight, they set up prison camps. Prisoners usually had only a blanket and a cup. There was little food.

Andersonville prison in Georgia was very overcrowded. The prisoners slept in holes in the ground and got hardly any food. Their water came from a stream that was also a sewer. Over a third of Union prisoners there died, mostly from disease.

At the Union prison in Elmira, New York, Confederate prisoners had no blankets to protect them from the cold. The pond was both a toilet and a garbage dump. The hospital was in a flooded basement. A quarter of the prisoners held at Elmira died.

Mark the Text

4. Underline items that Florida supplied to the Confederacy.

Think Critically

5. **Contrast** What was unique about Tallahassee during the Civil War?

_____

_____

_____

Mark the Text

6. Underline the location of a Confederate prison camp. Circle the location of a Union prison camp.

Show Your Skill

7. **Identify Cause and Effect** Why were prison camps set up?

_____

_____

_____

Take the Challenge

8. Research an area in your part of the state that was involved in the Civil War in some way. Learn three pieces of information about it to share with the class.

Think Critically

9. Evaluate What do you think was the greatest danger for soldiers during the Civil War?

_____

_____

_____

_____

10. Explain What does *habeas corpus* mean?

_____

_____

_____

Show Your Skill

11. Draw Conclusions Why did the New York City mobs turn against African Americans?

_____

_____

_____

_____

Wounded soldiers were treated in field hospitals near the battlefields. Bullets and cannonballs flew by as doctors worked and volunteers distributed, or passed out, bread and soup to the wounded.

Even in the camps, many soldiers got sick because they were crowded together and drank from unclean water supplies. Some regiments lost half their men to disease before they had a chance to fight.

Political and Economic Change

Both the North and the South faced rebellions. Food shortages in the South led to bread riots in Richmond, Virginia, and other cities. Protesters sometimes turned to rioting and looting.

In the North, the War Democrats did not like how the Lincoln administration was running the war. Peace Democrats wanted the war to end immediately. Many people viewed the Peace Democrats as dangerous traitors and called them Copperheads. A copperhead is a poisonous snake.

Habeas corpus was suspended in both regions. Habeas corpus is a legal process for making sure the government has the right to keep someone in jail. Thousands of Northerners went to jail without trial. Some were traitors, but others had only criticized the government.

Soon both sides had trouble recruiting enough soldiers. The Confederate Congress passed a **draft** law in 1862. A draft orders people to serve in the military during a war. In the North, the Union paid a **bounty,** or a sum of money, to encourage volunteers. Then, in March 1863, the Union also passed a draft law. In both the North and the South, a man could avoid the draft by paying a fee or hiring a substitute.

The draft law caused protests. Riots occurred in several Northern cities. In July 1863, people rioted in New York City. They attacked government and military buildings. They then turned against African Americans because many workers had opposed the Emancipation Proclamation. They were afraid that freed blacks would take their jobs. More than 100 people died.

In New York City, people rioted in the streets to protest what they felt were unfair draft laws that allowed the wealthy to avoid serving in the war.

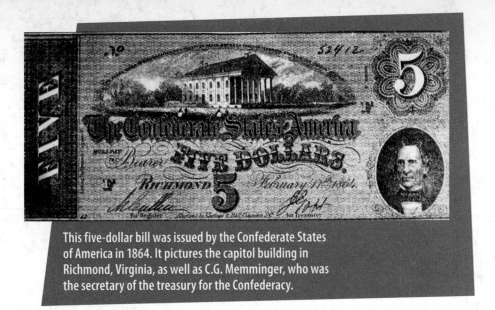

This five-dollar bill was issued by the Confederate States of America in 1864. It pictures the capitol building in Richmond, Virginia, as well as C.G. Memminger, who was the secretary of the treasury for the Confederacy.

The war strained the economies of both sides. The two governments had three ways of paying for the war:

1. They borrowed money.

2. They passed new taxes, including income taxes.

3. They printed money. Northern bills became known as **greenbacks** because of their color.

The North was better able to cope with the costs of the war. Northern industries made money by producing war supplies. Farmers also profited because they sold their crops to the armies. Goods were in demand, though, so prices rose faster than wages. This general increase in prices is called inflation. It made life harder for working people.

The South had bigger economic problems than the North. Many of the battles took place in the South, destroying farmland and railroad lines. The naval blockade stopped the shipping of trade goods. It also stopped important supplies from reaching the Confederacy. For example, there was so little salt that women scraped the floors of smokehouses to recover it.

The South also suffered much worse inflation. As early as 1862, citizens begged Confederate leaders for help.

 NGSSS Check How did life change for women and children during the Civil War? SS.8.A.5.6

_____

_____

_____

Think Critically

12. Explain What is *inflation*?

_____

_____

_____

_____

Mark the Text

13. Underline reasons why the economy in the South suffered.

LESSON 4

THE STRAIN OF WAR

NGSSS

SS.8.A.5.3 Explain major domestic and international economic, military, political, and socio-cultural events of Abraham Lincoln's presidency.

SS.8.A.5.5 Compare Union and Confederate strengths and weaknesses.

SS.8.A.5.6 Compare significant Civil War battles and events and their effects on civilian populations

SS.8.A.5.7 Examine key events and peoples in Florida history as each impacts this era of American history

Essential Question
Why does conflict develop?

Guiding Questions
1. What factors contributed to the early success of the Confederate forces?
2. What role did African Americans play in military efforts?
3. How was the battle of Gettysburg a turning point in the war?

Terms to Know

entrench
place within a trench, or ditch, for defense; place in a strong defensive position

flank
the side or edge of a military formation

When Did It Happen?

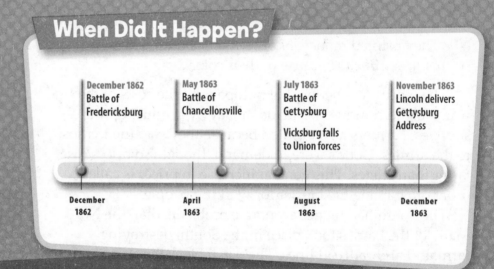

December 1862
Battle of Fredericksburg

May 1863
Battle of Chancellorsville

July 1863
Battle of Gettysburg

Vicksburg falls to Union forces

November 1863
Lincoln delivers Gettysburg Address

December 1862 — April 1863 — August 1863 — December 1863

What Do You Know?

Directions: Choose any four of the words below and write a sentence or two about the battles of the Civil War. When you finish the lesson, write another sentence using four different words from the list.

Lincoln	Gettysburg	Mississippi River	General Lee
General Grant	African American	France	battle
victory	Stonewall Jackson	loss	

Southern Victories

After Antietam, the Confederacy won a series of victories in the East because of the leadership of Generals Robert E. Lee and Stonewall Jackson. The Union commander, General Ambrose Burnside, began to march toward the Confederate capital at Richmond, Virginia. Lee moved his forces to Fredericksburg. They dug trenches in the hills and waited for the Union troops. When the Union soldiers arrived, Lee's **entrenched** forces fired down on them and pushed them back. Burnside's troops lost the Battle of Fredericksburg, and Burnside resigned.

Lee also had a brilliant plan at the Battle of Chancellorsville. He divided his troops. One group confronted the main Union force. Another group, led by Stonewall Jackson, attacked the Union forces on their **flank,** or side. Again, the Confederates won the battle, but Jackson was wounded and later died.

These Confederate victories showed the weaknesses of the Union generals:

- General McClellan was reluctant to do battle. He did not obey Lincoln's order to follow the Confederate troops after the Union's victory at Antietam.
- General Burnside lost at Fredericksburg. Lincoln replaced him with General Joseph Hooker.
- Hooker lost at Chancellorsville. Within two months, Hooker resigned, too.

Union Victories	Confederate Victories

African Americans in the Civil War

The Confederate army never accepted African American soldiers. Confederate officials believed that African Americans might attack their fellow troops or begin a revolt if they were armed.

At first, the Union army did not allow African Americans to enlist, either. Lincoln feared that allowing them to do so would anger people in the border states. By 1862, though, the North needed more soldiers. Congress allowed African Americans to

Copyright © by The McGraw-Hill Companies, Inc.

Mark the Text

1. Chart As you read this lesson, complete the chart to show Union and Confederate victories.

Think Critically

2. Explain What was Lee's strategy at Chancellorsville?

_____

_____

_____

_____

_____

_____

3. Evaluate What was General McClellan's weakness as a leader?

_____

_____

_____

_____

_____

Show Your Skill

4. Draw Conclusions Why did some people think Lee's strategy at Chancellorsville was brilliant?

_____

_____

_____

_____

_____

_____

_____

_____

_____

Show Your Skill

5. Make Inferences Why might African Americans have been eager to enlist and fight for the Union?

_____

_____

_____

_____

_____

Mark the Text ✏

6. Underline adjectives and phrases that describe what African Americans faced in the military. Circle phrases that describe the conduct of African American soldiers in the war.

enlist in all-black regiments. By the end of the war, African Americans made up about 10 percent of the Union army. They faced prejudice from other soldiers. They also faced fierce gunfire from Southern troops, who hated them.

Despite this, African Americans fought bravely and well. For example, the 54th Massachusetts served in the front lines of a battle to take Fort Wagner in South Carolina. The regiment suffered nearly 300 casualties. Their sacrifice made the 54th famous for its courage.

The Tide Turns

After the Confederate victory at Chancellorsville, Lee decided to invade the North. He hoped victories there would convince Britain and France to help the Confederacy.

On July 1, 1863, his forces entered Gettysburg, Pennsylvania, searching for supplies. There, they encountered, or met, Union troops. Outnumbered, the Union troops fell back to higher ground on Cemetery Ridge.

The next day, Southern troops tried and failed to force the Union troops from their positions on the hills.

On the third day, Lee ordered an all-out attack. Thousands of Confederate troops, led by General George Pickett, attacked Union forces on Cemetery Ridge. Half of those in Pickett's Charge were wounded or killed.

On July 4, Lee retreated. His army had suffered 25,000 casualties. Union troops had suffered almost as many.

Losing at Gettysburg ended Confederate hopes of getting help from Britain and France.

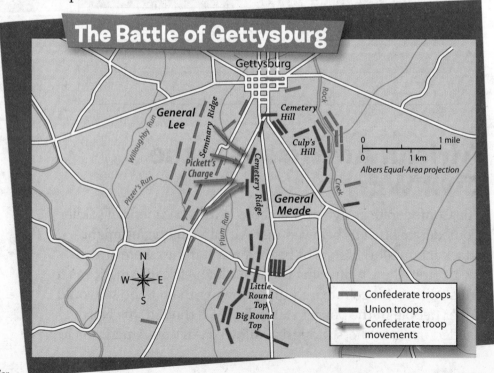

The Battle of Gettysburg

The Confederacy lost two other critical battles in July 1863:

- **Vicksburg** In April, Ulysses S. Grant had laid siege to Vicksburg, Mississippi. A siege is surrounding a place to keep it from receiving food or supplies. Both sides suffered heavy casualties. Vicksburg finally fell on the same day Lee retreated from Gettysburg.

- **Port Hudson** The Confederacy lost Port Hudson, its last stronghold on the Mississippi River a few days later. The Union had cut off Arkansas, Louisiana, and Texas from the rest of the Confederacy.

On November 19, 1863, people met at Gettysburg to dedicate the Soldiers' National Cemetery. First, the former governor of Massachusetts, Edward Everett, gave a two-hour speech. Then President Lincoln rose and spoke for just two minutes. He finished by saying, "It is rather for us to be here dedicated to the great task remaining before us—that from these honored dead we take increased devotion to that cause for which they gave the last full measure of devotion—that we here highly resolve that these dead shall not have died in vain, that this nation under God shall have a new birth of freedom, and that government of the people, by the people, for the people shall not perish from the earth." His powerful words became known as the Gettysburg Address. The words of the address are carved on the walls of the Lincoln Memorial.

The Gettysburg Address, which contains only ten sentences, is one of the most famous and beloved speeches in our country's history. Many people are familiar with the first words of the speech—"Fourscore and seven years ago. . . ."

 NGSSS Check What happened at Gettysburg, and why was it a turning point for the South? SS.8.A.5.6

_____

_____

7. Sequence Number the following events in the order they occurred, from 1 to 4.

_____ Pickett's Charge

_____ Union victories split the Confederacy in two

_____ Union and Confederate troops begin fighting in Gettysburg

_____ Grant lays siege to Vicksburg

Take the Challenge

8. Lincoln understood the power of a few carefully chosen words. Read the complete Gettysburg Address. Write a summary of the main points Lincoln makes. Use no more than 50 words in your summary.

LESSON 5

THE WAR'S FINAL STAGES

NGSSS

SS.8.A.5.3 Explain major domestic and international economic, military, political, and socio-cultural events of Abraham Lincoln's presidency.

SS.8.A.5.5 Compare Union and Confederate strengths and weaknesses.

SS.8.A.5.6 Compare significant Civil War battles and events and their effects on civilian populations

SS.8.A.5.7 Examine key events and peoples in Florida history as each impacts this era of American history

Essential Question
Why does conflict develop?

Guiding Questions
1. What events occurred at the end of the war?
2. What is total war?

Terms to Know

resistance
refusal to give in

total war
a strategy of bringing war to the entire society, not just the military

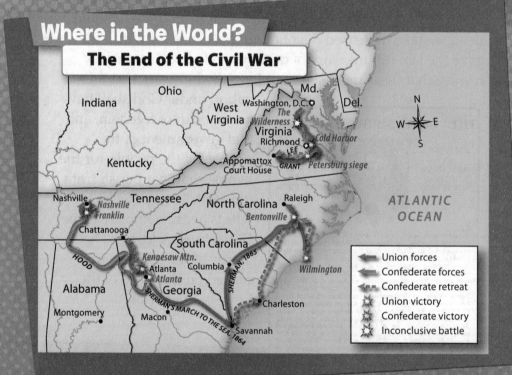

Where in the World?

The End of the Civil War

Ohio, Indiana, West Virginia, Virginia, Washington, D.C., Md., Del., The Wilderness, Richmond, Cold Harbor, LEE, GRANT, Petersburg siege, Appomattox Court House, Kentucky, Nashville, Franklin, Tennessee, Chattanooga, North Carolina, Raleigh, Bentonville, ATLANTIC OCEAN, South Carolina, Kennesaw Mtn., Columbia, SHERMAN, 1865, Wilmington, HOOD, Atlanta, Alabama, Georgia, Charleston, Montgomery, Macon, SHERMAN'S MARCH TO THE SEA, 1864, Savannah

Union forces
Confederate forces
Confederate retreat
Union victory
Confederate victory
Inconclusive battle

When Did It Happen?

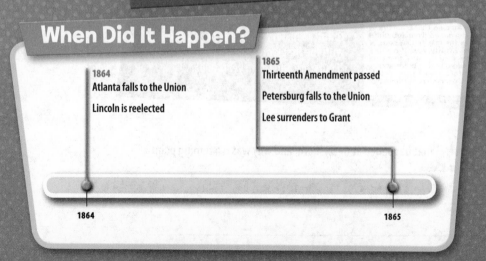

1864
Atlanta falls to the Union

Lincoln is reelected

1865
Thirteenth Amendment passed

Petersburg falls to the Union

Lee surrenders to Grant

1864 — 1865

networks Read Chapter 17 Lesson 5 in your textbook or online.

The Union Closes In

By 1864, Union forces surrounded the South, blocking its ports and controlling the Mississippi River. This cut off supplies to the South.

They also needed to cut off Florida's supplies from the rest of the Confederacy. Union forces landed in Jacksonville in February 1864. They moved into the center of the state. On February 20, the two armies fought a furious battle at Olustee Station. The Battle of Olustee, also known as Ocean Pond, stopped the Union advance. Union forces retreated to Jacksonville.

In March 1864, Lincoln put General Ulysses S. Grant in charge of all Union armies. Grant decided to attack from all sides. His armies would march to Richmond, Virginia, the Confederate capital. At the same time, Union General William Tecumseh Sherman would lead his troops through the Deep South.

Grant's troops met Confederate forces in three battles near Richmond:

1. **The Wilderness** The Wilderness lay about halfway between Washington, D.C., and Richmond, Virginia. Lee had only about 60,000 men, while Grant had more than 100,000. For two days— May 5 and 6, 1864—they fought in a dense forest. Fires raged through the forest. Both sides suffered huge casualties. There was no clear winner. Grant, who lost 17,000 men, cried in his tent at the end of the second day. On the third day, Grant moved his troops south toward Richmond.

2. **Spotsylvania Courthouse** From May 8 through May 21, 1864, the armies of Lee and Grant battled. Neither side won.

3. **Cold Harbor** On June 2, 1864, Grant's soldiers prepared by putting their names and addresses on their coats so people could identify their bodies.

From Cold Harbor, Grant moved his troops to Petersburg, Virginia. This city was a Confederate railroad center that moved troops and supplies. Grant wanted to take Petersburg to cut off Richmond from the rest of the Confederacy. Even without supplies or reinforcements, the Confederate troops in Petersburg held out for nine months.

In the meantime, General Sherman headed for Georgia. In July his troops surrounded Atlanta. General John Hood was in charge of Confederate forces there. His troops put up major **resistance.** Sherman laid siege, finally forcing Hood to give up the city on September 1. The mood in the South became desperate.

Think Critically

1. Explain What was Grant's strategy for winning the war?

_____

Show Your Skill

2. Interpret Information Why was the mood in the South after Sherman took Atlanta described as *desperate*?

_____

Copyright © by The McGraw-Hill Companies, Inc.

The War's Final Stages Lesson 5 **301**

3. Evaluate What is significant about the Battle at Natural Bridge?

_____

_____

_____

_____

_____

Mark the Text ✏️

4. Time Line On the time line, list the major battles and sieges that took place in 1864.

In August, David Farragut led a Union Navy fleet into Mobile Bay in Alabama. Despite strong Confederate resistance, he took control of the bay and blocked the last Southern port east of the Mississippi.

In March 1865, one of the last important Confederate victories of the war took place. Confederates won the Battle of Natural Bridge in southern Leon County, Florida. This stopped Union forces from taking the state capital, Tallahassee.

Civil War Battles of 1864

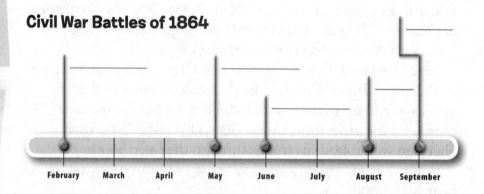

| February | March | April | May | June | July | August | September |

In early summer 1864, it looked like Lincoln would lose his bid for reelection. If Lincoln lost, the war would end, and the Confederacy would be recognized as an independent country. After the Union victories at Atlanta and Mobile Bay, though, Northerners felt that they could win. Lincoln was reelected in November 1864.

Lincoln interpreted his victory as a sign that voters wanted to end slavery. Congress passed the Thirteenth Amendment on January 31, 1865. It banned slavery in the United States.

When people visit the site of the Battle of Natural Bridge, south of Tallahassee, they will see this statue which commemorates the battle and those who fought in it.

The War Ends

Even though they seemed sure to lose, the Confederates kept fighting. The Union was determined to win.

After taking Atlanta in September 1864, Sherman's forces burned the city. Then they marched across Georgia to the Atlantic coast. As they went, the troops tore up railroad tracks and fields, burned cities and crops, and killed livestock. This was a strategy called total war. **Total war** is the planned destruction of an entire land, not just its army. The march became known as Sherman's March to the Sea.

When he reached the sea, Sherman continued his march through the Carolinas to join Grant's forces near Richmond. Wherever his troops passed, they left destruction behind them.

Thousands of African Americans left their plantations to follow Sherman's army. The troops gave them protection in their march to freedom.

On April 2, 1865, Petersburg finally fell to Grant's forces. Confederate leaders ordered weapons and bridges in Richmond burned and then fled the city. Two days later, President Lincoln walked the streets of the former Confederate capital.

The war finally ended on April 9, 1865. Lee surrendered to Grant in the town of Appomattox Court House, Virginia. The terms of the surrender were generous. Lee's officers could keep their small guns, and any soldier with a horse could keep it. Grant gave the Confederate troops food, and then they were allowed to go home.

More people died in the Civil War than in any other war in American history. More than 600,000 soldiers died. Much of the South was destroyed, and it would take many years to rebuild.

The North's victory had other results, too. It saved the Union and made it clear that the federal government was stronger than the states. It freed millions of African Americans from slavery.

It also left the nation with many problems to solve. How would the Southern states be brought back into the Union? What would be the position of African Americans in Southern society?

After the war—in the era called Reconstruction—it was difficult for Americans in both the North and South to find answers to these questions.

 NGSSS Check Why did General Lee finally surrender? SS.8.A.5.6

_____

_____

Copyright © by The McGraw-Hill Companies, Inc.

Show Your Skill

5. Make Inferences Why did Sherman burn and destroy the South?

_____

_____

_____

_____

Think Critically

6. Evaluate Do you think the North was too generous to the South or not generous enough in the terms of the surrender? Explain.

_____

_____

_____

_____

Take the Challenge

7. Take the role of a Confederate soldier at Appomattox. Write a letter home explaining how you felt when you heard the terms of the surrender.

ESSENTIAL QUESTION *Why does conflict develop?*

Reflect on What It Means . . .

Florida was one of the first states to secede from the Union before the Civil War, on January 10, 1861. It did not surrender to the Union until May 10, 1865.

To My Community and Me

Research how Florida's role in the Civil War developed. Then use your research to make a Florida Civil War time line in the space below. If possible, customize your time line for your own community, noting how the war progressed as seen from a local perspective. Note also any places you could go to see Civil War landmarks near you.

1860   1861   1862   1863   1864   1865

To the World

Find out about other countries that have experienced civil wars. Make a list in the space below of at least five other countries that have been through a civil war.

_____

_____

_____

TAKE THE CHALLENGE

As a class, put together a photographic history of the Civil War as it affected Florida, using resources such as the Florida State Library and Archives Web site. Put your photographic history on display in the lobby of your school and/or on your class Web site.

CHAPTER 18

THE RECONSTRUCTION ERA

ESSENTIAL QUESTION *How do new ideas change the way people live?*

Presbyterian minister Jonathan Gibbs traveled to Florida after the Civil War. He worked to improve the school system and started many schools for African Americans. The following is an excerpt from a speech Gibbs gave in the North during the War:

> "Your destiny as white men and ours as black men are one and the same; we are all marching on to the same goal. If you rise, we will rise in the scale of being. If you fall, we will fall. . . . Finally, let us . . . confidently predict . . . that the future will show that no efforts made in behalf of the bondman in this country were in vain. The sum of human happiness in this country will be increased . . . "

JONATHAN GIBBS

Keep in mind that this speech was given during the Civil War. What might Gibbs mean when he says that "If you rise, we will rise . . . If you fall, we will fall . . . "?

_____
_____
_____

bondman

Think of bondage as a clue. Write another word (synonym) for *bondman* below.

_____
_____

DBQ BREAKING IT DOWN

In the space below, write an outline for another speech for Gibbs—one that he could have given when he arrived in Florida. Write an outline that gives a persuasive argument about the importance of education for all people.

_____
_____
_____

McGraw-Hill
networks™
There's More Online!

PHOTO: Florida Photographic Collection

PLANNING RECONSTRUCTION

NGSSS

SS.8.A.5.8 Explain and evaluate the policies, practices, and consequences of Reconstruction (presidential and congressional reconstruction, Johnson's impeachment, Civil Rights Act of 1866, the 13th, 14th, and 15th Amendments, opposition of Southern whites to Reconstruction, accomplishments and failures of Radical Reconstruction, presidential election of 1876, end of Reconstruction, rise of Jim Crow laws, rise of Ku Klux Klan).

Essential Question

How do new ideas change the way people live?

Guiding Questions

1. Why did leaders disagree on the South rejoining the Union?
2. How did Lincoln's assassination change the plans for the South rejoining the Union?

Terms to Know

Reconstruction
the period of rebuilding the South and plans for readmitting Southern states into the Union

amnesty
the granting of a pardon to a large number of persons

When Did It Happen?

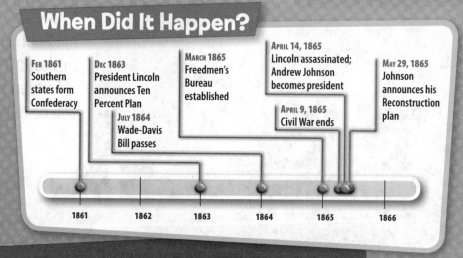

FEB 1861 Southern states form Confederacy

DEC 1863 President Lincoln announces Ten Percent Plan

JULY 1864 Wade-Davis Bill passes

MARCH 1865 Freedmen's Bureau established

APRIL 9, 1865 Civil War ends

APRIL 14, 1865 Lincoln assassinated; Andrew Johnson becomes president

MAY 29, 1865 Johnson announces his Reconstruction plan

1861   1862   1863   1864   1865   1866

What Do You Know?

Directions: In the first column, circle "True" if the statement is true or "False" if the statement is false. After the lesson, complete the last column.

Before the Lesson		After the Lesson
True False	The Freedmen's Bureau paid slave owners to give up their slaves.	True False
True False	The Radical Republicans wanted former slaves to vote in state elections.	True False
True False	Abraham Lincoln wanted to be less harsh on the Southern states than the Radical Republicans did.	True False
True False	Andrew Johnson became the president after Lincoln was assassinated.	True False
True False	Reconstruction paid for the rebuilding of the South.	True False

The Reconstruction Debate

The Civil War was fought from 1861 until 1865. The North, or Union, won the war. Now that the war was over, it was time for the country to be whole again. The states in the South needed to rejoin the states in the North. The Union needed to be rebuilt, or reconstructed.

The period of time that followed the Civil War is called **Reconstruction.** Reconstruction also refers to the plans for bringing the Southern states back into the Union. Northern leaders began forming these plans before the war even ended.

The president and Congress did not agree about how to bring the Southern states back into the Union. Some Northern leaders wanted to go easy on the South. Others wanted to punish the South for leaving the Union and starting a war.

President Abraham Lincoln wanted to go easy on the South. Lincoln's plan was called the Ten Percent Plan. He wanted to let the Southern states rejoin the Union if they agreed to these conditions:

- Voters in each Southern state had to take an oath of loyalty to the Union.
- When ten percent of the voters had taken the oath, the state could form a new government.
- The state would have to adopt a new constitution that banned slavery.

Lincoln went even further. He wanted to give **amnesty** to Southerners who would promise loyalty to the Union. Amnesty means a pardon, or forgiveness. Louisiana, Arkansas, and Tennessee agreed to Lincoln's requirements. However, Congress refused to accept their senators and representatives.

There were others who thought the South should be punished. They wanted a more radical, or extreme, approach. This group was called the Radical Republicans, or the Radicals. Thaddeus Stevens, a radical leader, said that Southern institutions "must be broken up or relaid, or all our blood and treasure will have been spent in vain."

These students and teachers are standing by a school in South Carolina that was built by the Freedman's Bureau.

Think Critically

1. Explain What are the two meanings of Reconstruction?

_____

_____

_____

_____

Show Your Skill

2. Make Inferences Who proposed the Ten Percent Plan, and why was it called that?

_____

_____

_____

_____

_____

_____

Mark the Text

3. Underline the definition of *amnesty*.

Radical Republicans in Congress passed their plan for Reconstruction in 1864. The Plan was called the Wade-Davis Bill. The Wade-Davis Bill would make it difficult for Southern states to rejoin the Union. The Wade-Davis Bill required the Southern states to do three things:

- A majority (more than 50 percent) of the state's white male adults had to promise loyalty to the Union.
- Only white males who swore they had not fought against the Union could vote for representatives to a convention to write a new constitution.
- All new states had to ban slavery.

The Wade-Davis Bill was harsher than Lincoln's Ten Percent Plan. The bill passed Congress, but President Lincoln refused to sign it. The bill did not become law. Plans for Reconstruction still had not been laid.

Meanwhile, Lincoln and Congress worked together to create a new government department called the Freedman's Bureau. The Freedmen's Bureau helped freed African Americans adjust to life after slavery. It provided food, clothing, and shelter. It set up schools and helped people find work. It also helped some people get their own land to farm.

Johnson's Reconstruction Plan

President Lincoln was assassinated on April 14, 1865, as he was watching a play in Washington, D.C. During the play, John Wilkes Booth snuck up and shot Lincoln in the head. Booth was an actor who sympathized with the South. African Americans and white Northerners mourned Lincoln's death.

Abraham Lincoln was assassinated at Ford's Theater. After being shot, he was carried across the street to the Peterson House where he died the next morning.

Vice President Andrew Johnson became president. He had different ideas about Reconstruction than Lincoln did. Johnson wanted to give amnesty to most Southerners. However, he would not give amnesty to Southern leaders unless they appealed to the president. Johnson wanted to humiliate these leaders. He thought they had tricked ordinary Southerners into the war. Johnson opposed equal rights for African Americans. He said, "White men alone must manage the South."

Johnson's plan for Reconstruction required Southern states to write new constitutions that banned slavery. However, he allowed only white men to vote for the delegates to the conventions that wrote these constitutions. Johnson's plan also required Southern states to ratify, or approve, the Thirteenth Amendment to the Constitution. The Thirteenth Amendment banned slavery throughout the United States.

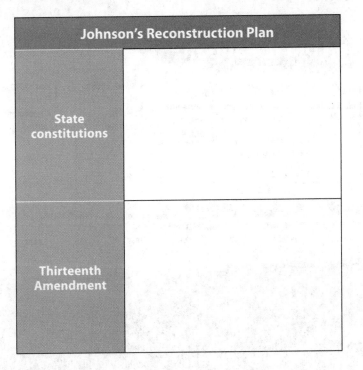

Johnson's Reconstruction Plan	
State constitutions	
Thirteenth Amendment	

NGSSS Check In what ways did Lincoln and the Radical Republicans disagree over Reconstruction and in what areas did they agree? SS.8.A.5.8

_____

_____

_____

_____

What was the importance of the Thirteenth Amendment? SS.8.A.5.8

_____

---

7. Make Inferences
How did Andrew Johnson become president?

_____

_____

_____

Mark the Text

8. Underline why Johnson wanted to humiliate Southern leaders.

Think Critically

9. Compare Was Johnson's Reconstruction plan more like Lincoln's plan or more like the Wade-Davis Bill? Why?

_____

_____

_____

Mark the Text

10. Chart Complete the chart to show what Johnson's plan would have required of Southern states.

Take the Challenge

11. Write a short news alert telling about the passing of the Thirteenth Amendment.

NGSSS

SS.8.A.5.8 Explain and evaluate the policies, practices, and consequences of Reconstruction (presidential and congressional reconstruction, Johnson's impeachment, Civil Rights Act of 1866, the 13th, 14th, and 15th Amendments, opposition of Southern whites to Reconstruction, accomplishments and failures of Radical Reconstruction, presidential election of 1876, end of Reconstruction, rise of Jim Crow laws, rise of Ku Klux Klan).

LESSON 2 — THE RADICALS TAKE CONTROL

Essential Question
How do new ideas change the way people live?

Guiding Questions
1. How did the North attempt to assist African Americans in the South?
2. What elements were included in the Radical Republican idea of Reconstruction?

Terms to Know

black codes
laws passed in the South just after the Civil War aimed at controlling freedmen and allowing plantation owners to take advantage of African American workers

override
to reject or defeat something that has already been decided

impeach
to formally charge a public official with misconduct in office

When Did It Happen?

1866 black codes passed

APRIL 1866 Civil Rights Act of 1866 passed

1867 Reconstruction Acts passed

JULY 1868 Fourteenth Amendment ratified

NOVEMBER 1868 Ulysses S. Grant elected president

MARCH 1870 Fifteenth Amendment ratified

1865 1866 1867 1868 1869 1870 1871

What Do You Know?

Directions: What would you like to know about Reconstruction after Lincoln was assassinated? Look at the information on this page. Write two questions you have about this time period. After you have finished the lesson, come back and see if you can answer the questions.

Protecting African Americans' Rights

In 1865 former Confederate states began creating new governments. States elected leaders to Congress, but the Radical Republicans would not seat them. They thought that Johnson's Reconstruction plan was too easy on the Southerners. Radicals wanted life to be difficult for the Southerners.

White people in the South were angry that they had lost the war. They were angry that enslaved people had been freed. To keep control of former slaves, Southern states passed laws called **black codes.**

The U.S. Congress was unhappy about the black codes. They wanted former enslaved people to be free and equal. Congress did two things in response.

David Shelby Walker was appointed as the governor of Florida by President Andrew Johnson.

Congress's Response to the Black Codes

• Empowered the Freedmen's Bureau to set up courts to try people who violated African Americans' rights

• Passed the Civil Rights Act of 1866

The Civil Rights Act gave citizenship to African Americans. It also gave the federal government the power to get involved in state affairs to protect African Americans' rights.

President Johnson vetoed both bills. He did favor punishing Southern leaders, but he did not believe in equal rights for African Americans. Radical Republicans in Congress were able to **override,** or overrule, each veto, so both bills became law.

Congress worried that the Civil Rights Act might be overturned in court, so it passed another amendment to the Constitution. The Thirteenth Amendment had ended slavery. This new amendment—the Fourteenth—made African Americans citizens. However, many Southern states would not ratify it. This made the Radical Republicans more determined than ever to treat the South harshly.

Think Critically

1. **Explain** Why would Radical Republicans not seat Southern senators and representatives in Congress?

_____

_____

Show Your Skill

2. **Interpret Information** Why do you think Southern states passed black codes?

_____

_____

Mark the Text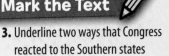

3. Underline two ways that Congress reacted to the Southern states passing black codes.

4. Underline the sentence that tells what the Fourteenth Amendment did.

5. Identify Cause and Effect
What allowed Radical Reconstruction to take place?

_____

_____

_____

_____

_____

Think Critically

6. Infer What was the main reason Radical Republicans wanted to remove Johnson from office?

_____

_____

_____

_____

_____

_____

7. Explain What did the Tenure of Office Act do?

_____

_____

_____

_____

_____

_____

Radical Republicans in Charge

Radical Republicans were a powerful force in Congress. They became an even more powerful force in 1866. It was an election year, and they won many seats in Congress. There was no way Johnson could stop them. A period known as Radical Reconstruction began.

The Radical Republicans passed the Reconstruction Acts. Read about what each one did.

Radical Reconstruction: The Reconstruction Acts	
Act	**What it did**
First Reconstruction Act	• said that states that had not ratified the Fourteenth Amendment must form new governments • divided ten states into five military districts governed by generals • banned Confederate leaders from serving in new state governments • required new state constitutions • guaranteed African American men the right to vote
Second Reconstruction Act	• empowered the army to register voters and help organize state constitutional conventions

The Southern states were now under the control of army generals. This angered Southerners. It also brought the differences between Radical Republicans in Congress and President Johnson to a boiling point.

The Radical Republicans in Congress had the majority. However, as president, Johnson was in charge of the army. He was in charge of the generals who were in charge of the South. This meant that he could control Reconstruction directly, and avoid Congress altogether, by giving orders to his generals.

Congress knew this. So, to keep President Johnson from becoming too powerful, they passed laws to limit his power. One such law was the Tenure of Office Act. It said that the president could not fire any government officials without the Senate's approval. They were afraid Johnson would fire the Secretary of War, Edwin Stanton, because he supported Radical Reconstruction.

This did not stop Johnson, however. He suspended Stanton without the Senate's approval. *Suspend* means to stop something temporarily. Radical Republicans in Congress believed that Johnson had violated the Tenure of Office Act.

The Radical Republicans reacted. The House of Representatives voted to **impeach** him—that is, formally charge him with wrongdoing. In 1868 the case went to the Senate for a trial. Not enough senators voted Johnson guilty, so he was able to remain president.

In 1869 Congress took one more major step in Reconstruction. The Thirteenth Amendment abolished slavery. The Fourteenth Amendment granted citizenship to African Americans. This new Amendment—the Fifteenth—granted African American men the right to vote. When the Fifteenth Amendment was ratified in 1870, many Americans thought Reconstruction was complete. However, there was still more to come.

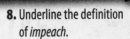

Mark the Text

8. Underline the definition of *impeach*.

9. **Chart** Complete the chart to show what each amendment accomplished.

Take the Challenge

10. How do you think Reconstruction might have been different if Lincoln had not been assassinated? Write a paragraph to explain your thinking.

Reconstruction Amendments	
Amendment	**What it did**
Thirteenth Amendment	
Fourteenth Amendment	
Fifteenth Amendment	

 NGSSS Check What action taken during Reconstruction do you think had the longest-lasting effect? Explain. SS.8.A.5.8

_____

_____

What action taken by the Radical Republicans did the most to punish the South? Explain. SS.8.A.5.8

_____

_____

_____

THE SOUTH DURING RECONSTRUCTION

NGSSS

SS.8.A.5.8 Explain and evaluate the policies, practices, and consequences of Reconstruction (presidential and congressional reconstruction, Johnson's impeachment, Civil Rights Act of 1866, the 13th, 14th, and 15th Amendments, opposition of Southern whites to Reconstruction, accomplishments and failures of Radical Reconstruction, presidential election of 1876, end of Reconstruction, rise of Jim Crow laws, rise of Ku Klux Klan).

Essential Question

How do new ideas change the way people live?

Guiding Questions

1. How were African Americans discouraged from participating in civic life in the South?
2. What were some improvements and some limitations for African Americans?

Terms to Know

scalawag
name given by former Confederates to Southern whites who supported Republican Reconstruction of the South

corruption
dishonest or illegal actions

integrate
to unite, or blend into a united whole

sharecropping
system of farming in which a farmer works land for an owner who provides equipment and seeds and receives a share of the crop

When Did It Happen?

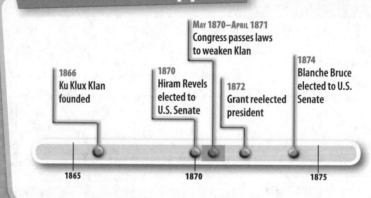

1866 Ku Klux Klan founded

1870 Hiram Revels elected to U.S. Senate

MAY 1870–APRIL 1871 Congress passes laws to weaken Klan

1872 Grant reelected president

1874 Blanche Bruce elected to U.S. Senate

1865   1870   1875

What Do You Know?

Directions: Use no more than three words to tell what you know about each of these terms. After you finish the lesson, adjust any of your descriptions if needed.

Reconstruction _____

Fifteenth Amendment _____

carpetbagger _____

segregation _____

Ku Klux Klan _____

Republicans in Charge

The Republicans were more powerful than the Democrats during Reconstruction. Generally, African Americans supported the Republican Party. The party helped African Americans participate in government. Reconstruction marked the first time African Americans participated in government. They participated both as voters and as elected officials. They served in state legislatures.

African Americans served at the national level, too. In 1870 Hiram Revels became the first African American elected to the United States Senate. Blanche Bruce was elected to the Senate in 1874. He was the first African American senator to serve a full term. Eighteen African Americans served in Congress between 1869 and 1880.

Most Southern whites opposed the Republican Party, but some supported it. They were usually business people who had never owned slaves. These people were called **scalawags** by other whites. The word means "scoundrel" or "worthless rascal." Some white southerners accused Reconstruction governments of **corruption**—dishonest or illegal actions.

Some who supported the Republican Party were called "carpetbaggers." Northerners who moved to the South during Reconstruction were called carpetbaggers because they sometimes arrived with their belongings in cheap suitcases made of carpet fabric.

Life during Reconstruction was difficult for African Americans. Most Southern whites did not want African Americans to have more rights. White landowners often refused to rent land to them. Store owners refused them credit. Many employers would not hire them.

HEROES OF THE COLORED RACE.

Mark the Text ✏

1. Underline the names of two African Americans from the South who were elected to the U.S. Senate.

Think Critically

2. **Analyze** What word for a white Southerner means "scoundrel" or "rascal"?

_____

_____

3. **Infer** Why did many Southerners resent scalawags and carpetbaggers?

_____

_____

_____

_____

_____

_____

Along with Frederick Douglass (center), Senators Revels and Bruce were considered heroes by many.

_____

_____

_____

_____

5. Draw Conclusions *Integrate* is the opposite of *segregate*. Segregate means "to separate." What does *integrate* mean?

_____

_____

Think Critically

6. Explain What "rent" did the farmer pay the landowner under the sharecropping system?

_____

_____

Take the Challenge

7. Choose one challenge faced by African Americans during Reconstruction. In 20 words or fewer, explain why you think this was the greatest obstacle that had to be overcome.

Even worse, African Americans were victims of violence. Secret societies like the Ku Klux Klan used fear and violence to intimidate them. Disguising themselves in white sheets and hoods, Klan members killed thousands of African Americans and their white friends. They beat and wounded many more. They burned African American homes, schools, and churches. Many Democrats, planters, and other white Southerners supported the Klan. They saw violence as a way to oppose Republican rule.

Education and Farming

African Americans started building their own schools during Reconstruction. Many white women and African Americans from the North came to teach in these schools. In the 1870s, Reconstruction governments created public schools for both races. Soon about 50 percent of white children and 40 percent of African American children in the South were attending school.

African American and white students usually went to different schools. A few states had laws requiring schools to be **integrated.** Schools that are integrated have both white and African Americans students

In addition to education, freed people wanted land. Having their own land to farm would enable them to feed and support their families. Sadly, most African Americans failed in their efforts to get their own land. Many freed people had no other choice but to farm on land owned by whites.

In a system called **sharecropping** a landowner let a farmer farm some of their land. In return, the farmer gave part of his crops to the landowner. The part demanded by landowners was often unfairly large. After giving landowners their share, sharecroppers often had little left to sell. Sometimes there was not even enough to feed their families. For many, sharecropping was little better than slavery.

NGSSS Check Name three ways that former slaves were discouraged from fully participating in Southern society. SS.8.A.5.8

_____

_____

NGSSS

SS.8.A.5.8 Explain and evaluate the policies, practices, and consequences of Reconstruction (presidential and congressional reconstruction, Johnson's impeachment, Civil Rights Act of 1866, the 13th, 14th, and 15th Amendments, opposition of Southern whites to Reconstruction, accomplishments and failures of Radical Reconstruction, presidential election of 1876, end of Reconstruction, rise of Jim Crow laws, rise of Ku Klux Klan).

LESSON

4

THE POST-RECONSTRUCTION ERA

Essential Question
How do new ideas change the way people live?

Guiding Questions
1. How did Democrats regain control of Southern governments?
2. Why did freedom for African Americans become a distant dream after Reconstruction ended?

Terms to Know

poll tax
a tax of a fixed amount per person that had to be paid before the person could vote

literacy test
a method used to prevent African Americans from voting by requiring prospective voters to read and write at a specified level

grandfather clause
a device that allowed persons to vote if their fathers or grandfathers had voted before Reconstruction began

segregation
the separation or isolation of a race, class, or group

lynching
putting to death a person by the illegal action of a mob

Where in the World?

Election of 1876

Hayes (Republican)
Tilden (Democrat)
Disputed Electoral Vote
Territories

When Did It Happen?

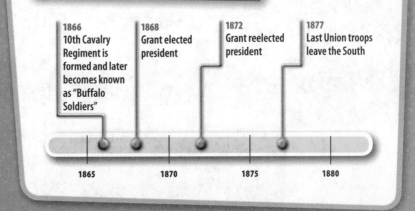

1866 10th Cavalry Regiment is formed and later becomes known as "Buffalo Soldiers"

1868 Grant elected president

1872 Grant reelected president

1877 Last Union troops leave the South

1865 · 1870 · 1875 · 1880

Read Chapter 18 Lesson 4 in your textbook or online.

Think Critically

1. Explain Why did Grant become an unpopular president?

_____

_____

_____

_____

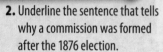

Mark the Text

2. Underline the sentence that tells why a commission was formed after the 1876 election.

Show Your Skill

3. Identify Cause and Effect What marked the end of Reconstruction?

_____

_____

_____

_____

Reconstruction Ends

As a general, Ulysses S. Grant had led the North to victory in the Civil War. He was elected president in 1868. He was reelected in 1872. Grant's presidency was one of corruption and dishonesty. Then, an economic depression struck: the Panic of 1873. The economy remained bad for years. These factors hurt the Republican Party, and Democrats made gains in Congress.

Democrats also made gains at the state level. Southern democrats who came to power called themselves "redeemers." They wanted to redeem, or save, their states from "black Republican" rule.

The presidential election of 1876 was extremely important. President Grant thought about running for a third term. The Republicans wanted a new candidate because Grant was unpopular. They nominated Rutherford B. Hayes. The Democrats nominated Samuel Tilden.

It was a very close election. It was so close that neither candidate got a majority of the electoral votes. To determine who should be president, Congress appointed a commission. A commission is a group of officials chosen for a specific job. The commission recommended that Hayes, the Republican, be named president. In return for this, the Republicans made many promises to Democrats. The most important was a promise to withdraw all troops from the South. The last troops left in 1877. This marked the end of Reconstruction.

With the end of Reconstruction, Southern leaders looked forward to a brighter future. They dreamed of a "New South." The New South would have industries based on the region's coal, iron, tobacco, cotton, and lumber resources.

River boats such as these on the St. Johns River near Jacksonville transported both people and supplies.

Indeed, the South did make great gains in industry in the 1880s. The tobacco, iron and steel, and lumber industries all boomed. The reasons for the success of Southern industry included abundant natural resources, cheap and reliable labor, and new railroads.

Southern industry grew, but the South was still mostly an agricultural region. Supporters of the New South hoped that agriculture would change, too. They hoped that smaller farms growing a variety of crops would replace huge cotton plantations.

Unfortunately, that is not what happened. Instead, the South became a land of sharecroppers and tenant farmers. Most of the sharecroppers were former slaves. They ran up debts to white landowners. Laws made them stay on the land until their debt was paid—which could take years, or even a lifetime. Thus, the sharecropping system was little better than slavery.

A Divided Society

Reconstruction was over. The Union troops that had protected the African Americans of the South left. The dream of freedom and justice for African Americans seemed far away. Southern government officials—the "redeemers"—passed laws that discriminated against African Americans. African Americans could do little about these government officials. The governments passed laws that made it nearly impossible for African Americans to vote. These laws enforced **poll taxes, literacy tests, and grandfather clauses.**

Restricting African Americans' Right to Vote in the South		
Method	**What it Was**	**How it Worked**
poll tax	a fee people had to pay to vote	Many African Americans could not afford the tax, so they could not vote.
literacy test	a requirement that voters must be able to read and write at a certain level	Most Southern African Americans had little education, so literacy tests prevented many from voting.
grandfather clause	A law stating that a voter could vote if his father or grandfather had voted before Reconstruction.	African Americans could not vote until 1867, so they could not meet this requirement. This also allowed poor white Southerners who could not read to vote.

4. Infer Complete this sentence: Despite the growth of

_____, the South's economy in the late 1800s still depended mostly on

_____ .

5. Infer How was sharecropping similar to slavery?

_____

_____

_____

_____

_____

_____

Show Your Skill

6. Draw Conclusions Why did white Southerners pass new voting laws?

_____

_____

_____

_____

_____

_____

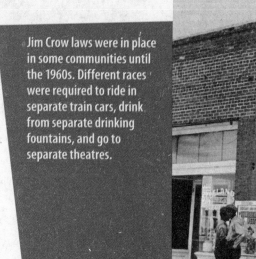

Jim Crow laws were in place in some communities until the 1960s. Different races were required to ride in separate train cars, drink from separate drinking fountains, and go to separate theatres.

PHOTO: Marion Post Wolcott/Library Of Congress/Getty Images

Mark the Text

7. Underline the definition of *lynching* in the text.

Think Critically

8. **Explain** What were Jim Crow laws?

_____

_____

_____

_____

Take the Challenge

9. Research some of the Jim Crow laws. Find three examples of Jim Crow laws to share with the class. Draw a picture to illustrate one of the laws.

Other laws also discriminated against African Americans. In the late 1800s, **segregation** was common in the South. Segregation is the separation of races. Public places were segregated by law. The laws that required segregation were called Jim Crow laws.

Even worse than segregation was the practice of lynching. **Lynching** is the killing by hanging of people by a mob. White mobs lynched many African Americans in the South.

Some African Americans managed to escape the South. Many fled to Kansas. They called themselves Exodusters after the biblical book of Exodus which describes the Jews' escape from slavery in Egypt. Other African Americans escaped the South by joining the army. They fought in the Indian Wars of the late 1800s. The Apache and Cheyenne named these African American soldiers "Buffalo Soldiers."

NGSSS Check List three ways state governments kept African Americans from voting. Tell what each did. SS.8.A.5.8

_____

_____

_____

_____

Reflect on What It Means . . .

Reconstruction was a time of healing, pain, rebuilding, destruction, violence, and growth. There is no single viewpoint that can express it all.

To the World, My Community, and Me

A time capsule often includes newspaper clippings, photographs, letters, and other objects that people hope will help future generations learn about them. You have just discovered a time capsule that was buried in your community during Reconstruction. What is inside? In the space below, show some of the items and explain how they touched the lives of individuals, the community, and perhaps the world. Include as many viewpoints as possible.

Keep Going!

TAKE THE CHALLENGE

As a class, produce a newspaper covering a key event during the Reconstruction years. Use as many types of newspaper devices as possible: letters to the editor, want ads, editorial cartoons, advertisements, and investigative reporting. Use the space below to create a draft of your contribution to the class Reconstruction newspaper.

NGSSS Inventory Test

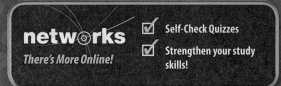
The state of Florida uses tests to measure your knowledge in different subject areas. The tests that you take will vary from year to year. However, the skills you need to perform well on standardized tests apply to every subject.

✓ Be Prepared

To do your best on test days, you need to take care of yourself beforehand. Try to get plenty of sleep for several nights before the test. Make sure to eat a good breakfast and lunch on test day. Then, be ready to do your best!

✓ What to Expect

The questions on your end-of-course tests will be multiple choice. Each question will be followed by four answer choices. Your job is to decide which of the four is the best possible answer.

Sometimes you absolutely know the answer to a question and the right answer leaps out at you. Other times you have to analyze the options and eliminate ones you know are wrong in order to zero in on the right answer.

✓ Pace Yourself

When you take an end-of-course test, it is important to pace yourself. If you work too quickly, you will be more likely to make mistakes. Instead, read each question and all of the answer choices carefully. If there's a question you can't answer, skip it and answer the next question. When you are done with the test, you can go back and reread those questions you did not understand.

✓ Read Every Word

Pay extra attention to every word in the questions. Just a word or two can change the meaning of the question.

✓ Make Your Best Guess

Make sure you go back and answer every question before submitting your test. Any question left blank will be marked wrong, so it's better to make your best guess. Remember to use the process of elimination to narrow the possibilities. Then make your guess from the remaining choices.

✓ Check Your Work

After you finish the test, go back to the beginning and check your work.

NGSSS Inventory Test

Directions: Circle the best answer.

1 In 1644, Roger Williams established the colony of Rhode Island in order to create a place where

A people of all faiths could worship freely.

B women could vote.

C slavery was illegal.

D English colonists could live peacefully with Spanish colonists.

 SS.8.A.2.4 Identify the impact of key colonial figures on the economic, political, and social development of the colonies.

2 Why did the Pennsylvania colony have better relations with Native Americans than the other British colonies?

A the colonists who settled there were Catholic and wanted peace with them.

B Native Americans worked with Spain to negotiate a treaty with William Penn.

C William Penn paid the Native Americans for the land he settled.

D the Native Americans migrated to South America.

 SS.8.A.2.5 Discuss the impact of colonial settlement on Native American populations.

3 One consequence of the French and Indian War was that

A Spanish holdings in North America increased.

B the British worked with France to win Spanish lands in North America.

C France gave up all of its claims to land in North America.

D Native Americans gained power in the colonies.

 SS.8.A.2.6 Examine the causes, course, and consequences of the French and Indian War.

4 American colonists objected to British taxes because

F they did not see the benefit from paying taxes.

G the taxes would encourage people to buy goods elsewhere.

H taxes were immoral and should never be imposed.

J they felt that the tax laws were violating their rights as British citizens.

 SS.8.A.3.2 Explain American colonial reaction to British policy from 1763-1774.

5 Which Founding Father served in the American Revolution as a military leader?

A George Washington

B Thomas Jefferson

C Benjamin Franklin

D James Madison

 SS.8.A.3.3 Recognize the contributions of the Founding Fathers (John Adams, Sam Adams, Benjamin Franklin, John Hancock, Alexander Hamilton, Thomas Jefferson, James Madison, George Mason, George Washington) during American Revolutionary efforts.

6 During Jefferson's presidency, U.S. territory increased through
F gains during the French and Indian War.
G the Louisiana Purchase.
H the passage of the Embargo Act.
J land acquired during the War of 1812.

 SS.8.A.3.14 Explain major domestic and international economic, military, political, and socio-cultural events of Thomas Jefferson's presidency.

7 Alexander Hamilton helped build a strong national economy by
A encouraging George Washington to set up a cabinet of advisors.
B arguing that the United States should refuse to pay its war debts.
C stopping the United States from imposing protective tariffs.
D asking the United States Congress to create a national bank.

 SS.8.A.3.12 Examine the influences of George Washington's presidency in the formation of the new nation.

8 The letters *X*, *Y*, and *Z* in the XYZ affair refer to
F three French agents.
G three members of the Adams cabinet.
H the laws known as the Alien and Sedition Acts.
J the Democrats, the Republicans, and the Federalists.

 SS.8.A.3.13 Explain major domestic and international economic, military, political, and socio-cultural events of John Adams' presidency.

9 In the early 19th century, shipping goods by steamboat from New York City to Detroit was made easier by the construction of
A canals.
B the turnpike system.
C the transcontinental railroad.
D the national road.

 SS.8.A.4.5 Explain the causes, course, and consequences of the 19th century transportation revolution on the growth of the nation's economy.

10 In *Gibbons* v. *Ogden*, the Supreme Court upheld the power of the federal government
F to print money.
G to form a navy.
H to regulate interstate commerce.
J to negotiate with foreign governments.

 SS.8.A.4.13 Explain the consequences of landmark Supreme Court decisions (*McCulloch v. Maryland* [1819], *Gibbons v. Ogden* [1824], *Cherokee Nation v. Georgia* [1831], *Worcester v. Georgia* [1832]) significant to this era of American history.

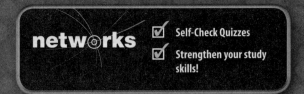
11 The demand for women's suffrage was included in the Declaration of Sentiments issued by the Seneca Falls Convention. Suffrage refers to

A the right to own property.

B the right to vote.

C the right to run for political office.

D the right to an education.

SS.8.A.4.14 Examine the causes, course, and consequences of the women's suffrage movement (1848 Seneca Falls Convention, Declaration of Sentiments).

12 One challenge faced by the Continental Congress was that

F the Continental Congress did not know how to prepare for a war

G the economy was in the middle of an economic downturn.

H the colonies had no foreign allies.

J it did not have all the powers of a nation.

SS.8.A.3.8 Examine individuals and groups that affected political and social motivations during the American Revolution.

13 French exploration of North America differed from the Spanish conquest of territory because

A the French did not care whether they made any money in the Americas.

B the French were mostly interested in trade and trade routes.

C the Spanish were interested in exploring and finding trade routes.

D the Spanish were nonviolent in their exploration of the Americas.

SS.8.A.2.1 Compare the relationships among the British, French, Spanish, and Dutch in their struggle for colonization of North America.

14 Abolitionists tried to persuade Americans to oppose slavery by

F buying enslaved people out of slavery.

G speaking out about the living conditions of enslaved people.

H attempting to incite violent rebellions and revolts.

J working to reduce Southern dependence on cotton.

SS.8.A.4.11 Examine the aspects of slave culture including plantation life, resistance efforts, and the role of the slaves' spiritual system.

15 The Mayflower Compact was significant because

A the Pilgrims agreed to govern themselves democratically.

B the Pilgrims were being suppressed by Queen Elizabeth of England.

C the Pilgrims were in favor of the colonies becoming independent.

D the Pilgrims refused to accept a democratic government.

SS.8.A.1.5 Identify, within both primary and secondary sources, the author, audience, format, and purpose of significant historical documents.

16 To analyze changes in population distribution in the United States after the construction of national roads and turnpikes, the best tool for a geographer to use would be

A primary sources.

B physical maps

C census data.

D political maps.

 SS.8.G.4.2 Use geographics terms and tools to anylyze the effects throughout American history of migration to and within the United States, both on the place of origin and destination.

17 One of the weaknesses of the Articles of Confederation was that

A the Articles made the national government too strong.

B the Articles made the national government too weak.

C the Articles did not give equal rights to all adults.

D the Articles did not explain how power should be divided.

 SS.8.A.3.9 Evaluate the structure, strengths, and weaknesses of the Articles of Confederation and aspects that led to the Constitutional Convention.

18 One reason New England colonial merchants resisted British taxation policies was because they were concerned about

A growth of trade unions.

B scarcity of raw materials.

C lowered demand for British goods in American markets.

D losing profits.

 SS.8.E.1.1 Examine motivating economic factors that influenced the development of the United States ecomomy over time including scarcity, supply and demand, opportunity costs, incentives, profits, and entrepreneurial aspects.

19 The War with Mexico began in 1846 when

A Mexico invaded Texas.

B Mexico invaded a disputed area.

C the United States invaded a disputed area.

D the United States invaded Mexico City.

 SS.8.A.4.1 Examine the causes, course, and consequences of United States westward expansion and its growing diplomatic assertiveness (War of 1812, Convention of 1818, Adams-Onis Treaty, Missouri Compromise, Monroe Doctrine, Trail of Tears, Texas annexation, Manifest Destiny, Oregon Territory, Mexican/American War/Mexican Cession, California Gold Rush, Compromise of 1850, Kansas Nebraska Act, Gadsden Purchase).

20 The mechanical reaper, invented by Cyrus McCormick greatly increased

A factory production.

B the speed of steamboat engines.

C the amount of grain a farmer could harvest.

D the rate at which cotton could be cleaned.

 SS.8.E.2.1 Analyze contributions of entrepreneurs, inventors, and other key individuals from various gender, social, and ethnic backgrounds in the development of the United States economy.

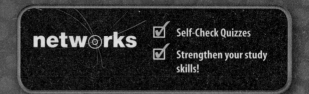

21 The president acts as Commander in Chief of the U.S. armed forces

A because the Supreme Court will not allow Congress to control the military.

B because the president is elected and members of Congress are not.

C because almost everyone looks to the president for leadership.

D because the president is given that role in the U.S. Constitution.

SS.8.C.1.5 Apply the rights and principles contained in the Constitution and Bill of Rights to the lives of citizens today.

22 Which of the following acts would violate the "due process of law" clause of the Fifth Amendment to the Constitution?

F jailing a person for a long period without a trial

G forcing people to pay taxes that they did not vote for

H using government money to help a business or corporation

J breaking the law by committing a crime

SS.8.C.2.1 Evaluate and compare the essential ideals and principles of American constitutional government expressed in primary sources from the colonial period to Reconstruction.

23 What did President Lincoln do to keep the support of border states during the Civil War?

A He allowed those states to stop paying taxes.

B He allowed those states to continue slavery.

C He tried to prevent battles from being fought in those states.

D He agreed to deny African Americans the right to fight in the war.

SS.8.A.5.3 Explain major domestic and international economic, military, political, and socio-cultural events of Abraham Lincoln's presidency.

24 Which of the following factors did Southerners hope would work to their advantage during the Civil War?

F The North did not have an organized navy.

G Native Americans in the South supported the Confederacy.

H The South controlled much of the worldwide supply of cotton.

J The Confederacy could rely on enslaved people to fight the war.

SS.8.A.5.5 Compare Union and Confederate strengths and weaknesses.

25 The post-Civil War Congress wanted to use Reconstruction to

A redraw state boundaries.

B ensure civil rights for African Americans.

C preserve the plantation system.

D establish labor unions.

SS.8.A.5.8 Explain and evaluate the policies, practices, and consequences of Reconstruction (presidential and congressional reconstruction, Johnson's impeachment, Civil Rights Act of 1866, the 13th, 14th, and 15th Amendments, opposition of Southern whites to Reconstruction, accomplishments and failures of Radical Reconstruction, presidential election of 1876, end of Reconstruction, rise of Jim Crow laws, rise of Ku Klux Klan).